D1426550

SCHUBERT

SCHUBERT

by

George R. Marek

ROBERT HALE · LONDON

Robert Hale Limited
Clerkenwell House
Clerkenwell Green
London ECIR OHT

British Library Cataloguing in Publication Data
Marek, George R.
  Schubert.
  1. Schubert, Franz   2. Composers – Austria
  – Biography
  I. Title
  780'.92'4   ML410.S3

ISBN 0-7090-2592-0

Printed in Great Britain by
St Edmundsbury Press, Bury St Edmunds, Suffolk
Bound by Hunter & Foulis Limited, Edinburgh

CONTENTS

ILLUSTRATIONS

ACKNOWLEDGMENTS

A BIOGRAPHER IS HELPED BY THE QUICK AND THE DEAD. OF THE SCHOL-
ars who have examined the life and works of Schubert, the indispensable
digger was Otto Erich Deutsch, for whose work I extend thanks in the
Introduction, and here thank again. I could not have written without
him. As Donal Henahan points out (in *The New York Times* of September
4, 1983), it is curious that Deutsch did not set out to be a musician or
to examine Schubert, being at first interested in a biography of the painter
Moritz von Schwind, "but he soon found himself wrapped up in the
composer's life and work." When I used a document Deutsch quotes, I
have marked it "DQ"; when I quote Deutsch himself, the excerpt is
marked "D." Other authorities no longer with us were Maurice J. E.
Brown and Alfred Einstein, who concerned himself more with the music
than the man.

Of the current Schubertians, Dietrich Fischer-Dieskau wrote a fine
study of Schubert songs; he examines them from the viewpoint of the
executant artist, and I learned a lot from the book. A few quotations I
used from it are marked "FD."

Other of the many sources I have read are listed in the Bibliography;
they range from dry documents to highly fanciful ones, of which the
most amusing is a little book by one Elly Ziesel (*Schubert's Death and
Burial*), which asserts that Schubert was poisoned by the Freemasons,
who are "prevailingly a Jewish organization." Perhaps it is unnecessary
to add that this "scientific" conclusion was published in Germany in
1933.

For the research undertaken freshly for this biography—most of it done in the Vienna archives—I am grateful for the help given to me by Christian Simonis, a conductor of Vienna, and to Isabella Schuppanz, a researcher of Vienna. And to Dr. Harald Goertz of the Österreichische Gesellschaft für Musik, Dr. Helmut Leitner of the Institut für Geschichte der Medizin, Vienna, Dr. Lorenz Mikoletzky of the Österreichisches Staatsarchiv, Dr. Fritz Cocron, formerly the head of the Austrian Cultural Institute in New York, Mr. Robin Price of the Welcome Institute of London, Ms. Else Radant, historian in Vienna, H. C. Robbins-Landon, the eminent Haydn authority, Charles Gerhardt, a Schubertian of London, Henry Pleasants, critic of the International *Times,* Adelbert Schusser of the Historic Museum of the City of Vienna, etc. These Leporello-like lists are meaningless to most readers, but courtesy demands them and in this instance they are given gladly, because everybody was most willing: mention Schubert, and the response is a warm smile.

I am most grateful to the prudent and judicious guidance of Alan Williams of Viking, who is what has become a rarity: a truly dedicated editor.

Is there such a thing as a "definitive" biography? I doubt it. A biography must be rewritten. I can only hope that this one will stimulate further inquiry. Whatever the longevity of the book, it is certain that Schubert will be around on his two-hundredth anniversary, provided of course that civilization will be around.

George R. Marek
New York, 1983

To Muriel

I know nothing more paltry under the sun
Than You, you Gods!
How sparsely is your glory nourished
By the breath of prayer
And the ritual of sacrifice!
You would starve, were it not for
Children and beggars,
Those hopeful fools.

—SCHUBERT, "Prometheus"
(FROM GOETHE, *Prometheus*)

INTRODUCTION
The Legendary Schubert

WHO IS SCHUBERT, WHAT IS HE, THAT ALL MUSIC'S FRIENDS COMMEND him—yet know little of his total work and little of him as a man?

Of his six hundred and three songs, fewer than a tenth are in general usage; of his symphonies, only two form a firm part of the orchestral repertoire; of his fourteen extant string quartets, four or five are regularly played; of his fifteen completed piano sonatas, five or six alone are frequently presented, though his smaller piano pieces, the marches, impromptus, and waltzes, have done obedient service for the young who, still brought up in the genteel tradition, learn, willingly or not, to play the piano. His fifteen operas lie buried full fathom five, and to hear a live performance of one of his five masses constitutes an exceptional event. Yet what remains is greatly beloved, and the measure of that love is proportionate to our love for all music.

Schubert? Yes, those who have only a casual interest in music know that he wrote some pretty songs, such as "Serenade" and "Who Is Sylvia?" and "Ave Maria." He composed an unfinished symphony called the *Unfinished*. Those whose interest delves deeper respond to and are thrilled by the embracing C-Major Symphony, the *Trout* Quintet, the C-Major Quintet, the *Death and the Maiden* Quartet—all glories of chamber music—and the last three piano sonatas. Perhaps the songs mean most to those who can understand the texts, though even those who cannot are able to hear the murmur of the song cycle *Die schöne Müllerin* or feel the frosty desolation of *Die Winterreise*. It was he who lifted the expressiveness of the lied to a height where Schumann, Brahms, Wolf, Richard Strauss, and Mahler would follow.

[xiii]

Whether one knows little or much of Schubert's music, one agrees that he was a great composer. What was he like as a man? How do we see his personality? How can one explain him as a human being? It is curious, but in my opinion no famous composer has been more falsely presented. The colors of his portrait coalesce vaguely and are clotted until we no longer discern the lines. His biography is at best "half-legend, half-historic," as Tennyson wrote in *The Princess*. Nineteenth-century biographers, while dropping a tear or two on their manuscripts, have done nothing to weed out the sodden underbrush around his monument, the thicket of "heartbreaking" anecdotes which so often grows around the stories of genius.

The romantic view of Schubert which is generally accepted is this: He was desperately poor, often did not have enough to eat, was almost totally ignored, was an "unconscious genius" (whatever that may mean) shaking one song after another from his sleeve, scribbling them on any piece of paper that lay handy, writing on the back of a menu or on a bill he had no intention of paying, never—or hardly ever—making preliminary sketches or correcting what he had composed, one reason being that he didn't own a piano and had to go to a friend's house to try out his works. He was quite uneducated, not only musically, his talent being "instinctive," but in other ways: he read few books and could not diagnose the worth of the texts he put to music, choosing them haphazardly. He knew nothing of politics and was not cognizant of what was happening in the world. Pictures and statues, ancient and contemporary, he passed by with an unseeing eye. He just kept on composing. Few of his compositions were published during his lifetime. Virtually nobody bought the things that were published. But he didn't care much, being a happy-go-lucky fellow, as most Viennese are. He spent his free time in the coffeehouses, wine cellars, inns, restaurants of the gay city, drinking too much. He was often inebriated. With his friends he liked to play games, charades or guessing games, or childish pranks, such as performing his "Erlkönig" by blowing through a comb. Personally he was unprepossessing, his hair disordered, his linen not quite clean. He was very nearsighted. He was shy, painfully so, and had no inkling of his importance. He was unsuccessful with the female sex. Peter Altenberg, one of the group of Viennese writers at the end of the nineteenth century (a group to which belonged Hofmannsthal, Schnitzler, Bahr), wrote a prose poem about Schubert which reflects the then-prevailing impression. Translated, it reads something like this:

Viennese Ballad: Franz Schubert

If you are chubby and plump
If your legs are short
If your neck is short
If you are short of breath
If you have thick unruly hair
If you have small fat paws—
Then your having written "The Erlking" or "The
    Trout" or "The Post" or *"Du bist die Ruh'* " or
    even "By the Sea"
Is of no help with charming, pretty girls.
Nobody wants to sleep with a fat lark!
Poor, poor Franz!

Poor, poor Franz! A Viennese Rodolfo without a Mimi. He suffered from the cold. He never earned a decent sum of money. He died a pauper's death, like Mozart (who too has been falsely portrayed). Vienna forgot him. Even as late as 1978 an Austrian writer, Horst Osterheld, wrote in his biography:

Schubert was incredibly undemanding. A bed, a table, one chair—often that is all he could call his own. In bitter winter his friends found him sitting in a half-lit, dank, unheated cubbyhole, clad in a threadbare robe. He froze— and composed.

Franz Schubert Schicksal und Persönlichkeit

Was he, then, a one-chambered, one-track hermit, unaffected by anything but music? As a French writer, Marcel Schneider, put it: "Those who only know Schubert through his legend . . . see him as a creature of sentiment, naive, pure and somewhat foolish, a sort of Parsifal of the *Lied*, in short a heavenly simpleton who produced his melodies as a tree bears its fruit."

And, as Maurice J. E. Brown, who wrote the Schubert article in the current edition of *Grove's Dictionary,* asks, does Schubert's story contain "no climax of recognition of his genius, or acknowledgement of it, [which] breaks the continuous obscurity of his years"?

Other descriptions show him, and in speaking of him many imagine him, as "leading a rowdy life among the plebs" or as the Schubert "of the new wine," almost a neighbor across the vineyard of that other Viennese, Johann Strauss, Jr. Still another nineteenth-century viewpoint is the patriotic one: we are asked to believe that the Viennese always cherished "their" Schubert. In point of fact, it took forty-four years after his death before they erected his monument in the City Park. There it stands near the (much better) Johann Strauss monument: it is a wretched hunk of marble (by Karl Kundmann) and there he sits, comfortable in an armchair, corpulent, wrapped in an elegant cloak, looking like the Chairman of the Board. Is this man who seems so pleased with himself really Schubert?

This book is an attempt to correct the legend, and by examining his life and character afresh to arrive nearer the truth. Truth, especially biographical truth, the portrayal of a personality, is relative. Shift your point of view and the subject appears in a different light.

Superficially it seems easy, actually it is difficult, to write about Schubert. Easy, because some of his friends wrote copious reminiscences of him, and during his last years and after his death some serious appraisals began to appear. Difficult, first, because most of the friends wrote what they wrote long after and wanted to speak of him only in loving tones, their memories rose-tinted and often inaccurate; second, because Schubert wrote very few letters—only seventy-one are extant—while in revealing himself he was least like Rousseau; third, because some documents have been treated carelessly and one arouses suspicion: a page of the usual Protocol of his death seems to have been torn away. (Deutsch lists the Protocol as XX, dated December 2, 1828.) In addition, at least three diaries kept by contemporaries of Schubert's are lost, those of Anselm Hüttenbrenner, Leopold Sonnleithner, Johann Baptist Jenger, "all of which were clearly destroyed intentionally" (D). A further difficulty: during the Vienna uprising of 1927 the Palace of Justice was burned; some material was rendered illegible or burned completely.

I tried to walk between the sad Schubert and the carefree Schubert. I sought answers to such questions as: Was he really as little-known as he is often made out to be? Was he as poor as the proverbial church mouse? Was he, similar to what Cézanne said of Monet—"Just an eye, but what an eye!"—just an ear? Were the publishers as mean to him as has been reported? Did he really live in a gray garret? How good or bad was his literary judgment? Was his disposition nearer to that of Poe or of Pope?

Considerable fresh research was undertaken to help answer these questions. Yet anybody writing about Schubert owes a fundamental debt to Otto Erich Deutsch (1883–1961), who gathered research for many years.* The original title of his work—*Franz Schubert: Die Dokumente seines Lebens und Schappens*—has been loosely translated as *The Schubert Reader*, and under this title was published in the United States in 1947 (in 1944 in England under the misleading title *Schubert, a Documentary Biography*). The English-language version is corrected and fuller than the German version, since Deutsch had to flee from Hitler's invading hordes, and lived long enough to be able to complete his labors undisturbed in Cambridge. Deutsch was to Schubert what Alexander Wheelock Thayer was to Beethoven, with the difference that Deutsch did not attempt a biography. He says in his Preface, "This is a book of facts . . . a fairly complete collection of all the known biographical raw material." Many of the facts given by Deutsch and others are cribbed for this book. The facts, not the interpretation.

I have attempted no technical analysis of Schubert's music; such a task would be beyond my capacity. What I *have* attempted is to draw a clear picture of the man, using not only published facts but other data found through research in the Vienna and other archives. For that purpose I have spent much time in Vienna and other "Schubert locations." If I have succeeded, the portrait will make it easier to understand the melancholy and introspection which mark much of his music. Yet the portrait will not be that of a prophet with beetled brow: a smile is there.

I have loved his music since I first hummed "Heidenröslein." I have come to love him as a man. This is not an objective biography.

---

*Later he performed the same service for Mozart, earlier for Handel.

I

The Twelfth Child

HOWEVER AUTHORITARIAN THE REIGN OF AUSTRIA'S GREAT QUEEN, HOW-
ever awesome her voluminous hoopskirts, to which clung all citizens,
and however stiff her religious and moral precepts, Empress Maria Theresa (1717–1780) knew the value of education. She planned a thorough
reform of the Austrian school system around 1740, founded the presti-
gious "Theresanium" in 1746, which served as an educational institution
for the sons of the aristocracy, and dotted her realm with schools ranging
from humble huts instructing the ABCs to Vienna's University. She demanded that even the lowliest teacher pass an exam, and these were
usually supervised by a local bishop. Many clergymen, from Jesuits to
Piarists, were themselves teachers. Maria Theresa's son, Joseph II (1741–
1790), continued her zeal for education, with greater liberalism and much
idealism, struggling against the ostracism of the Jews, the excessive wealth
of cloisters and abbeys, the simony of the Vatican, the superstitions of
the ignorant.

To be a teacher you could not be an out-and-out ignoramus. To be
sure, you had to be a good Catholic, dragging your little charges to
church on dark winter mornings no matter how sleepy you and your
pupils were. Why did anybody want to become a teacher? Teachers were
badly paid. Respectability and security were the answers. Once hired,
you became part of the Austrian bureaucracy, an "official"; you wore a
uniform (how much a uniform added to your self-esteem!); if you behaved
yourself you could not be dismissed; as you entered the classroom the
pupils rose to stand at attention; and after many, many years—usually
thirty—you received a pension, small but sufficient to let you retire per-

haps in "Pensionopolis," in Graz, where life was cheaper than in Vienna.

For such reasons Franz Theodor Florian Schubert, born in Moravia in 1763, decided to become a schoolteacher. Like so many young fellows, he emigrated to Vienna and at the age of twenty-two became a "school assistant" in a suburb called Liechtental. Lady Mary Wortley Montagu described it in her elegant travel letters of the 1760s as "containing pretty palaces which quite obliterate from vision the small, poor buildings." Had Lady Mary looked a little closer, she would have seen how poor these buildings really were. All the same, the district had its own pretty little church, called the Church of the Fourteen Apostles, and a few meters to the right stood a park, built by Prince Adam Liechtenstein, which, even if commoners were not allowed to enter, wafted its fragrance over the smelly streets. The crowning glory of that park was, and is, the Liechtenstein Palace, one of Vienna's finest palaces. (As a child I played in that park and saw my first Rubens there. The gallery has been transferred to Vaduz near Zurich, and its most famous possession, the *Ginevra de' Benci* by Leonardo, is now in Washington's National Gallery.)

Schubert soon rose to be a full-fledged teacher and moved to a house and school in the Himmelpfortgrund, which was part of the Liechtental. The name means "Heaven's Portal," but there was little heavenly either about the setting or about Schubert's house, which was called "The Red Crayfish." In eighty-six houses and no more than nine streets huddled some three thousand inhabitants, including no end of noisy children, some tenth of whom the young schoolmaster had to tame.

Franz had married in 1785 a girl three years older than he, Elisabeth Vietz, a cook. Her famous son has left us only a vague impression of her as a gentle and submissive woman.

Franz the father was by no means a stupid man, and the description of him based on an execrable portrait as a "bullet head with its wooden features [which] exhibits barely enough intelligence to belong to a stagecoach driver" (Robert Haven Schauffler) is unjust. His career, which ascended to principal, then to owner of a large, successful school, proves it, if nothing else does. He was merely a conformist, fitting smoothly into the groove of Austria's system, a somewhat righteous moralist taking God's help for granted and believing everything he heard in church. But he was not a dolt, and neither Shakespeare's "short-armed ignorance" nor "tedious poverty" prevailed in Schubert's home.

The twenty-five-year-old Franz Sr. became a father even before he married Elisabeth, showing that however strong were his morals his sexual instincts were stronger, and suggesting that the hasty marriage was a matter of social necessity. This first child was called Ignaz, his birthday March 5, 1785. (In a document of 1818 Ignaz's birth year was falsified, for obvious reasons.) Judging by a portrait, Ignaz grew up to be a man with compressed lips and timid eyes; judging by a few letters, he was conscious of his bastardy and was apparently treated with less affection than the other children. He was a hunchback, unprepossessing, yet had a good mind and a love of music. He admired his brother Franz and was a bit envious of him.

From his first adult days to his last, Franz Sr. kept a punctilious family chronology, as if he knew that somebody would some day be interested in examining these bare names and dates of too many births and too many deaths. In the twenty-seven years the marriage lasted (Elisabeth Vietz died on May 28, 1812), fourteen children were born, all in an alcove next to the courtyard. Of the fourteen only five survived infancy. Only five—statistically not a very good but not an unusual average for eighteenth-century child survival. But who cares about statistics as one reads "Karl, born April 23, 1787, 1:30 P.M., died February 6, 1788, 7 A.M." or "Petrus, born June 29, 1792, 1:15 A.M., died January 14, 1793, 5:30 A.M."? Again and again the swaddling clothes had to be changed for a funeral blanket, the mother saw her hope vanish, the father called in a useless doctor, the infant's cries shrilled through the night, the acrid odor crept through the house at dawn.

The twelfth child was a boy, born January 31, 1797, and baptized Franz Peter. The boy lived. The thirteenth child was a girl, born December 17, 1799, and named Aloisis Magdalena. She lived only one day.

The composer's brothers and sisters who did reach maturity include (in addition to Ignaz) Ferdinand, three years older than Franz and his favorite brother, who became a very successful teacher; then Karl, two years older than Franz, who developed into a reasonably good though not very original landscape painter (the creative trace was there); and a sister, Maria Theresia, four years younger than Franz, who married a school principal.

Hardly a year after Father Franz's first wife died, he married again. (He did not wait out the traditional year of mourning.) Evidently he could not live without a woman. In 1813 he was forty-nine; the girl he chose, Anna Kleyenböck, was twenty years younger. The name is not Austrian; it suggests a Dutch origin. Her father was a silk manufacturer, and it is probable that she brought a little dowry into the marriage. From this union five children were born, four of whom survived. Anna seems to have been a charming girl, and nearer in spirit to her husband's children than to her husband. No animosity existed between Elisabeth's and Anna's children; they all got along, Anna's youth and lightheartedness bringing laughter to the miscellaneous brood and its rather austere progenitor. More than once she slipped young Schubert a florin or two of pocket money.

In 1801 the elder Schubert had enough money—or enough credit—to purchase the small home attached to his school. The school was expanding and gaining in reputation. The house was called "The Black Stallion"—Viennese houses had names before the advent of street numbers—and the purchase price was 3,200 florins, which would represent about $40,000 in today's purchasing power. Obviously, Franz Sr. was not a pauper, though he needed to husband every florin and every kreuzer to provide for the five plus four plus one family. Yet there was not a day when young Franz didn't have enough to eat, not a Sunday on which he could not be dressed in a clean shirt, not a winter when he could not wrap himself in a coat. "Tedious poverty"? Schubert as a child was never as poor as young Brahms, or the cobbler's son Hans Christian Andersen, or the grocer's son Claude Monet, who literally starved.

As the nineteenth century marched in, inflation marched with it. Bread and milk and shoes cost more. It was the usual progression. In 1801, the very year Father Schubert bought the house, he was suddenly taxed an additional twenty-five florins fifty-eight kreuzer "for the army—for the defense against Napoleon." It wasn't all that much, but it was an indication that the tax collector would call again and soon. All the same, one managed, and money was not the chief topic of the household. They were interested in music. Franz Sr., first teaching the older sons, and Ferdinand, especially, loved music. Then, reading. To judge by the easy casualness with which both Ferdinand and Ignaz mentioned current authors, there were books in the house or in the school. Exciting new things appeared in Vienna's bookstores or in the newspapers, which, short on news, were long on literature. In the year Franz Jr. was born, A. W. Schlegel began his translations of Shakespeare; in 1800 Novalis published his *Hymns to the Night*—written after the death of his bride—and people quoted the verses and wept copiously; in 1801 Schiller gave the world his dramatic masterpiece, *Maria Stuart*.

The twelfth child, Franz Peter, went to his father's school. Being under a father's tutelage is difficult for a little boy, but Franz seems to have done well, as shown by his later school certificates. The subjects taught were, in order of importance as shown on the semester reports, first and foremost, Religion, then Reading Printed German, Reading Written German, Writing, Calligraphy, Arithmetic in Four Versions. Calligraphy was especially stressed; Schubert's manuscripts are exceptionally neat, like Mozart's.

As a little boy he marched over to the piano which stood in the Schubert home and played. Did the Schuberts have a piano? They did: Ferdinand said so clearly—for example, in an article he wrote for the Leipzig *Neue Zeitschrift für Musik* (in April 1839) describing their early life—and Ferdinand's reports can be trusted. The widely circulated story that Schubert did not have a piano at his disposal and had to go to a friend's house to try out his compositions is a sentimental invention. And where could he possibly have learned the technique of piano composition *without* a piano?

2.

Music is the art in which talent shows itself at an astonishingly early age. Not always, but often enough. We don't hear much of child-prodigy painters and nothing of child-prodigy novelists. The history of music, however, is replete with stories of the wunderkind. The explanation lies obviously in the nature of music itself, the art having the least connection with the outside world, the art which resides entirely in imagination and is disassociated from "real" life, that life for the grasping of which some measure of experience and maturity is required. Music cannot use ships or cabbages or sealing wax as symbols. It creates its own symbols, self-contained, the first meaning of which is emotional. W. H. Auden observed: "A verbal art like poetry is reflective; it stops to think. Music is immediate, it goes on to become." That is not to suggest that music is freed of the requirement of reasoning, contemplation, growth in craftsmanship; it is merely to suggest that the experience of living is not the spark which ignites the fire. The endowment is present in the child; it may or may not develop—yet remarkably often it gives proof of its presence even before the child can add two and two or write an orderly sentence. Schopenhauer, in *The World as Will and Representation*, cited the early arrival of musical talent as an argument for his view that music is the most elementary of the arts.

Who can explain Mozart? Nobody can explain Mozart. One reads in an old account:

> We fall into utter amazement on seeing a boy aged 6 at the clavier and hear him, not by any means toy with sonatas, trios and concertos, but play in a manly way, and improvise moreover for hours on end out of his own head, now *cantabile*, now in chords, producing the best of ideas according to the taste of today; and even accompany at sight symphonies, arias and recitatives at the great concerts. —Tell me, does this not exceed all imagination? —And yet it is the simple truth! . . . I was also present in person when a clavier player on several occasions played a few bars of melody for him, which he then repeated and had to fit a bass to of his own; and every time he carried this out so beautifully, accurately and well that everybody was astounded.
>
> *Augsburger Intelligenz Zettel*, May 19, 1763

How is it possible that at the age of eight Mendelssohn knew all of Beethoven's symphonies by heart, that he began to compose at the age of six, that by the time he was fourteen he had set thirteen little symphonies, a brace of concertos, and a quantity of chamber music on paper, and that at the age of sixteen he composed the glorious Octet? Paganini at nine played miraculously, so well that it moved Rossini to say that he had wept only three times in his life: once when his first opera failed, once when on a boating excursion a turkey stuffed with truffles fell into the water, and once when he first heard Paganini play. Saint-Saëns began composing when he was three and was called "a child lacking in inexperience."

Schubert began composing at the age of five, though he was not a child prodigy, able to perform astonishing feats on the piano or the violin. He came to music by way of song. While the song is of course a natural expression of musical talent, and there is hardly any composer, early or late, who has not written songs, it assumes a special chair at Schubert's board, the chair of the host. Had a reporter from Augsburg written about a boy named Schubert, he might have exclaimed in "amazement" at some early song attempts of which no trace remains. The earliest songs extant ("Hagars Klage" and "Des Mädchens Klage") date from his fourteenth year. Both songs are romantically teary. Reasons may be cited for this predilection: the Romantic Age was blooming and expressing itself in verse and fairy tale. Goethe was omnipresent, and Jakob Grimm was only twelve years older than Schubert. As a schoolmaster's son he must have heard and read these things. Then, too, and as already indicated, while he experimented with instrumental music early, he was not a priori an instrumental musician—not at the beginning—and he wanted to produce music he himself could use.

He was one of the very few major composers one can think of who were *not* performers—Beethoven and Mozart, Brahms, Schumann were pianists, Bach and Handel organists, Mendelssohn, Tchaikovsky, Berlioz, Wagner conductors, etc. His lack of interest or his inability in performing professionally did influence his career and circumscribe his fame. He learned to play the violin and the viola well enough, and the piano better than well enough, but on none of these instruments was he a master. When he did play, accompanying his songs or presenting one of his piano compositions, it was chiefly in a home. A concert performer's fame was denied to him—or more probably he denied it to himself.

He began as a boy soprano. The opportunity offered itself when he was just past ten years old. The Imperial-Royal Seminary was an educational institution located near the Vienna University; it was run by the Piarists. The school prepared boys for entrance to the University; it had an active music department, the pupils being given an opportunity of forming a choir. That choir was especially important since it included boys from the Court Chapel of the Palace and even some mature voices. It sang at religious and other ceremonies and once in a while gave a recital in the Seminary itself. The school principal was a Dr. Innocenz Lang, himself an enthusiastic music lover, and the selection of the boys was entrusted to no less a panjandrum than Antonio Salieri, the official Imperial-Royal Court Composer. Schubert was a little over ten years old when there appeared in the *Wiener Zeitung* a notice announcing that positions were open for two boy choristers. Applicants were to present themselves for a competitive examination, bring their school marks with them, have the parent prove that the young candidate not only "has been well instructed in singing" but was "fit to enter the first Latin class . . . as also that he is past the danger of smallpox." (How could anybody prove *that*? Or did it mean that the candidate had had the disease already? Schubert escaped it.) Should the boys selected then "distinguish themselves in morals and studies, they are to remain there; otherwise they are to leave after mutation of the voice" (May 28 and August 3, 1808).

Schubert had been "well instructed" and not only in singing: in his home his father, Ignaz, and Ferdinand sometimes played chamber music and sometimes Franz was given lessons in violin playing. In a memoir Franz Sr. wrote shortly before he died, he remembered those first instructions:

> In his eighth year I taught him the essential first principles of violin playing, and brought him along to the point where he could play easy duets tolerably well. Then I sent him for singing lessons to Herr Michael Holzer, the Liechtental choirmaster, who repeatedly assured me with tears in his eyes that never before had he possessed such a pupil. Said he: "If I wanted to teach him something new—he had already mastered it. Consequently I could not give him any real instruction, but could only talk with the lad and quietly admire him."

Did Michael Holzer, long-time choirmaster and organist, really shed tears over an eight-year-old? Possibly. But however sentimental the father's postfame memoir may be, it is a further indication that Schubert's home was not a place of ignorance.

At any rate, two boys showed themselves as worthiest of becoming early models for the Wiener Sängerknaben: one was Schubert, the other Franz Müllner. A third boy was accepted as well, an alto named Maximilian Weisse, who became a famous astronomer and for whom Schubert wrote one of his earliest compositions, an "overture for pianoforte" (now lost). The appointment of the three boys was confirmed by documents as grave as if the matter concerned a peace treaty, involving memoranda to and from Lang, Salieri, Count Ferdinand Kuefstein, the "Court Music Official," and "His Serene Highness, Prince Ferdinand von Trauttmansdorff-Weinsberg, Supreme Court Chamberlain, Knight of the Golden Fleece." All these paper conferences, all this bigwig fuss—while Napoleon stood outside the door of Vienna!

Franz Schubert, choirboy, got his certificate and his uniform, which consisted of a three-cornered hat, a coat with a small epaulet at the left shoulder, a white cravat, knickerbockers, shoes with ornamental buckles. The boys marched in formation, they sang in formation. In addition, as Lang reported to Kuefstein and Kuefstein reported to Trauttmansdorff, the boys formed a little orchestra, instructed by, among other teachers, a Wenzel Ruzicka, who was the official Court Organist and so dedicated a teacher that, even as the French soldiers were swarming over Vienna and consuming every ounce of flour and butter they could find, he "continued with his usual commendable zeal, even in this troubled half-year [1809], to give special instruction in the various branches of music by means of extra lessons." This although Ruzicka "was under no obligation to work at anything beyond the pianoforte" (memorandum by Kuefstein). Ruzicka conducted the school orchestra, with his "commendable zeal," and Schubert soon played the first violin. Josef von Spaun, who was to become one of Schubert's intimate friends, played the second. Presently, when Ruzicka had to be absent, it was Schubert who conducted. Whether or not Ruzicka did say that "Schubert learned it from God," this teacher was one of those idealists who awaken idealism in a young mind and who perceive talent when talent is as yet hidden behind innocent eyes. Schubert studied music almost to his last days; surely a man like Ruzicka nurtured this curiosity, extending it to the past as well as to the contemporary. Genius helps himself to what is there.

What was there in 1809—in addition to the legacy of Mozart now recognized—was all of Haydn's great work, as well as Beethoven's first six symphonies, the first version of *Fidelio,* the Violin Concerto, all five piano concertos, such sonatas as the *Moonlight,* the *Appassionata,* the *Pathétique,* the *Kreutzer,* the three *Rasoumovsky* Quartets—all not as a "marbled mansion" but in the immediacy of new growth, heady, still disputable and disputed. Musical creativity was there—all around Schubert. But trouble was there as well.

In 1797, the year Schubert was born, Napoleon had scored significant victories over Austria in Italy, and Austria signed a tricky and dishonorable peace treaty with France (at Campo Formio, October 17, 1797). It was only the beginning of trouble. The Corsican ogre would not rest. Two years later war with Austria was resumed; he drove eastward to humble Austria decisively. In 1805, when Schubert was eight and after Napoleon had defeated the Austrian army at Ulm, he invaded Vienna, inviolate for centuries.

The French troops swarming into the city passed the house where the Schuberts were living. The boy must have looked at the blue uniforms with some fright, some curiosity, and small comprehension.

Napoleon ordered the army to treat the Viennese as kindly as possible. One of the Viennese inhabitants, who left a record of what life was like in those days, was a certain Josef Carl Rosenbaum, a cultivated man passionately interested in music, an acquaintance of Haydn's, and mar-

ried to Therese Gassmann, a well-known opera singer. He kept a diary*—
as who did not?

Wednesday, November 13th, 1805: . . . At about 11:30 o'clock, a crowd of
people streamed in at the Burg Thor, all shouting the French are coming! . . . May they soon leave Vienna in just as friendly a way! . . . At the
Mehlmarkt people are almost fighting to the death over a quarter-pound of
flour; there is virtually nothing to be found at the other markets, for no one
brings anything to sell.—

Friday, 15th: St. Leopold's Day: A beautiful day. . . . There is nothing at
the market; yesterday a pound of butter cost from 2 to 3 gulden. —No one
risks bringing anything, since it will be confiscated, and the horses unhar-
nessed and taken. In the villages there have been instances of excesses; they
want inplausibly good service, make many unusual demands, such as coffee
several times a day, poultry, special wines and bread. . . . At about 11 o'clock
mid-day in the Laimgrube, a Frenchman, whose shoes were torn, seized a
journeyman and attempted to take his boots off by force. When he resisted,
the Frenchman slashed him across the mouth with his sabre. Some of our
people came running immediately, disarmed the Frenchman . . . and led him
off to the nearest guard-room. . . . Except for whores, one sees very few
women at the theaters.

Sunday, 17th: . . . Up to now, the town council has had to deliver 50,000
portions of bread, meat, wine, oats, hay, etc. each day. . . . Everyone fears
a famine. —The burden caused by quartering is implausibly heavy.

Wednesday, 20th November: Today, at the Theater an der Wien, there is
the premiere of Beethoven's opera *Fidelio oder eheliche Liebe*, in 3 acts,
loosely based on a French source, by Jos. Sonnleithner. . . . In the evening
I went to the W. Th. to hear Louis Beth's opera. . . . The opera has pretty,
ingenious, difficult music and a tedious libretto of little interest. It had no
success and the theater was empty.

Nevertheless, and characteristically, theater performances continued
during the first occupation. Karoline Pichler, a Viennese writer, described
one of them:

*The Rosenbaum diary, 1770 to 1829, has been excellently edited and elucidated by Elsa
Radant (Vienna, 1968).

We found the galleries full of noisy French soldiers and gaudy uniforms. The curtain had not yet risen, for they were waiting for the Emperor [Napoleon]. After this had gone on for some time, enabling me to contrast it with the punctuality of our kind ruler, who was always careful not to keep the public or officials waiting, about eight o'clock there was suddenly heard a furious drumroll which announced the Emperor's arrival. And again I could not help comparing this unfriendly din to the alarm signals we use for exceptional and tragic happenings such as outbreaks of fire. . . . He went into his box and sat down, a pamphlet in his hand; behind him stood his aides de camp, or something of the sort. So this was the man who had made the earth tremble, the man who shook all the thrones of Europe and had overturned more than one of them. What was he going to do next, this man to whom nothing seemed impossible, in whose hands all our destinies lie?

The "kind ruler" was Francis I, Emperor of Austria. He was an egregious fake. He played the role of "father of his people," close in kindly kinship to the smith and the weaver. He had learned to speak a low Viennese dialect, acted folksy, and suppressed any sign of disgust when he kissed a Viennese child with a running nose. The truth was that he much preferred speaking French and he couldn't have cared less about the fate of the "mob." Whatever emotion he felt, this cold and calculating ruler, was concentrated on the crown. For the sake of preserving it he knuckled under to Napoleon's edicts. He had to resign as the head of the Holy Roman Empire, marking its demise (1806), and, though unwillingly, he bestowed his daughter Marie Louise on Napoleon, who wanted to "copulate with a belly" (Napoleon's words) when Josephine produced no children. He destroyed most of Joseph II's reforms and was supposed to have said, "I don't need university professors—I need loyal subjects." Francis was a coward—but when Napoleon was finally beaten he returned riding a white charger and claimed credit. Haydn had apostrophized him in the fine hymn "Gott erhalte Franz den Kaiser." The people sang the hymn and cheered. Schubert lived his life under Francis's reign. The royal Francis totally ignored the fact that another Franz existed, one who wrote some good music.

Four years later, in 1809, Vienna was once again occupied. This time all pretense of clemency disappeared, because Francis foolishly decreed that the city was to be defended. An insane decision. Francis's brothers Maximilian and Archduke Rudolf pleaded its uselessness, while Francis, his Empress, Maria Ludovica, and his daughter Marie Louise hied themselves hence to safety. Rudolf accompanied them—which gave Beethoven the occasion to compose the Sonata op. 81a, which we know as *Les Adieux*.

Rosenbaum's diary:

Thursday, May 11th, 1809: . . . It was only just quarter past 9 o'clock [in the evening] when the French began . . . the bombardment; there was heavy firing until midnight, then it slackened until 3 o'clock. As dawn began to break, they . . . stopped. Our batteries fired only very little, for they were without effect. . . . The fires that broke out were dreadful to see. . . . The poor city suffered great damage, for no one was prepared, no one conceived of such misfortune. . . . One cannot walk about due to the broken glass. . . . At our house . . . everyone fled to the cellar. . . . I had nothing but my light dressing gown, and consequently froze. . . . With a thousand consolatory arguments . . . I attempted to calm . . . the wailing group. . . . From time to time I went out on the street, onto the Graben to see how far the ravaging flames had advanced and how our house was to be saved. . . . I called everyone together; we carried water . . . and in this way managed to save our house.

Friday, 12th May: . . . Vienna capitulated . . . early in the morning we burned all 3 of the Tabor bridges. —This was an ineffectual act, for we ourselves will only have to build them again. At midday, once the capitulation had been concluded, the white flag was hoisted on the Rotenthurm Bastion . . . then all the artillery and munitions carts . . . all timber . . . all armatures and places of equipment were abandoned.

Saturday, 13th May: The entry of the French during the forenoon. . . . Now we are to pay an additional 20 million [florins]. . . .

On the very night Rosenbaum describes, that of May 11, the building of the Seminary was hit by a howitzer grenade. It was only by luck that the twelfth child was not killed in his twelfth year. The Seminary had been evacuated, classes discontinued, Schubert had gone home. Vienna was now under French jurisdiction.

But schools and seminaries must continue. By the end of October of that year music study had been resumed and the director of the Seminary added to Schubert's second-term report card (which ranged from "good" in Morals to "very good" in Pianoforte) a note reading, "A special musical talent."

3.

1811—Schubert was fourteen years old. A grim year broke over Austria. The state, once prosperous, but now lamed by the burden of the levy Napoleon put upon it (a sum which would be equivalent to almost $200 million in today's purchasing power), staggered and went bankrupt. Austrian currency was drastically devalued by new paper money called Wiener Währung (Viennese currency), worth about one-fifth of the old money. Worse followed: even the "W.W." (which the people called "Weh, Weh!") slid downward as the people and the banks lost faith in government-issued paper. Beethoven's friend Therese Brunsvik wrote in her memoirs: "The man who went to bed in March 1811 with the comfortable feeling of being a capitalist, having provided for his wife and children, got up in the morning as a beggar." She was right. People who owned jewels, silver, antiques, etc., were not so badly off. But those dependent on salaries, the teachers, the government employees, the factory workers, were rubbed raw. More than one family sat on the street in front of the house around a little table on which a plate had been placed, hoping that somebody would drop a few kreuzer in the receptacle. Princes dropped fortunes—and stopped supporting music. Kinsky, Palffy, Lobkowitz—when Schubert grew to manhood they could no longer be the generous patrons that they had been in Beethoven's best days. Some of the candles in some of the palaces were snuffed out.

Yet now, for those ensconced within the Seminary, musical enthusiasm and study continued to function—though the records show that every possible economy was practiced and hungry boys were hungrier than ever. This does not contradict my belief that Schubert did *not* starve. The "hunger" here refers to growing boys who are always hungry, especially in school. Schubert's drive toward expression became stronger. It was an audible heartbeat. He began to compose in earnest, trying his 'prentice hand at several string quartets, overtures to be played by the school orchestra, symphonic fragments, and a song or two. Most of these compositions are lost; one song already mentioned, "Hagar's Lament" ("Hagars Klage"), is extant; he composed it in March 1811, the very month of the devaluation of the currency. The song is sentimental, and one could hardly predict that its author would soon revolutionize the lied, but then predictions about a genius are as unreliable as predictions about the weather. According to Schubert's friend Spaun, it was the Hagar song which drew Antonio Salieri's attention to the youth and decided Salieri to give him lessons. He was too busy to devote time to systematic instruction, but he looked over Schubert's youthful manuscripts and gave him good technical advice, as is indicated by Schubert's writing "Salieri" on several of them; on one (a quartet in D major of 1813) Salieri himself added after his name "Premier Maître de Chapelle de la Cour Imp et Royale de Vienne." It is amusing to note that Beethoven's friend Anton Schindler, that left-handed historian, denied that Salieri functioned as a teacher: ". . . we know for certain that Salieri never gave regular lessons, etc." Schindler was jealous of anybody who touched Beethoven's life; he suppressed the fact that the pianist Moscheles, when he was in Vienna that very year, called on Salieri and found a note on his table which read, "The pupil Beethoven was here."

As to the pupil Schubert, there is no doubt that, formally or informally, Salieri helped. He was a better man than his present reputation. Johann Rochlitz, chief critic of the Leipzig *Allgemeine Musikalische Zeitung*, spoke of him as "friendly, obliging, benevolent, full of the joy of life, witty, inexhaustible in anecdote and quotation"—and, we may add, more than a bit on the conceited side in that resplendent uniform of "Maître de Chapelle." Salieri understood best the music of his compatriots; he loved Italian melody, Monteverdi, Scarlatti, Vivaldi, and, contrary to some reports, he did approve of Mozart. *Don Giovanni* fascinated him, except that it was "too dissonant." Salieri's enthusiasm for Italian dulcet sounds was not lost on Schubert.

Except when he specifically wrote piano compositions Schubert rarely used the piano. His friend and fellow seminarist Albert Stadler wrote that Schubert asserted that a piano merely hampered the freedom of his thoughts. He would sit bent over a little table, scribbling away, his right hand now and then marking an unheard rhythm. Spaun, nine years older than he and well-to-do, supplied him with "reams and reams of music paper," which Schubert accepted with equanimity. A doubtful fact!

Schubert was supposed to have been very nearsighted. He was supposed to have been unable to see anything clearly without his spectacles. These have been preserved in the Vienna Schubert Museum. I took their measurements (minus 3.75 Dioptrin spherically) to New York and submitted them to a well-known ophthalmologist, Dr. Dianne Aronian, New York Hospital, without telling her to whom the glasses belonged. After examining them she indicated "somebody with a slight myopia, nothing more." So the extreme nearsightedness, too, turns out to be myth.

Early he changed from boy to man, at least in his looks; if one compares youthful portraits to later ones, one finds little difference, except that his hair receded a bit and his forehead appears larger. That forehead was the most remarkable feature of his face; above it rose a wilderness of thick, soft, dark hair, of which he was vain, and from which two sideburns descended to the *Vatermörder* collar, forming an oval which framed his countenance in a "touch-me-not" line. More than one of his friends said that with all of Schubert's sociability they could not reach his true self; they never knew what was going on in his head. He wore his glasses constantly whether there was anything to see or not, perhaps because unconsciously they gave him a sense of separation. According to Spaun, he sometimes slept with them on and in the morning, hardly dressed and after only the scantiest of toilets, he went to the table and began composing.

His head, owlish rather than leonine, was supported by a squat body: he was only about five feet tall. The Viennese were not very tall, and Schubert's brother Ferdinand was not much taller than he. Though his appearance was not imposing and he was certainly not handsome in any conventional sense, he had a forceful personality, his determination balancing his modesty—the "timid Schubert" is another myth. His smile charmed, lit by a nimbus of veiled friendliness. He was interested in other people, to an extent which almost contradicts his personal abstraction. People liked him. Except when he was thinking of music—which to be sure was much of the time—he could be pleasantly convivial. He loved to walk, as most Viennese do, he loved to sightsee, and above all he was as enamored of discussion as a French *philosophe.* He would talk about anything and everything, sometimes far into the night, about politics, literature, philosophy, the state of the world—but also about the latest scandals. When music filled him, he resembled Thomas Mann's musician in *Buddenbrooks,* a man whose thought "rested on the far-away . . . that glance of the musician which seems vague and empty because it lingers in a realm of logic which is profounder, purer, freer of dross and more inexorable than anything we can express by spoken concepts and thoughts."

His eyes were blue-gray; his friends said that their color changed with Schubert's mood, being more often gray than blue. His teeth were white and regular (according to the conductor Julius Benedict). He neglected them; in later years he was a passionate pipe smoker and he smelled of tobacco. Yet on the rare occasions when he appeared in the salon of a countess, he did take great care of his toilet. He wore clean linen and polished his hat. He was never plain slovenly. A Viennese usually enjoys being well dressed and Schubert was a real Viennese, speaking Viennese dialect with his cronies, *Hochdeutsch* with the countess.

He was pudgy but not fat, contrary to legend. His nickname 'Schwammerl"—meaning either "little mushroom" or "little sponge"—used by biographers and fiction fabricators, was *not* often used by his friends. It is mentioned in a letter of 1823 in which Anton Doblhoff, later Austrian Minister of Commerce, asks about "our dear Schwämmelein." The nicknames his friends most often bestowed on him were "Butschel" and "Bertel," and of course "Franzl."

Franz kept composing, quite undisturbed by the din of his fellow seminarists, their disputes and their rackety arguments about the food. As Mozart could write his music down while a game of billiards was being played in the same room, so could Schubert compose amid a school's clatter.

Yet with all his enthusiasm for music he was able to master other subjects taught in the Seminary, a testimony to the flexibility of his mind. His report cards showed straight "ones" in Morals (meaning behavior), Application, Religion, Latin Language and Style, Geography and History, and Greek. "One" was the second-highest mark, the highest being "EM," meaning "eminent." Only in Mathematics did he sink to a "two." So good a record would fit him into the family profession. So his father thought.

Not so the son. Even as a teenager, singing in his soprano voice the sacred and the patriotic songs of his day, he knew what he wanted. He wanted to become a composer.

One may hazard the guess that Schubert would have become a composer had he been born in Paris or Moscow or in the Oberpfalz. He is called a Viennese composer. Yet what does that mean? Every artist of every art shows some national influence, some expression of his mother tongue. Yet to call Schubert Viennese is to overemphasize one aspect and to limit another. It conjures up a false idea of three-quarter time; though he produced many waltzes, he produced no "Blue Danube." His major works walk freely over national boundaries and characteristics and are not Viennese, just as *Madame Bovary* is not exclusively French, its precise ambience of French provincialism notwithstanding, or *Sense and Sensibility* is not confined to a parson's England. Like most great music, Schubert's adheres to no flag.

Musical talent seems to occur in clusters like grapes, nobody knows why. Between Schubert's birth and his teens were born Donizetti, Lortzing, Berlioz, Glinka, the elder Strauss, Mendelssohn, Chopin, Nicolai, Schumann, Liszt, Wagner, Flotow, Verdi. Italian, German, French, Russian, Hungarian—none, except Strauss, Viennese.

Still, Schubert's birthplace was the city in which music played a vital role. What was the savor of this city, what were the attributes of its people, which left so strong an impress?

2

Vienna, "City of Dreams"

IN MOMENTS OF PRIDE THE VIENNESE CALLED THEIR CITY "THE MOTHER of genius." The truth was that the outpost on the Danube, a crucible of German, Hungarian, Italian, Czech, and Oriental elements, was less a mother than a seductress, less a Cornelia than a Messalina, more a Lorelei than a Griselda. She attracted men and women of artistic bent because as a city she herself seemed a work of fiction in which the necessity of earning one's living—quite as hard and humdrum there as anywhere else—was overlaid by fairy tales. The frog of an underpaid bureaucrat turned into a prince, the plain Jane became a beauty at midnight. It didn't happen, but the Viennese dreamed that it could happen. Their favorite two-word sigh was "If only—," and they were forever lighting a flame of wish-fulfillment under the pot of everyday; they were forever making believe. It was a theater town, in and out of the theater; if a Viennese was a failure, it was not his fault but bad luck. He had chosen the wrong profession, he knew the wrong people. "If only—." He looked for the amaranthine flower or, unable to find the fabled blossom, he at least looked for the four-leaf clover. "Are all the people who come to Vienna bewitched so that they have to stay here? It rather looks like it," wrote Mozart's father.

Vienna claimed to be the city of music. True, to an extent. Young girls from "good families" were expected to be able to sight-read and play the pianoforte. Soulfully! In quite a few homes chamber music was played, if not well then enthusiastically. Beethoven's greatness was recognized. But Haydn had to go to London to become really appreciated, Mozart though famous was woefully underpaid, Bach was practically unknown, and Handel, familiar to few, was considered less consequential than Salieri. As against one *Zauberflöte* there were ten Schikaneder farces which filled his theaters and threw snickering jokes and raunchy ditties at pleased audiences. Rasoumovsky and a dozen friends liked the *Rasoumovsky* Quartets. But how many others could have heard them, or having heard them cared a florin about them? One must subtract something from the propaganda that "every" Viennese loved great music.

Still, music was the art which evoked a particular response in Vienna's mind and heart; one could be bemused by it, laugh at Rossini's capers, be inspired by the organ at St. Stephen's Cathedral, the tones of which were so powerful that one could feel them graze one's skin; and best of all one could sing, sing a varied repertoire of longing and love, sing in praise of the city when one had drunk rather too much of the new wine. "Wien, Wien, nur du allein / Wirst stets die Stadt meiner Träume sein. . . ."

No sooner was Mozart dead (on December 5, 1791) than a Count Joseph Deym appeared at the house, took his death mask in wax, and asked Constanze for one of her husband's suits. This Count Deym—a shady character*—owned a "Gallery of Statues," something like Madame Tussaud's, which displayed reproductions of the Belvedere Apollo and the Medici Venus, as well as famous personages of history, from Alexander the Great to Josef II. Now Mozart "in the habit as he lived" joined the celebrities. One could view the effigy while a mechanical contrivance played a solemn strain which Mozart had composed for a curious instrument, the *Orgelwalze*. So Mozart *was* a celebrity, worthy of representation in a gallery which the Viennese paid to visit. Yet *Figaro* and *Don Giovanni* were better appreciated by the audiences of Prague, those "provincials."

What happened to Mozart was to happen to Schubert. There is a pattern here: Vienna has derogated or chased away more than one of her talented men, from Schubert to Mahler to Karajan, from Freud to Wittgenstein to Schiele, as well as the physicians who at one period made Vienna the "Mecca of Medicine," from Rokitansky to Semmelweis to Tandler to Lorenz, only to name streets after them once they were safely dead.

Vienna was a city of gaiety. Was it? When the sun went down, "ev-

---

*Pretending to be wealthy, he wooed and married Countess Josephine Brunsvik, with whom Beethoven had been in love. Deym expected a substantial dowry; he didn't get it. The marriage proved unhappy.

erybody" stopped walking and started dancing. Did everybody? This reputation, which Schiller made famous, speaking of Vienna as "the land of the Phaeacians" (referring to the blessed island Ulysses visits) and observing that here "Sunday is perpetual," this definition wreathed in smiles, needs correction. It is a one-seventh view, a *Fledermaus* view. Of course a Viennese could be gay and waltz on a Sunday evening and crack jokes—here the overused word *gemütlich* enters on cue—provided that times were beneficent. But times were rarely beneficent. And a closer look reveals that the temperament of a Viennese is fundamentally inclined to resignation and melancholy. The superficial bonhomie should not fool us; soon the dark strain rises to the surface. The wit he uses covers his melancholy: it is supercilious, can be both charming and caustic, and is spoken with a shrug of his shoulders, exuding a "What's the use?" He luxuriates in resignation as if it were a warm bath. He belittles his own ability. Loudly. But let a friend agree, if only cautiously, and he explodes.

There are historic reasons for such insecurity: life was hardly ever "safe," being menaced by the Bohemian King Ottokar in the thirteenth century, by repeated onslaughts of the Turks—Vienna being the gateway to the Western world—by marauding Hungarian hordes, by Frederick the Great in the eighteenth century. And in the early nineteenth came Napoleon.

Vienna's great writer of comedies, Ferdinand Raimund, a contemporary of Schubert's, is marked "by a deepseated melancholy beneath his wit" (W. E. Delp, *The Oxford Companion to the Theater*). Franz Grillparzer, Austria's national poet, another contemporary of Schubert's, wrote:

> What is earthly fortune?
> A shadow!
> What is earthly fame?
> A dream!*

Near the end of the Austro-Hungarian Empire, Rainer Maria Rilke wrote: "Who speaks of victory? To survive is everything." Dusk, parting, death, the transitoriness of friendship, the fleetness of love, the seduction of a mood, the vanity of struggle—these November themes pervaded Viennese poetry.

---

*Was ist der Erde Glück?
 Ein Schatten!
 Was ist der Erde Ruhm?
 Ein Traum!

What does one do? One complains. A Viennese *raunzt*, to use a favorite slang word: he bitches. Nothing and nobody is right, not the director of the Royal Imperial Opera, not the cobbler who tries to make the pair of shoes last longer, not the official who squints at the petition and pronounces "Impossible!" Every Viennese knew that "Impossible" was only the first answer in a delaying tactic. The petitioner kept trying and usually got what he needed. If he could ascertain what the official's hobby was— anything from philately to lepidoptery—and could discuss it with him, he could be twisted around. Bribery wouldn't do it: Viennese functionaries were remarkably honest.

In short, life being full of holes, one walks around the holes. One "arranges" oneself. The straightforward way rarely appeals to the Viennese mentality. One has to have "connections." If one wants a job, one does not simply ask for it, one tries to find somebody who knows somebody who knows somebody who is a cousin of the boss.

If you were a merchant, you strove to obtain the *Kaiserlich-Königlich* stamp: the nod from the "Imperial-Royal" House of Hapsburg was all-important. *All* titles were helpful, even if you were a barber. (You could become a *K.-K. Ober-Friseur.*) The government employee slowly climbed a ladder where his title became ever more polysyllabic. Hardly any physician was just a plain "Dr.": he was a *Dozent,* a *Professor,* a *Medizinalrat.* Even if you were a musician, a connection with the K.-K. helped your career. Salieri made it in full panoply. Mozart made it late and was given the distinction only as a sop. Alas, Schubert tried and was found wanting. In a restaurant you never called for just "the waiter": you addressed the lowest waiter as "Herr Ober." Except the busboy, who was called "Piccolo." If the man talking to you knew your position, he automatically promoted you to the one above that to which you were entitled. A vice-president was addressed as "Mr. President." If you hired a *Fiaker* (a cab with two horses), the driver looked you over; if you were poorly dressed, he called you "Herr Doktor," if you were decently turned out you were "Herr Baron," and if your sartorial opulence was evident, he called you "Herr Graf" or even "Your Excellency."

Conversation, even with good friends, was as liberally dotted with polite phrases as a good rice pudding is with raisins. Schubert's letters and those of his friends are spiked with courteous formulas. Any woman above a charwoman was greeted with "I kiss your hand, gracious lady," and this was followed by a peck on the hand. Pious people kissed the hand of the priest, children the hands of their parents, a girl the hand of a married lady. When two people met on the street, they burst forth in a torrent of questions, asking each other the state of "your precious health" and that of "your highly honored gracious lady." The questioning gave you time to try and remember who for God's sake it was you were talking to.

Yet, and in spite of the time wasted in politeness or in daydreaming, Vienna's men worked hard and long. When Schubert was a child, the workday began at 5 A.M. and lasted till 7 or 8 P.M., including Saturdays. When Schubert grew up the workday was shortened by an hour. (Child-labor laws did not exist.) Enthusiasm for what they were doing prevailed as an exception rather than as a rule. The historian Otto Friedländer wrote: "A Viennese lives for his leisure occupation. That is the true goal of his life. . . . The relationship in which men stand to their work is one of lukewarm convenience—not one of passion." Artists, however, proved an exception; they possessed the passion. The big topic among bourgeois employees was, "Where shall we go for our vacation?"

Careers were interrupted by compulsory military service, usually lasting two years. Many young men loved it, both because the uniform attracted girls and because the discipline obviated the need for thinking. More hated it; one of the advantages of being a teacher was that you could be excused from serving. Government functionaries went from house to house examining the men. A document is extant about Schubert, showing that he was excused because he was not tall enough.

2.

As was true of Paris or London, Vienna society was a layered structure, with the difference that the top layer was very thin—and very snobbish. (Well, perhaps all so-called aristocratic societies are snobbish.) Lobkowitz, Palffy, Kinsky, Schwarzenberg—as great a difference lay between such names and those of recent nobility as between an antique commode and a modern reproduction. No more than two hundred families in the entire Empire could claim to belong to *die Adeligen,* "the noble ones" of long lineage, whose males paraded in shining uniforms designed by themselves, or slouched in torn hunting clothes and mud-stained boots, while their women would either spend a fortune on jewels and Paris gowns or roam the palace in a dress their maid would disdain to put on. In the eighteenth century these *Adeligen* would build palaces, for their own and Vienna's glory. Prince Eugene of Savoy, the dour, bellicose Italian bred at Versailles who never mastered the German language, commissioned Johann Lucas von Hildebrandt to design two palaces for his summer retreat. They were connected by a sloping garden, laid out in the French style. On top of the hill stands today this dazzling abode, the Upper Belvedere, crowned by the kind of white statuary that seems to communicate with the sky. The palace was used for great festivals and functions and resembles Blenheim Castle, the palace of the Duke of Marlborough. Below he built an outwardly plain house, its interior offering a fabulous voyage through endless rooms, paintings on the ceilings, marble supporting the carved doors, gold everywhere. That is the Lower Belvedere and Eugene lived there.* During the winter he resided in the inner city at another masterpiece of a palace, a collaboration of Fischer von Erlach and Hildebrandt, the entrance of which showed Aeneas rescuing his father (right) and one of the labors of Hercules (left). It is now the Ministry of Finance, but it is still one of Vienna's most beautiful buildings.

Prince Franz Joseph Lobkowitz, Knight of the Golden Fleece, built his four-square palace in the very center of the city and asked the superb sculptor and architect Fischer von Erlach (a pupil of Bernini's) to design its portal. On the roof baroque statues remind the sightseer of the Bernini tradition. Yet one cannot look at the Lobkowitz Palace without thinking of Beethoven and all it meant to him: there the Fourth Symphony was first performed. Fischer von Erlach was responsible as well for the design of the Karlskirche, St. Charles's Church, with its two ostentatious columns and the huge dome, covered with a patina which diffuses a bright green light on sunny days.

The palace of Ferdinand Prince Kinsky of Wchinitz and Tettau was a work of Hildebrandt; it faced the "Scottish Church." (Falsely named, being administered by Irish monks. The church served as an asylum for fugitives; once you reached it you couldn't be arrested.) Kinsky's widow, Charlotte, was the hostess of an evening when Schubert accompanied a singer who sang his songs; all the guests praised the songs and the singer, nobody noticed the accompanist. (Spaun's *Reminiscences,* though he gives no date for the evening. He reported Schubert as saying that he didn't

---

*The Upper Belvedere is now Vienna's Museum of Modern Art, the Lower Belvedere a museum for medieval art, while the garden is kept in pristine condition. Bernardo Bellotto painted the garden with its splendid view of Vienna.

mind; indeed he "quite liked it, he felt less embarrassed." A doubtful anecdote.)

One of Vienna's most fascinating houses was (and is) the Pallavicini Palace, which faces the Imperial Library and the statue of Joseph II. Four female figures, a work of the sculptor Anton Zauner, guard the entrance. In the courtyard the eldest tree of Austria, an acacia tree, still blooms. The palace belonged originally to Moritz Reichgraf Fries. He and his wife were such beautiful people that two painters, Vigée-Lebrun and Gérard, painted them. The house contained a private theater, on the curtain of which were inscribed the words *Gayeté et Indulgence,* a definition of aristocratic Vienna. Schubert dedicated his Op. 2, the heartbreaking song "Gretchen am Spinnrade" (Goethe), to Fries. Fries lost his fortune and died poor and forsaken in 1823 in Switzerland. The house was bought by Marquis Alphons Pallavicini.

The Lobkowitzes and the Kinskys hardly nodded to the men whose patents of nobility denoted that they had earned them themselves and fairly recently, by deeds beneficial to the Court, or money spent for a public cause, or by a bit of adroit bribery. Hofmannsthal limns the distinction in *Der Rosenkavalier:* Octavian Rofrano and the Marschallin belong to the true aristocracy; von Faninal is a parvenu, "von" or not; Ochs, though a nobleman, is a "provincial."

In these palaces the new music was heard and supported—as long as the owner's money remained plentiful. The Faninals, grown rich, were less interested in music than in display of themselves in ostentatious abodes, filled with silver-buttoned servants. The families of these servants lived where most of the poor people lived, in pressed-together habitations of the inner city, in rooms which were documents in humility.

Vienna had a population of 230,000 in the war years when Schubert was a boy, rising to 290,000 in 1825, when Schubert was twenty-eight. As many as 5,000 held government jobs, state, county, and municipal. Industry developed more slowly in Austria than in other European countries: glasses were still hand blown, chairs carved one by one, wool spun at home.

The city was fortified, a semicircle bounded on one end by the Danube Canal, an artificially regulated branch of the river, the Danube itself flowing outside Vienna proper. The Danube seemed far away* and excursions were organized to bathe and picnic there. In spring, swollen by

*Actually about six miles from St. Stephen's, as the crow flies. But it seems farther.

Alpine thaws and overflowing its banks, it could prove dangerous, but most of the time it was a placid stream, now silvery, now gray, now green, never blue. The city was protected by a wall, whose Bastion and a moat called Glacis were local landmarks. Bastion and the broad and pleasant Glacis were where the Viennese loved to stroll; they were built in the Middle Ages, a bulwark of Christendom against the Ottoman Empire. Joseph II had planted trees on the Glacis and furnished them with lanterns. In good weather Schubert often used them as places under which to sit and cogitate. The wall embraced the city—but also hampered its expansion. Later a second wall was built to enclose the outlying districts; they called it the "Line Wall." Napoleon ordered the destruction of the inner wall—located where today the famous Ringstrasse executes its tree-shaded sweep—and the Viennese wept, while secretly determining to rebuild it as soon as they could get rid of the monster. They did not rebuild—fortunately—but a remnant can still be seen facing the University, where stands the home which once belonged to Baron Pasqualati, friend of Beethoven. Ludwig lived there relatively often in his unstable moves around Vienna.

The great houses shone with hundreds of candles, while the little houses were as poorly lit as they were in any big city, perhaps more so. Streets were unpaved and narrow. The dust, agitated by traffic and thickened by the process of chipping at the wall, permeated the ground floors and the courtyards. There stood the walls from which you fetched your water, pumping and heaving, the water often emerging brown. One breathed in dust, one drank it—and one sneezed and coughed. Outhouses were communal in buildings where as many as thirty families lived. Most poor families made do with two rooms: a fair-sized kitchen which served as the living room, and a bedroom where father, mother, and all the children slept and where they could gaze at a little print of the Madonna, illuminated by a tiny red taper which was never allowed to be extinguished. The odor of life enveloped everything; a smell of cooking, of the dung of horses, of mortar, of urine, of wash drying on a line mixed with the incense of the churches. In winter the smells were inescapable, carried by the wind which blew almost continuously down from the surrounding mountains.

As soon as the snow melted, Vienna took to the streets. The children played ball and hide-and-seek and they bothered the customs officials who, clad in white uniforms and smoking long white clay pipes, sat by the eleven portals which led from the Bastion to the suburbs. The soldiers chased them, they sneaked back; it was more or less a good-natured game. Peddlers wandered through the city, crying out their wares: you met the "pretzelman" who supplied fresh *Kipfel* (the croissant in the shape of the Turkish flag, which according to legend was invented by a Viennese baker to celebrate the victory over the Turks), *Beigln* (bagels), and *Brezen* (pretzels). You could buy from the *Bandlkrämer* (ribbon-hawker), the *Lavenderweib* (lavender girl), the *Lorbeermänner* (laurel-men), *Teekräutler* (tea herbists), or a *Krapfelweib* (doughnut woman). If on a hot day you were thirsty, you could find relief at a "lemon hut," which dispensed not only lemonade but oversweet, unhygienic ices. On cold days you burned wood in plump iron stoves; only the well-to-do could afford the handsome tile stoves. Chimneys had to be cleaned frequently. If you met a chimney sweep on the street, it meant you were going to be lucky.

If you needed an errand done in a hurry, you called to a "runner" (*Schnelläufer*), who was clad in a long sweater hung with little bells. A blind organ-grinder sang a ditty dealing with the latest murder, while an old woman with him offered little pictures of the affair for sale. A weary knife-grinder pushed from house to house, chanting "Knife sharp" in a high voice. The laborers sang at their work, as did the merchants when business was slow and they stood in front of their tiny shops. When their lady customers did appear, they always came in pairs; it was not respectable for a woman to shop alone. The popular songs Schubert heard dealt with the usual subjects, usually in the Viennese dialect, such as "Let's go, you brave masons . . . spring is here," or "My loved one, come to the window," or again the melancholy "If I have to leave my Vienna. . . ."

The men who had a bit of change to spare met in the coffeehouses, where they would linger for hours over "a small black" coffee, get a free glass of water, and could read such newspapers as were passed by the censor. Bachelors had their breakfast there: rolls and coffee, each roll charged separately. The Vienna *Kaffeehäuser* were unique institutions, unlike those of London: they served as warm, smoke-filled refuges for husbands who wanted to get away from their wives and children or indulge in a little game of cards. In Schubert's time, nearly a hundred coffeehouses flourished and each had its particular clientele. The Kaffee Daum, for example, was a meeting place of the military, the Kaffee Kramer attracted the literati; others were favored by delegates, or minor functionaries, or bricklayers, or students who studied there to save the expense of heating. Business deals were discussed in loud voices, politics in whispers. The waiter knew and retailed the latest gossip. You tipped him. When you got ready to leave you called for the "pay-waiter" (*Zahlkellner*); you told him what you had consumed and you tipped *him*.* In Vienna you tipped everybody, the letter carrier, the chimney sweep, the coachman, and, if you were invited to a meal, the serving maid.

As soon as a man earned enough money, he tried to move himself and his family into one of the suburbs. There you drew a freer breath, or imagined you did. Immediately beyond the wall and connected with the inner city by portals lay a series of parishes, each an entity with its own church, its own school, and its own tradition. By and large the inhabitants of the suburbs lived a bit more comfortably than those in the city, since houses and flats were roomier and often a tiny garden could be brought to life behind the house. The *Vororte*—thirty-four of them, comprising some 7,000 houses—acted as intermediaries between the overstuffed city and the free country. Sometimes the country squeezed tempting wedges between the street and alleys, a tree here, a path of meadow there. Though during Schubert's life a few omnibuses began to form a link to the city, most men still went to work on foot; the distances were not all that great.

Bureaucracy was active in the suburbs as well, many of them having their own mayor, complete with dignity, beard, and a quasi-gold chain. But the central member of the community was the old priest, white haired and rosy cheeked. Everybody knew him and he knew everybody's problems. When he took his walk, his head covered by an old cylinder, his black cassock strewn with tobacco crumbs since he was still taking snuff, the janitor standing before the door took the pipe out of his mouth, the housewife out marketing bowed, and both asked after the health of "Your Dignified Highness." He gave the children little colored pictures of the saints and offered lozenges to the women. His day began at five o'clock in the morning and ended late at night, and he worried about everything in and outside of the church, the orphan asylum, the organ music, the funeral arrangements, the goings-on at the inn, the unwed girls, the fullness of the collection box. He was supervised by a bishop who reported to a delegate responsible to Rome. Austria at a certain period was virtually though unofficially a possession of the Vatican. The church

---

*A few of these coffeehouses are still in business, such as the famous Mozart Kaffee, but most have been replaced by espresso bars.

delivered value for value received, with masses, processions, and festivities.

Three suburban theaters catered to the thirst for amusement: one, fairly new, the Theater an der Wien (the Wien is a small tributary of the Danube), was built by Schikaneder; the Leopoldstadt Theater; the Josefstadt Theater. All three performed spoken plays, mostly comedies, and farces with music. They were smaller and more vulgar versions of the two court theaters in the city, one near the imperial residence (Hofburg), the Burgtheater, which cultivated classic plays and where an exemplary German was spoken, and the Kärntnertor Theater, an opera house in which ten Italian operas were given to one native product. Most people, suburban or city dwellers, could afford an evening at these theaters only infrequently. Prices of admission were high, and afterward one had to trudge home through unlighted streets.

Life in Vienna, then, was no bed of roses. Could that not be said of most cities? But Vienna's health record was worse than most, typhoid and tuberculosis being endemic diseases. The weather was not of much help: very cold in the winter, very hot in the summer, and always the wind, often of menacing force.

And yet—

Why was it that its people loved the city so ardently that being away from it was tantamount to banishment? Why was it that Vienna—"it alone"—remained "the city of my dreams"? Why was it that neither Mozart nor Beethoven nor Schubert thought of leaving it, though Prague was mad about Mozart, and London offered Beethoven lucrative terms if he would but deign to settle there? Schubert was honored by Graz and had influential well-wishers in that charming city. But as to moving there? Not to be considered.

Two factors, one psychological, the other geographical, explain a love which often stretched to absurdity. That love is still true today. A Viennese—let's call him Franzl because that is a popular Viennese name—is a member of a private society, a club, a clan, as surely as are Freemasons or Rosicrucians. The rules are unwritten, but they are there, forming a union which holds them all. Only another Viennese can understand the mixture of nonchalance and darkness which travels up and down Franzl's bloodstream. If he is successful he may yet be gloomy, if he is a failure he may yet be jocund. Hence the popular Viennese saying: "The situation is tragic, but not serious." Hence the Viennese language, a dialect which few outsiders can unravel and which states everything in a mocking diminutive. Hence the sniggering satire which is leveled at foreigners, the French, the Germans, and the Jews, whom they consider strangers however long they have lived in Vienna and whom they secretly envy for their forward-going, optimistic attitudes. Aren't they all part of life's joke? Only one fact is serious: Vienna is the place to live. Five miles away "the province" begins, and Franzl can lay a kilo of contempt into the word "provincial." In the provinces one starves—mentally and (at least in the belief of nine out of ten Viennese) literally.

Food is an all-important concern to Franzl. How he loves to eat! And how good Viennese cooking is! There are no fewer than thirty-two varieties of boiled beef (*Tafelspitz*) available, served with a creamy chive sauce or applesauce laced with horseradish. Schnitzel and a special fried chicken (*Backhend'l*) are other favorites. Meals usually end with a warm rich dessert. Here variety is triumphant, including such creations as *Palatschinken* (crepes), *Kaiserschmarrn* ("the Emperor's trifle"—broken-up crepes), *Marillenknödel* (dumplings stuffed with apricots), and various forms of strudel—apple, poppy seed, cheese, etc. A special round yeast cake, the *Gugelhupf,* is the heraldic emblem of Viennese gourmandizing.

Franzl's wife (or the maid she hires) has to be a first-class cook. Lunch, the day's main meal, has to be ready at noon precisely: it and the opera performance are the only events which start on time. Viennese housewives often had to serve five meals a day: coffee for breakfast; a ten-o'clock "fork breakfast" (*Gabelfrühstück*); *Mittagessen*; *Jause*—a five-o'clock tea, but it was coffee and pastry, not tea; finally a light supper. The rolls baked in the morning would not do for supper. No, they were not fresh enough: Franzl had to have the 2 P.M. batch. If the food does not please Franzl, he is capable of tearing the tablecloth off the table and breaking the dishes.

Today Viennese life has become simpler, the young people resembling American or British youngsters. In Schubert's day the Viennese loved to dress up, but even today our imagined Franzl is more formally attired when he goes to the opera than is either Frank or François, his predecessors of the 1820s, when all but the poorest wore the stovepipe hat and a high stiff collar which was called a "father killer" (*Vatermörder*). If he could afford it, he sported fancy embroidered waistcoats. They were expensive; the girls admired them. Before he got married Franzl had a liaison with "a sweet young thing" (*ein süsses Mäd'l*), but it was understood by both that the union was not to be permanent. When he did get married he usually—not always, but usually—remained faithful to his wife. She was always subordinate to her husband. He embodied for her the wisdom of the world, especially in political matters, of which she understood little and for which she cared less. On the other hand, she advised him on artistic matters, especially on what was good in the theater. Franzl preferred women who were *mollert,* soft, blond, and not too thin. As such women grew older, they sometimes became dictatorial to the help, giving them inferior food, and locking up everything with a big bunch of keys which they carried at the waist.

One of the main reasons for Vienna's magic was the ease with which you could get away. City and country stood in amicable proximity. A little effort and the dust was behind you. The leaves began to rustle, the lights brightened. Schubert and his friends could walk, and did. The country, beautiful, beneficent, verdant, was always near, reminders of its presence being wafted into the center of the city by the wind on balmy days. In the suburbs you had as it were just to stick your nose out of your window to feel a neighbor to nature. In the city you had just to look around to see the hills beckoning, gentle giants which stood guard in a green haze, here the Kahlenberg, there the Leopoldsberg. The city was cradled in a basket, the rim of which consisted of leaf and blossom. The rain in the spring fell with clear soft water, and after that all the surroundings looked clear and soft and seemed stage-managed for a holiday.

The Vienna Woods were the public parks, open to poor and rich and without fences. They were alive with the sound of thrushes and quails, full of surprises offered by glimpses of rabbits, foxes, and deer, playful with changes of sunlight and the deep shadows created by the tall pines huddled together. The ground was as pliant to your steps as a Persian carpet. Daisies, violets, gentian, bluebells, anemones grew in such profusion that everybody could, and did, take a little bouquet home. Walking was the sport of the Viennese; virtually the entire population was out in the woods on Sundays, yet there was no crowding. One could always find the hidden spot alongside a noisy brook and eat black bread and pale cheese. This countryside in which one constantly ascended or descended was never dull, yet never spectacular. It was a place for dawdling and lolling, for strolling and sauntering, equally accommodating when one raised one's glance to exchange a message with a cloud as when one bent down to find a hidden mushroom. Save that here and there a little inn could be found—what would Vienna do without a handy place for refreshment?—the woods seemed untouched; yet something about them denoted tameness. Nature seemed to be expressly arranged for the utilitarian purpose of serving a city. Whoever put the woods there knew what he was doing: for the sake of such succor the Viennese could endure Monday to Saturday. Near and far one could reach little settlements, quite countrified, and melodiously named, such as Dornbach or Neuwaldegg or Cobenzl or "Am Himmel" or Nussdorf, which Beethoven liked so much. Invariably a glass of inexpensive wine was waiting.

Vienna's great men perfected their thoughts outdoors. Schubert, later Mahler and Freud, Wittgenstein and Otto Wagner, Klimt and Kokoschka walked, and not only on Sundays. It really didn't matter where they walked—the daisies were everywhere.

This is no longer true, since Vienna has expanded, become an industrial city; automobile roads have cut through the Vienna Woods. The birds have fled, the flowers become scarce. Yet even today this "City of Dreams" conjures up a romantic aura. "Ah, Vienna, how charming it is!" exclaims the tourist, having eaten an excellent schnitzel, observing only the city's bright aspect and knowing nothing of its struggles, its streaks of cruelty, its political cowardice. Vienna did not always remain the same. It rose to periods of greatness and sank to periods of atrophy and decadence.

During Schubert's time it experienced a new direction, during which political power, previously held by emperor, church, and aristocracy, gradually began to shift toward the new bourgeoisie, eager to make money, less sure of itself—and less interested in music. These changes were not drastic—not at least until the great revolution of 1848, which Schubert was not to witness—yet a reshuffle of the trump cards was being prepared. Schubert's fate was adversely influenced by these changes.

One quality remained unchanged, the fixation of the Viennese on Vienna. As Hofmannsthal was to write, many years later: it is a "city easier to love or to hate than to understand—or to leave" ("Stadt, die eher zu lieben und zu hassen, als zu begreifen und zu verlassen ist").

3

The First Masterpieces

WE HAVE PLENTY OF EVIDENCE THAT SCHUBERT WAS A GOOD BOY IN the Seminary. A *very* good boy, as the Professor of Grammar, the Teacher of Religion, the Professor of Geography and History noted. Ignaz Mosel, Director of the Seminary, sent a memorandum to his immediate superior, Ferdinand Count von Kuefstein, detailing the progress, or lack of it, of the various pupils. Kuefstein in turn "had the honor of forwarding, according to regulations," this memorandum to Prince Trauttmansdorff. The memorandum was then interred in the government files. That is where most of the elaborately calligraphed missives expired; they dealt with a stream of picayune matters which could have been decided by a word or two if anybody had been willing to make a decision or assume responsibility. But it was easier to forward, file upstairs, and forget. Nothing was thrown into the wastepaper basket. Never: thus we are able to read that Schubert's talents were recognized early. Referring, as an example, to Mosel's report—he suggested that

> . . . Hellmesberger is to be given an emphatic rebuke in the name of the Lord High Steward's Office for insufficient application to his studies; to Franz Schubert, on the other hand, an expression of the satisfaction felt here with the excellent progress he has shown in all subjects . . . [September 28, 1811; DQ].

Why didn't Mosel himself do this? That would have been contrary to regulations.

Regulations forbade the Seminary boys to take part in public concerts. An exception was made for a celebration on December 18, 1811, honoring the memory of Heinrich von Collin, the poet, for whose play *Coriolan* Beethoven had written an overture, and to raise money for a Collin monument. Schubert sang, and we may be allowed to imagine that he sang with all the fervor of his fourteen years, and that the occasion, held in the large hall of the University, which allied music with poetry, spurred his desire to make music his life's content.

His life and progress in the Seminary, then, where he remained until he reached sixteen, are well documented. We are on less-certain ground when we try to describe his turning from boy to young man, from a prescribed and regulated course to the necessity of making decisions. Here—that is, from about 1812 on—we meet conflicting stories; we find it difficult to separate fact from rumor.

Rumor "blown by surmises, jealousies, conjectures" takes over and relates that no sooner had Father Franz learned that his son was thinking of devoting himself to music as a career—and evidently without becoming a virtuoso—than he waxed incensed and cried the traditional "How are you going to earn a living?" A row ensued, Franz Jr. was banished from the parental home, father and son did not speak; only after his mother died at the end of May 1812 was the rupture repaired and was he allowed to return to shed a tear over Elisabeth's grave and be embraced once more by a father softened by sadness.

A touching tale—but what evidence is there that it is true? None which will stand biographical scrutiny. The story does not fit the character of Father Franz, who, however prosaic he may have been and however practical-minded, was not a tyrant. Franz Jr. was never close to his father, never shared his father's attitude of trust-in-God-and-obey-the-Emperor, but neither he nor his intellectual brother Ferdinand mocked the old man; brother Ignaz a little more so, with more reason. The relationship of the sons to the father was not that of a warm and smiling intimacy, but it was respectful. It accepted—Schubert accepted—the nineteenth-century view of the father as the paterfamilias. Had a quarrel or a banishment occurred, young Schubert or later Ferdinand, who wrote reminiscences of his brother, would certainly have mentioned it. Here is rumor at work, the story being based chiefly on one biographer's (Walter Dahms) interpretation of a sentimental effusion Schubert wrote more than ten years later and which he called "My Dream." These are some excerpts from it, as given by Deutsch and translated by Eric Blom:

I was the brother of many brothers and sisters. Our father and mother were good people. I was deeply and lovingly devoted to them all. Once my father took us to a feast. There my brothers became very merry. I, however, was sad. Then my father approached me and bade me enjoy the delicious dishes. But I could not, whereupon my father, becoming angry, banished me from his sight. I turned my footsteps and, my heart full of infinite love for those who disdained it, I wandered into far-off regions. For long years I felt torn between the greatest grief and the greatest love. And so the news of my mother's death reached me. I hastened to see her, and my father, mellowed by sorrow, did not hinder my entrance. Then I saw her corpse. Tears flowed from my eyes. . . .

Then my father once more took me to his favourite garden. He asked whether I liked it. But the garden wholly repelled me, and I dared not say so. Then reddening, he asked me a second time: did the garden please me? I denied it, trembling. At that my father struck me, and I fled. And I turned away a second time, and with a heart filled with endless love for those who scorned me, I again wandered far away. For many and many a year I sang songs. Whenever I attempted to sing of love, it turned to pain. And again, when I tried to sing of pain, it turned to love.

Thus were love and pain divided in me [DQ].

Whatever psychoanalytical interpretation one wishes to apply to this soliloquy—I think it is a fruitless task to place a dead man on the couch— it is certain that the style of "My Dream" is a copy of the romantic style which was blossoming in every poetic nook and cranny. It is close to the style of Novalis in *Hymns to the Night*. He was a romantic German poet who created the mystic "blue flower," the flower none could pluck, which became a symbol of the romantic movement. Schubert had read Novalis, admired him, and set several of his hymns to music. As Deutsch pointed out, Schubert's "Dream" reads like a "figment," a piece of imitative literature naively written, and "the description of his father's school first as a place of revelry and then as a pleasure garden carries no conviction." Yet it furnished Dahms and posterity with a do-not-darken-my-door-again episode, a surmise which hardened into fact, a scene of an out-and-out break in the relationship between father and son. No such scene is traceable. Father and son remained father and son—and strangers.

The fact is that the year 1812, when young Schubert was practically finished with his singing at the Seminary, carried its own special threat. Metternich, now in ascendancy, had reported to Emperor Francis on

December 28, 1811, that "the moment had arrived, long envisaged by Napoleon, which makes the last battle unavoidable, the battle of the old order against his plans of topsy-turvy-dom." That battle, Metternich knew, was to be fought against Russia, and he believed that Napoleon would conquer Russia. If he did, Austria's position would be desperate and it could mark the end of the Hapsburgs.

In the spring Napoleon convoked to Dresden the heads of the tributary nations. They came as he had bidden, including Emperor Francis. It was the first time in history that a Hapsburg emperor had to cede precedence in entering a meeting: Napoleon entered first. He told the assembly that he would hold them strictly to their commitment to furnish soldiers for the Grande Armée. Everybody sighed. Everybody bowed. On May 28— the day Schubert's mother died—Napoleon left Dresden and headed east. "Within a week I'll have the Russians at my feet," he wrote to Caulaincourt, his Russian ambassador. Kaiser Franz went to Teplitz to take the water cure. He needed it.

Schubert was not truly aware of the extent of the Corsican's threat, in spite of his fondness for talking politics. He could not have forgotten the bomb that had fallen on the Seminary four years previously, nor the financial mess that followed. Yet he gave no more sign that he understood what a Napoleonic victory would mean to Vienna, to Europe, to the world, to *him*, than Mozart understood the changes in his time, he who never once in his letters mentioned the French or the American revolutions. Perhaps the thinking of certain geniuses—Turner, Keats—is so overdeveloped in one direction that they have little to spare for, or are deficient in, the understanding of all matters not directly connected with their work. A chamber of their mind is closed. Others—Leonardo, Goethe— are able to roam and explore.

The young Schubert in search of expressing the music which sounded in his brain made endless explorations of which many are lost, but even those which have been preserved (mostly by his father—which extracts another nail from the story of the father's supposed enmity) are sufficient to prove his impassioned concentration on one subject only. In 1813 he produced a quantity of trios and canons, an octet for wind instruments (two movements only are extant), a "drinking song" for solo bass with male chorus, two minuets and German dances for orchestra, in addition to some thirty minuets for piano (ten of which are lost)—and his First Symphony.

Most of these are student works, derivative of Haydn and Mozart. But in the caressing slow movement of the D-Major Symphony we first hear Schubert's own voice.

The question remained: How was Schubert going to earn his livelihood from music? Who was going to care about music, anyway, at a time when Napoleon's victory over the Czar seemed certain and at a moment of such financial turbulence that even Prince Lobkowitz defaulted on Beethoven's annuity, paltry though the contracted sum was? By September 7, after their defeat at Borodino, the Russians abandoned Moscow. A week later Napoleon entered the city. The Russians set fire to it, and flames consumed much of the holy city. On October 19 Napoleon's historic retreat began. Not till after that date, not till winter, when the Russian guns decimated the Grande Armée as it fled across the Berezina, could anybody believe the unbelievable: the Corsican was vulnerable.

Schubert was no longer happy at the Seminary. His voice was undergoing mutation. In July a notice was placed in the *Wiener Zeitung*: another competition would be held in September for the admittance of two new boys, since two places needed to be filled for the coming school year. Schubert knew it. In one of the manuscript parts used for a performance of Peter Winter's First Mass—no doubt the sheet from which Schubert sang—Schubert wrote: "Schubert Franz crowed for the last time on July 26, 1812."

In November, he reported to his brother Ferdinand in a half-jocular, half-complaining note:

November 24, 1812

Straight out with what troubles me, and so I shall come to my purpose the sooner, and you will not be detained by any beating about the bush. I have long been thinking about my situation and found that, although it is satisfactory on the whole, it is not beyond some improvement here and there. You know from experience that we all like to eat a roll or a few apples sometimes, the more so if after a middling lunch one cannot expect anything better than a miserable evening meal. . . . The few groats I receive from Father go to the devil the very first days, and what am I to do for the rest of the time? "Whosoever believeth on Him shall not be put to shame." Matthew, iii, 4. I thought so, too—How if you were to let me have a few kreuzer a month? You would not miss it, while I in my cell should think myself lucky, and be content. I repeat, I lean upon the words of the Apostle Matthew, where he says: "He that hath two coats, let him give one to the poor," &c. Meanwhile I hope that you will give ear to the voice that calls unceasingly to you to remember

> Your
> loving, poor, hopeful
> and again poor brother
> Franz [DQ].

It is the first Schubert letter which has been preserved. Was it for fun that he mixed up the Bible quotations—or from carelessness? The first Matthew quotation is actually St. Paul's and the second St. Luke's. Schubert's humor when expressed in music was adroit and charming, as well formed as a pretty girl. Schubert's humor when expressed in words was often clumsy. To a fragment of the Octet for wind instruments he added a postscript:

Finished wi' th' *Quartet*, the which has been composed by Franz° Schubert, Chapel Master to the Imp. Chinese Court Chappppelll at Nanking, the world-famous resident of His Chinese Majesty. Written in Vienna, on a date I can't tell, in a year which has a 3 at the end, and a oner at the beginning, and then an eight, and another oner: that is to say—1813 [DQ].

He did not have to leave the Seminary. They recognized that he had talent, one not found every day. A scholarship was offered him for further education, both musical and general, provided only he would improve in mathematics. But he had had enough. He was tired of the uniform, tired of the routine. To him now "Denmark was a prison." No matter what the alternative offered, he insisted on leaving. His father approved the decision; he was anxious that his son enter a "regular" profession, in the tradition of the family. Schubert went home. Franz Sr. insisted that the sane and safe course lay in becoming a teacher. "You will have time to do your composing in the evening." That at the moment seemed the prudent step to take, and he enrolled in a training school for assistant teachers located in the center of the inner city, in the Annagasse, near the opera house. This training school, established by Maria Theresa,*

*For Maria Theresa's reform of the educational system, see Edward Crankshaw's fine biography, *Maria Theresa* (1969): "She saw the need for greatly improved elementary education if all her peoples were to be employed to the advantage of the realm." "There were to be three sorts of school: the *Normalschule*, which was the model, set up in each Land; the *Hauptschule*, of which there was at least one in every district; the *Trivialschule*, one in every small town and in every rural parish. All children of both sexes had to attend from between the ages of six and twelve. In the country children up to eight years old enjoyed a good reputation, though its location was hardly suitable, the Annagasse being one of the centers of prostitution. For eight months he marched almost daily from the suburb to the Annagasse, to emerge with a certificate which enabled him to teach in his father's school (salary seventy gulden per year, about $700). A seventeen-year-old school-teacher—he was, if we can trust one or two reminiscences of his pupils, *not* a good teacher, impatient and uncomprehending and bored with all but one subject. He knew what he wanted to do. He knew he did not want to breathe chalk or point the teacher's ruler at a recalcitrant child, but he did not have the courage to follow his heart. Not quite yet. For some two years he scribbled on the blackboard that two and two make four, but all the while his head was preoccupied with the four pulses of the common rhythm, or with the infinite combinations which four string instruments could produce, or with melodies which one plus one, the human voice and the piano, could conjure.

2.

Napoleon was finally beaten (or so it seemed), forced to abdicate, banished to Elba. A sigh of relief went up, a "Te Deum Laudamus," the length and breadth of Europe, from Agrigento to Malmö, from London to Vienna. In the autumn of 1814, or about the time that Schubert assumed his seat at the teacher's desk, the triumphant Metternich invited the European nations to the Congress of Vienna. The purpose of the Congress was to establish an equilibrium among the nations which would prevent further arrogation of power and its disastrous wars. A fine ideal! That it was not achieved, that on the contrary the meeting for peace threatened at one time to break into a new war, that tricks and secret deals crept into the proceedings—that was due to the fact that neither Metternich for Austria, nor Talleyrand for France, nor Hardenberg for Prussia, nor Castlereagh for Britain, nor decidedly Alexander for Russia could forget national interests in favor of humanity. Metternich succeeded in tightening the reins of the Hapsburg Empire in retrogressive moves, as if the French Revolution had never made its impact on people's minds;

---

attended the summer school, from Easter to the end of September, while all from eight to twelve attended the winter school, from December 1st to March 31st, so that they could help with the farm work in the summer. There were special refresher schools—two hours each Sunday after Mass for youngsters between thirteen and twenty." "Naturally, as in most reforms, the situation looked better on paper than it did in practice. The shortage of teachers with the right qualification was chronic."

the Czar gobbled up a large part of Poland, and Britain remained ruler of the waves.

The Congress has been much maligned: "Congress dances." There *was* a lot of dancing, yet a prodigious amount of serious work was accomplished in such matters as freedom of river shipping and abolition of the slave trade, and the Congress finally did succeed in preventing major European wars for half a century. At the very least the Congress kindled new hopes, those hopes burning brightest in Vienna, the center, if only temporarily, of all the excitement. Not that the Congress improved economic conditions there; on the contrary, the luminaries and their satraps had to be fed and entertained to the tune of some 500,000 florins a day, a sum which Vienna could ill afford, and which was partly raised by new taxation. But what could one do? One had to take care of an assembly which included two emperors, two empresses, four kings, some 250 members of reigning families, all with their entourages, plus generals, diplomats, technical experts, bankers, cartographers, journalists, cooks, barbers, valets, ladies' maids, coachmen, equerries, interpreters, a chorus of spies—not to forget wives, mistresses, and select prostitutes.

All in all, some 10,000 people streamed into Vienna. To transport the more important ones, 1,400 horses stood in the stalls of the Hofburg; they too had to be fed. As Talleyrand put it, "The Czar makes love, the King of Denmark drinks, the King of Würtemberg eats, the King of Prussia thinks, the King of Bavaria talks, and the Emperor of Austria pays." Yet with all the paying and the crowding, a new mood of optimism pervaded Vienna and was arguably a congenial background, not only for Schubert's composing more in 1814–15 than in 1813, but for his daring to undertake more ambitious works. The seventeen-year-old finished, in time to celebrate the centenary of the church at Liechtental, a Mass in F Major, which he conducted and for which Michael Holzer served as choirmaster, brother Ferdinand presided at the organ, and Therese Grob sang the soprano solo (October 16, 1814). It was the first time a work by Schubert was performed publicly and—writes Deutsch— "there is no doubt that this performance was attended by several foreigners who were in Vienna for the Congress." Not a small compliment, really. Salieri was present as well. Schubert's father was said to have given his son a gift of a piano at the time—he was that proud of his son.

Summer and winter, in the schoolroom or out in the Vienna Woods, inspiration never dried to a trickle; it was a river fed by reliable tributaries, its flow steady. He was in good health, the times were apt, he had confidence in himself—it is significant that he dated his compositions punctiliously—and putting notes on paper was easy for him, after he had "composed" them in his head. Three string quartets belong to this period, as well as a little piano sonata. The sheer volume of Schubert's output has astonished the world and has given rise to the myth that he never revised, never rewrote, but put it all down without, as it were, drawing breath. At the end of the first movement of the Quartet in B-flat Major (September 1814) he wrote: "Done in 4½ hours." It is a boastful remark of a very young genius. For he *did* revise and he did change when dissatisfied. He did not compose in a happy-go-lucky fashion. He worked fast, but, viewing the totality of his output, we must remember that in his mature years he had nothing else to do—nothing whatever except to compose. The neat notes give no inkling of how long or how hard his head cogitated before he entrusted them to paper. His fecundity does remain astonishing: is it more astonishing than Mozart's producing the three last symphonies between the end of June 1788 and the beginning of August?

As Mozart composed three symphonies at the age of eighteen (Köchel 199 to 202), so did Schubert compose two symphonies in the early part of 1815, one in B-flat major (No. 2) and one in D major (No. 3), the first of these taking approximately four months to complete, the second hardly two months.

The Second Symphony is superior to the First, and the Third, more concise, is superior to the Second. The Second Symphony's first movement is robust, a young man's plunge into the midst of life. It varies between a heady staccato and a charming cantabile. This movement owes something to Beethoven's Second Symphony. The second movement consists of an andante in five simple variations which do not venture far from the theme. The third movement, the minuet, is perhaps a bit too boisterous, and of the last movement (presto) Einstein says that it is "full of dynamic surprises, dropping often to sleep as it were and then waking up with a start." Brahms loved this symphony.

The Third Symphony presents an unmistakably Schubertian theme which he was to use again. In fact, it is not difficult to hear intimations of the *Unfinished* throughout the movement. Its best movement is the finale, a presto packed with fun.

Though these symphonies are worth hearing and enjoying—especially by Schubert admirers—they are not masterpieces. Too many godfathers stand around the cradle: Beethoven, Mozart, Haydn. They are not even true symphonies in the sense of being built on themes to be developed and sent on dramatic quests. It was as if Schubert, writing a symphony, was at the same time thinking of something else—melodies of songs.

Before the completion of the symphonies and along with them, there began that miracle of music, the Schubert lied.

3.

Every Hans and Liesl, even if only half-educated, reads *Faust* at least twice: once when young, when he or she savors the music of its verse, is moved by the tragedy of the abandoned Gretchen, and wishes for the attainment of so sophisticated a worldliness as Mephisto displays; once again when older, when the flashes of Goethe's reflections shine more clearly, when the true meaning of Faust's contract is understood, and the hunger for the unattainable is felt as a personal experience.*

As is true of most poetry, it is especially true of Goethe's lyric verse that it is untranslatable. The effect lies not only in its rhythm, the precise word and the position of the word within the meter, but in its musicality, its *sound*. How do you render into another language

> Füllest wieder's liebe Tal
> Still mit Nebelglanz
> Lösest endlich auch einmal
> Meine Seele ganz

or that poem, seemingly so simple,

> Über allen Gipfeln ist Ruh
> In allen Wipfeln spürest Du
> Kaum einen Hauch . . .

which ends with

> Warte nur
> Balde ach balde
> Ruhest Du Auch.

*I am speaking of *Faust, Part I*. The second part is far more difficult, comprising the fields of science, philosophy, mythology, economics, and often it becomes turgid. This in spite of some great scenes and the incomparable poetry Goethe wrote in his old age. Surely more than half of the people who know Part I lose their bearings in the second part, if they read it at all.

with its contrasting dark *ü*'s and the resolution in bright *a*'s and the last three words returning to a consolatory dark tone on the word *Ruhest*, as quieting as Hamlet's "Rest, rest, perturbéd spirit!"? Or those sharply changing sea-pictures, which gave Mendelssohn the basis for the Overture *Calm Sea and Prosperous Voyage*, the rhythm so precisely divided that it alone conveys the ideas:

Tiefe Stille herrscht im Wasser,
Ohne Regung ruht das Meer,
Keine Luft von keiner Seite!
Todesstille fürchterlich! . . .

Die Nebel zerreissen
Der Himmel ist helle,
Und Aeolus löset
Das ängstliche Band.

An adagio followed by an allegretto.

Schubert fashioned his song "Meerestille" from the first part of the poem (as did Beethoven in a choral setting). It is a masterpiece of a menacing seascape, its vague broken chords suggesting "a painted ship upon a painted sea."

The major part of Goethe's poetry is confined to those whose native tongue is German. It is largely nonexportable. Only music can carry it beyond the Rhine and the Danube. Only music can render it duty-free, internationally. Only music can "translate" the feel and sound of his words into an experience valid even for those who do not understand German. Of all the composers of whatever nationality—French (Berlioz and Gounod), Finnish (Sibelius), Russian (Tchaikovsky), Italian (Boito), Austrian (Hugo Wolf, Mahler), Hungarian (Liszt), German (Schumann, Spohr, Wagner, Busoni, etc.)—it was Schubert who most beautifully transmuted him, it was Schubert who was most greatly inspired by him, it was Schubert who returned in equal value the stimulation he received, it was Schubert who made the poetry the property of those who had never read *Faust* or had never met the Erlkönig.

Goethe is Schubert's debtor, but Schubert is Goethe's debtor. We can date Schubert's greatness from the moment when, on October 19, 1814, he set to music "Gretchen am Spinnrade" ("Gretchen at the Spinning Wheel"), one of her soliloquies from *Faust*. It was an epoch-making song

it the *Tragic* (the title is his, not grafted on, like *Emperor* or *Moonlight*) cannot be explained by the circumstances of his life, but derives from its melancholy adagio introduction and its slow movement, which contrasts agitation against a Goethean resignation and hope for rest.

No. 5 is a chamber work for the performance of which Schubert could have called together a small group, with the help of his brothers Ferdinand and Ignaz. No trumpets or drums are required. Even the most casual listener could enjoy it on a Sunday afternoon, while a more attentive listener would observe that Schubert had perfected his skill in writing instrumental music. He is still taking a pinch from Mozart, a teaspoon from Haydn, but it is integrated Schubert. And delectable. Donald Tovey called it "a pearl of great price."

1816 was a beneficent year for the world and for art. For Schubert it had its ups and downs. He was expanding his gifts, as the world was expanding, composing symphonic music, chamber music, piano music, and always returning to his first love, the song. His desire for education was exemplified by Friedrich Froebel's establishing an educational community in Thuringia. There were indications of a bright light breaking through post-Napoleonic suffering. 1816 was a good year for art; painting broke away from the cool classicism of David's *The Oath of the Horatii* and turned to the romanticism of young Géricault. Rossini produced *The Barber,* Coleridge published "Kubla Khan," Byron "The Siege of Corinth," while "Emma" (equal in its combination of charm and seriousness to Schubert's combination of charm and seriousness) came from Jane Austen.

Goethe's influence on Schubert continued: he was sunk in the reading of *Wilhelm Meisters Lehrjahre,* the "novel of education" which was preceded by Defoe's *Robinson Crusoe,* Fielding's *Tom Jones,* and Fénelon's *Télémaque.* Of Wilhelm Meister's Mignon, Schiller wrote:

> Everything you have created with this figure, living and dead, is extraordinarily beautiful. In her isolated appearance, her mysterious existence, her purity and innocence . . . she leads one to a clarified sorrow, a truly human sadness, precisely because she represents the essence of humanity.
>
> Letter to Goethe, January 7, 1796

Schubert set Mignon's song "Nur wer die Sehnsucht kennt" to music six times over eleven years. Similarly he experimented with the Harper's songs, the most famous of which is "Wer nie sein Brot mit Tränen ass." Dietrich Fischer-Dieskau, in his comments on Schubert's songs, has written:

> The voice is choked by tears, is forced to break off again and again, and the harp is left to play the interludes alone. Individual stanzas are repeated, thus creating the requisite "mood of fantasy." Schubert re-created every detail exactly, without giving the impression of having slavishly followed the text. Everything fits, freely and unforced. . . .

Even today, when we are wont to derogate the melting mood, these songs have not lost their appeal. It is safe to call them immortal.

4.

Schubert loathed being a schoolteacher, dealing drudgingly with the three R's in the lowest class of his father's school. Not that he was totally uninterested in the task of education; rather, he was weary of depending on his father, who paid him a pittance. What could he do to improve his earnings and to get away? The songs, now becoming known and admired by his friends, carried as yet no remuneration. On February 17, 1816, he read an announcement in the *Wiener Zeitung,* specifying that a "Music Master's Post" was open at the "German Normal School" in Laibach in the province of Carniola (now Ljubljana in Yugoslavia). Emperor Francis was trying to force German into the non-German parts of the Hapsburg Empire, and this gave rise to severe intramural quarrels. The Croatians, Serbians, Hungarians, Czechs did not *want* to attend German schools. The salary was attractive, some 500 florins per year, about six times what he was then earning. Applications were to be submitted by March 15, with "authentic testimonials" to the applicant's musical knowledge and teaching capacity.

Schubert very much wanted this post. Yet it was not till April 9, more than three weeks late, that he sent an application, lamely worded:

Right Hon. I. & R. Captaincy of the Civic Guard,

The undersigned most submissively begs that the vacant post of Musical Director at Laibach may be graciously assigned to him.

He supports this request with the following reasons:

1. He is a pupil at the I. & R. Seminary, ex-choir-boy of the I. & R. Court

Chapel and composition scholar of Herr von Salieri, first I. & R. Court Musical Director, on whose benevolent advice he desires to obtain the said post.

2. He has gained such knowledge and skill in all branches of composition, in performance on the organ and violin, and in singing that he is declared to be the most suitable among all the applicants for this post, according to the enclosed testimonials.

3. He promises to use his qualifications in the best possible way to do the fullest justice to a gracious consent to his petition.

Franz Schubert
at present assistant teacher at his
father's school in
Vienna, 10 Himmelpfortgrund.

Who can explain the delay in Schubert's application? Who can explain that he exaggerates his proficiency "on the organ and violin" and does not mention one—just one—of his compositions? On the same day—again too late—Salieri wrote a short note, supporting the application. It counted for something, but not for enough. Schubert's dilatoriness and the ignorance of the Laibach authorities about his work combined to throw the selection on one Franz Sokoll, a musician of the region, called a nonentity by Schubert's biographers. No doubt a nonentity—but perhaps a more suitable teacher than Schubert.

The vote against Schubert came in August. A severe blow, and yet Schubert that month set to music eight poems by Johann Georg Jacobi, a German anacreontic poet; "Die Perle" ("The Pearl") is one of the most lighthearted songs he composed.

Two months previously Schubert had an occasion to observe how sweet fame can taste. The fiftieth anniversary of Salieri's residence in Vienna was being celebrated. It was a Sunday in June, the sky was cloudless. Early in the morning Salieri and his four daughters were summoned to the Italian Minorite Church, which was filled with white flowers strung on silver bunting and from whose steeple a high bell tolled. There they heard mass. Then they proceeded to the *Burg,* where the Lord High Chamberlain, Prince Trauttmansdorff, awarded him, in the name of His Imperial Royal Majesty Francis I, the "Civil Gold Medal of Honor." Count Kuefstein and the entire staff of the Court Chapel were present. In the chapel Salieri himself conducted high mass, with music he had composed. This was followed by a formal lunch. In the evening the celebration moved to Salieri's home. His pupils gathered around the sixty-six-year-old man, dressed in official court splendor, his medals shining. He sat at the piano on a golden chair, his handsome face, from which now more than one tooth was missing, smiling on one and all. Past and present pupils, twenty-six of them, twelve men on the left, fourteen women on the right, had each brought a composition newly finished for the occasion. Schubert was one of them. They made music, beginning with a hymn composed by Salieri and ending late at night with an excerpt from one of his oratorios. Schubert's offering was, in addition to a perfectly terrible little poem, a trio for voices and piano.

That the occasion made a great impression on Schubert is attested by his describing it in his diary late that very night. He wrote:

June 16, 1816

It must be beautiful and refreshing for an artist to see all his pupils gathered about him, each one striving to give of his best for his Jubilee, and to hear in all these compositions the expression of pure nature, free from all the eccentricity that is common among most composers nowadays, and is due almost wholly to one of our greatest German artists; that eccentricity which joins and confuses the tragic with the comic, the agreeable with the repulsive, heroism with howlings and the holiest with harlequinades, without distinction, so as to goad people to madness instead of dissolving them in love, to incite them to laughter instead of lifting them up to God . . . [DQ].

"One of our greatest German artists" is undoubtedly Beethoven, and one hears the echo of a pronouncement that Salieri gave forth. It proves, too, if proof were necessary, how little one can trust a diary scrawl, a fleeting impression. Schubert actually revered Beethoven. However, on that evening, looking at Salieri's medals, hearing Salieri's music—so predictable yet so orderly and easy—his judgment was led astray. Probably he was trying to free himself from the influence which pressed upon him too heavily for his own creative freedom in the early years. For the moment, but only for the moment, he hit out. He was to return to Beethoven almost at once.

The next day Schubert noted in the diary: "Today I composed for money for the first time." It was a cantata for the name day of Professor Josef Watteroth, a jurist who was to become a good friend to Schubert. The fee was 100 florins, a fairly generous one. (The cantata is lost.)

Only a few sheets of Schubert's diary have turned up, but at any rate he was never methodical in keeping one. We do have his impression of a musical evening of that year:

A light, bright, fine day this will remain throughout my whole life. As from afar the magic notes of Mozart's music still gently haunt me. How unbelievably vigorously, and yet again how gently, was it impressed deep, deep into the heart by Schlesinger's masterly playing. Thus does our soul retain these fair impressions, which no time, no circumstances can efface, and they lighten our existence. They show us in the darkness of this life a bright, clear, lovely distance, for which we hope with confidence. O Mozart, immortal Mozart, how many, oh how endlessly many such comforting perceptions of a brighter and better life hast thou brought to our souls!—This Quintet is, so to speak, one of the greatest of his lesser works.—I too had to show myself on this occasion. I played variations by Beethoven, sang Goethe's "Restless Love" ["Rastlose Liebe"] and Schiller's "Amalia." Unanimous applause for the former, less for the latter. Although I myself think my "Restless Love" better than "Amalia," I cannot deny that Goethe's poet's genius contributed much to the success [DQ].

The "success" took place in a private home. Perhaps these occasions, along with his being paid for a composition "for the first time," encouraged him. In the autumn of that year he quit the hated business of schoolteaching, he made the vital decision, he left his parental home, and on the invitation of his friend Franz von Schober moved in with him, to remain for most of his life the constant visitor.

Soon after his decision to be a composer first and last, Schubert tried to make himself known beyond the wall of Vienna. What better sample of his skill could he show than the "Erlkönig"? He sent a copy of the manuscript to Breitkopf and Härtel in Leipzig, one of Germany's leading publishers. The only Franz Schubert they knew was a composer of church music living in Dresden. Accordingly they sent the manuscript to him with a refusal. Not interested! In return they received a spluttering note from the Dresden Schubert. He begs "to state that this cantata was never composed by me. . . . Who sent you that sort of trash?" He intends to "discover the fellow who has thus misused my name." Did the Dresden Franz ever discover the true author? History sayeth not.

4
Love and Friendship

No Mathilde Wesendonck or George Sand or Constanze Weber appears in Schubert's life. No letter to an "Immortal Beloved" hidden in a secret drawer has been found to intrigue the scholars. Indeed, Schubert did not write a single love letter; or if he did—which is improbable—it has disappeared.

Anton Holzapfel was a fellow student of Schubert's at the Seminary, where he remained for twelve years, eventually studying law and becoming a municipal councillor in Vienna. He wrote some reminiscences in which he recalled that Schubert, then eighteen years old, told him that he had fallen in love with and was "inclined" to marry Therese Grob, a girl two years younger than he, daughter of a neighbor's family friendly with the Schuberts. Therese had sung in the performance of Schubert's First Mass. Holzapfel knew Therese, was supposed to have liked her, and described her as "not by any means a beauty, but well shaped, fairly buxom, with a fresh childlike little round face." But when Holzapfel heard that the gifted Franz—who had already given proofs of his gift by such songs as "Gretchen am Spinnrade" and "Heidenröslein" and a symphony—was thinking of binding himself in marriage, he firmly grasped a pen and told his friend that the idea was ludicrous. The sketch for this letter, written in 1815, was still in Holzapfel's possession in 1858. Since then it has been lost, and so has the letter itself. Assuming that Holzapfel's recollections were accurate, they still give no inkling how earnestly Schubert meant it. Was it but a momentary mood after Therese sang so prettily? Consider—he was a very young eighteen, she sixteen. Much later Schubert was supposed to have told his friend Anselm Hüttenbrenner the same story, more or less, adding that he had hoped for three years to marry her but he "could not find a post that would support us both." He described Therese as "not really pretty, and had a pockmarked face—but she was an angel."

In her portrait, painted in later life, she does not look much like an angel, with a schoolmarm's face, thin lips, a severe bun on top of her hair.* Hüttenbrenner reported Schubert as saying that since then he had never met anyone whom he could love.

Any reminiscence by Hüttenbrenner needs to be taken cautiously, since he besprinkled his facts with liberal portions of fiction. Is it believable that Schubert closed his heart and his normal sexual instinct—at the age of eighteen? Is it possible that he who, unimpressive though his appearance may have been at first glance, was welcomed in the homes of pretty Viennese women and by dark-eyed Hungarian girls should have remained untouched? There is evidence to the contrary. True, Schubert was not a man in whom the sex drive was strong. True, his inspiration was not rooted in, or driven by, the feminine, as was Wagner's or Goethe's or Byron's. He wrote love songs, some of them very loving, but predominantly they are more charming than erotic, more playful than libidinous, except of course when they deal with love's tragedy. He reserved his profoundest feelings for the portrayal of the outcast, the lonely, the humble, the homeless, the man who feels that "there where I am not, there resides fortune." His most wonderful songs are those of restlessness and renunciation, the riddle of the soul in uncertainty, such as Heine's "Der Doppelgänger," Müller's "Der Leiermann"—which is almost too agonizing to be endured—and Müller's "Der Lindenbaum," a song which hides longing for peace and death behind an easygoing melody. (Thomas Mann used it to end *The Magic Mountain*.) But to believe that the composer of "Sylvia," "Laura," the two Suleika songs of Goethe, and the three versions of "Serenade" (Grillparzer, Shakespeare, Rellstab) could be impervious to women's nature is to believe the impossible.

Schubert's first biographer, Heinrich Kreissle von Hellborn (Vienna, 1865), claimed that he was "too timid" to form relationships with women. Well, perhaps—but the explanation doesn't sound convincing. He was certainly not aggressive; on the other hand he was not psychopathically

---

*She married a master baker and lived prosperously ever after. She died at the age of seventy-seven. "She never told her love"—if love it was. Her niece inherited her collection of some early Schubert songs in autographs. She did not pursue a singing career and seems to have been an altogether dull lady.

withdrawn. He enjoyed playing games,* charades, picnics where girls were present, and he was tireless in playing the piano for dancing. Shortly after the "Erlkönig" he became something of a salon celebrity; girls fussed over him, and if there was no overt wooing on his side, there certainly was plenty of covert flirting on their side. He did not hide from women; on the contrary, there were instances when he was on perfectly easy terms with them. And in some letters he hints—just hints—of being in love with a young Countess Caroline and of having a brief affair with a chambermaid; her name was Pepi Pöckelhofer (imagine whispering "Pöckelhofer") and she worked on the estate of this same Countess Caroline Esterházy in Zseliz, Hungary. But *le grand amour* was missing from his life, and for this lack we need to look for causes other than shyness, or without invoking that psychiatric platitude, ye olde Oedipus complex, Schubert hating his father and being in love with his mother, for which not a shred of evidence exists.

Ill luck had something to do with it: he never found the right woman. But he never looked for her. I believe that the chief reason was an almost frantic desire for freedom, a wish to remain emotionally unencumbered. He was fond of many people, but he did not love—love wholeheartedly and with the complete dedication of his being—anyone. Not his parents, not his friends, much though he needed them, not his teachers. His brother Ferdinand was the exception; Schubert came nearer to fraternal kinship with him than with his other brothers. Ferdinand, who understood music and even had some ambition as a composer, understood Franz. What was more important, he loved Franz and Franz loved him. The letters Schubert wrote his friends, and vice versa, give the impression that their relationships were more ardent than they actually were, at least on Schubert's part. Romantically extravagant expression was the style in which people wrote each other at that time. Some of the plumed phrases read almost like love letters, without having the slightest homosexual basis. Schubert to Anselm Hüttenbrenner: "I felt as I kissed you good-bye that you would not soon return. . . . Where are the many hours I spent so happily with you?" (January 21, 1819). Schubert to Schober: "Still my longing for you to some extent at least by letting me know how you live and what you do" (November 30, 1823). Schober to Schubert: "Love me well. We shall certainly be united again" (December 2, 1824). Cer-

*A game called "Words" was popular. It consisted of making poems of a given number of words. Similarly, "Dots" had to be formed into pictures. Schubert was once asked to compose a dance from disconnected notes.

tainly—Schubert appreciated and valued his friends and they recognized his quality as man and artist; yet at the core he needed to remain free in order to be vessel for, and vassal to, his imagination.

Part of this drive for freedom derived from a revolt against the discipline and regimentation to which he was subjected from the age of ten. He had no real childhood. As an adult he became an emotional drifter, while discipline continued to inform and shape his work. Even physically he was a drifter, living in various lodgings with one friend or another. He was often poor enough so that saving rent was a godsend. But quite as often he did have money and never once did the thought occur to him that he might use his money to establish a home, with a woman to take care of it. He did not even want to walk arm in arm with a woman. Over and over again he spoke of his wish to be "unobstructed." And so, two years after the Therese episode, Schubert wrote in his diary: "For a free man, these days, marriage is a fear-inspiring thought. He identifies it either with sadness or with lust." A pontificating statement, not typical of him, in which we hear the voice of self-justification, perhaps with an overtone of regret.

How, then, did Schubert still his sexual needs? He followed the practice of the young men of his time who, too poor to get married or even to entertain a long-lasting liaison, sought satisfaction by climbing into bed with a girl one night and then saying good-bye. These girls were not all prostitutes, though the statistics—which may be exaggerated—estimate that there were 10,000 plying their trade in the Vienna of the 1820s. The whores promenaded not only in the dark side streets, the Annagasse being a favorite, but in the bright and elegant Graben as well (the Viennese called them "Grabenymphs"), and their health was unwatched until a decree of 1827 demanded that they be inspected for venereal infection. Such inspection was undertaken all too casually. They had competition from the nonprofessionals, "girls and women who wanted to earn a little money on the side, or fulfill their sexual longings, without being averse to accepting a small gift" (Richard Waldegg, *Moral History of Vienna*).

The nabobs of the Congress of Vienna had done their part in accentuating sexuality, with the beautiful Princess Bagration—who was reputed to be not only Czar Alexander's mistress but also Metternich's—displaying her extreme décolletage publicly; they called her "the naked angel." The Czar enjoyed a liaison as well with a Demoiselle Morel, who was the mistress of the Grand Duke of Baden. The Czarina was easily consoled, since she herself found in Prince Constantin Czartorisky an adequate lover. Frederick VI, King of Denmark, became popular with the Viennese because he had an affair with a simple, plump Viennese girl who loved to dance; they called her "The Queen of Denmark." Dance halls for plain people, inexpensive or charging no admission, became the rage, and they served as places where young men could make their arrangements. The most popular was the Mehlgrube (Flour Cave), where Mozart had played. (It was located where today the Hotel Ambassador stands.) To preserve decorum, available girls visited it in company with a male "friend." The young men stood against the wall and if one followed a girl with a smiling glance, and she responded with a smile, the two approached each other at the end of the dance. Other dance halls were the Sperl, which was certainly too expensive for Schubert, the Apollo Hall, and one called Elysium, which opened in 1823, the first to be illuminated by gaslight instead of candlelight; it was inexpensive and featured nightly masked balls, the girls often appearing in "Turkish" costumes, "Turkish" stemming from no farther than Vienna's suburbs. Another suburban hall was the White Swan, where Josef Lanner, forerunner of Johann Strauss Sr., got his start.

Obviously no documentation exists to show when or how often Schubert frequented these girls. That he did is suggested by the reminiscences of his more conservative friends, who claimed that Franz Schober (see below) "led him astray." In addition, and setting aside that prissy phrase, we have a written statement from Wilhelm von Chézy, son of the authoress of the play *Rosamunde,* who assuredly was not a prude: "Unfortunately Schubert's thirst for life had lured him into byways from which there is usually no return, at least no healthy return." (*Memoirs,* 1863).

While the ministers and deputies of the victors snatched at frontiers trying to wrest still another square of earth from a neighboring nation, while British bankers extracted the gold coins which still lay in French vaults, while Austrian furniture-makers finished their cabinets by affixing to them brass plates showing a snake coiled around a laurel wreath— Metternich's signet—and while Archduke Rudolf tried to interest his brother in developing the ironworks of Bohemia—while this was going on Schubert worked with the fullness of young power. In 1815 he composed 145 songs, including "Heidenröslein" and "Erlkönig," along with four operas. In 1816 came over a hundred songs, including "An Schwager Chronos," the Harper and Mignon songs, and the "Wiegenlied," plus two symphonies and some dances for piano. In 1817, aside from seven piano sonatas, almost sixty songs were composed, including the master-pieces "Der Tod und das Mädchen," "Ganymed," "An die Musik," "Die Forelle."

Because he was young and working he was content—or as content as he ever managed to be—and for relaxation he sometimes took long walks in the Vienna Woods, where, the Viennese say, "God stretches his arm out."

I took an evening walk for once, as I had not done for several months. There can be scarcely anything more agreeable than to enjoy the green country on an evening after a hot summer's day, a pleasure for which the fields Währing and Döbling seem to have been especially created. In the uncertain twilight and in the company of my brother Karl, my heart warmed within me. "How beautiful," I thought and exclaimed, standing still delightedly. A graveyard close by reminded us of our dear mother. Thus, talking sadly and intimately, we arrived at the point where the Döbling road divides. And, as from the heavenly home, I heard a familiar voice coming from a halting coach. I looked up—and it was Herr Weinmüller [a bass who had sung Rocco in *Fidelio* in 1814], just alighting and paying us his compliments in his cordial, honest voice.

Schubert's diary, June 14, 1816

The year after, he met another singer, one who was to change his life. Johann Michael Vogl was an anomaly, an intellectual opera singer. He was a huge man from whose huge mouth issued an astonishing voice, a baritone flexible and smooth, capable of stentorian and of gentle tones. He was well over six feet tall, strong, not paunchy, so imposing in appearance that he could have served as captain of the Pope's Swiss Guards. He was lordly in movement, lordly in stride, quite conscious of his importance, and only a bit uncomfortable because of his outsize flat feet. He was born in 1768, and when Schubert met him he had been a star of the Vienna Opera for some twenty years, singing such roles as Orestes in Gluck's *Iphigenia*, Agamemnon, Sarastro. In 1814 he sang Pizarro in the revised *Fidelio*. As a character he was the antithesis to that one-dimensional villain: having been brought up in a Jesuit college, he never lost a tendency toward self-analysis, a moral skepticism applied to himself and to the world. When he was not singing he was reading, and when he was not reading he was cogitating and examining systems of philosophies. He would sit during an opera's interval in his dressing room and read Marcus Aurelius or Homer (he knew almost the whole of the *Iliad* by heart) or Plato, as well as modern authors such as Scott and Byron. He was fluent in several languages, preferred English, and translated parts of Epictetus into four languages. Yet he was not a bookworm and as often as he scoffed at it just so often did he enjoy applause and notoriety. His diary abounds with thoughts, both worldly and unworldly, as for example: "Happiness consists in beholding, not in possessing" or "To bear is more difficult than to act" or "If people do not want to learn from us (which is almost always the case), we have to learn from them" or the practical "If you want to succeed, don't tell anybody your plans," his own observations being interspersed with quotations from and notes on Montaigne, "a wise old man. . . . It's good company hard to find in real life." These thoughts he discussed with Schubert later. Somebody described him as "an actor ascending the pulpit," but he was a mundane preacher, by no means devoid of humor. He had his clothes made by the best tailor in Vienna.

The meeting of Vogl and Schubert came about through Schubert's friend Franz Schober, who had some connection with the opera house through his sister, who had married the singer Siboni, a favorite of the Empress. But Siboni was no longer in Vienna, the sister had died, Vogl disliked being approached and having his reading disturbed, and Schober needed persistence and persuasion to manage to speak to the famous man, whom the writer Bauernfeld characterized as a "hermit" and a "peculiar customer." What happened when Vogl met Schubert in February or March 1817 was fully described by another member of Schubert's circle, Josef Spaun.

Spaun wrote several reminiscences of Schubert, one essay in 1829 shortly after Schubert's death, one in 1858, one in 1864. Spaun was a truthful man and his reminiscences, though tinged with sentimental streaks, may be taken as truthful:*

> Schubert, who had to sing his own songs himself, frequently expressed the wish to find somebody who could sing them. And several times he mentioned how much he would like to meet Court-Singer Vogl. Our little circle then decided to try to acquaint Vogl with Schubert's work. It was a difficult task, since Vogl was well-nigh unapproachable. . . .
>
> Schober, fired by a glowing enthusiasm, told Vogl of Schubert's beautiful

*Deutsch printed the 1829 version (under "Obituary Notes, XXX"). The version given here is that of 1864, an original manuscript clearly copied by Spaun's niece, unpublished as far as I know. I translated it and am using it in preference to the earlier version because it is fuller and livelier.

compositions and asked him to sample them. Vogl replied that he had had enough of music, it was coming out of his ears, and that he was attempting rather to forget it than to hear anything new. A hundred times had he heard talk of "new geniuses." He had always been disappointed. He was sure that would be the case with Schubert. "Leave me in peace. I don't want to hear any more about it." We all felt hurt by his refusal. All except Schubert; he had expected such an answer and found it natural.

Yet Schober continued to storm at him, and finally Vogl promised to come one evening to Schober's to find out what it was all about.

At the appointed hour he entered gravely, and as the little insignificant-looking Schubert made him an awkward bow, thanked him for the great honor, and in his embarrassment stammered a few nonsensical phrases, Vogl lifted his eyebrows. A bad beginning! Vogl said, "Well, what have you here? Accompany me," and took a sheet of music paper lying on the piano. It contained the song "Augenlied," a pretty but not an especially important song. He hummed rather than sang. "Not bad," he said somewhat coldly. But then he perused "Memnon," "Ganymed," and other songs; singing with half-voice he became friendlier. He departed without committing himself. Before he left he tapped Schubert on the shoulder. "You do have talent," he said, "but you are too little the actor, too little the charlatan. You are too prodigal with fine thoughts, without developing them."

With this parting shot Vogl was gone. Schubert thought the interview had been a failure. Unexpectedly soon, Vogl returned. The songs he had sung and the songs he had seen had not let him rest. An idea had come to him: he was now nearing fifty, an age which presaged the end of an operatic career. But here, with the work of this young man, a possibility of a new career opened. He would become an interpreter of these extraordinary songs which required not only singing but acting, the interpretation of music and poetry in a new homogenous style.

In fact, Vogl became the first full-fledged lieder singer. He became as well Schubert's proselytizer, the medium through which the songs became known. And Vogl's second career came to be as fruitful as his first.

Spaun wrote:

After only a few weeks, Vogl sang Schubert's "Erlkönig," "Ganymed," "Der Kampf," "Der Wanderer," etc., to a small but delighted audience and the enthusiasm with which this great artist performed these songs was the best proof of how moved he was himself by them. But this magnificent singer had the greatest effect on the young composer himself, who was overjoyed to see his long-nourished hopes fulfilled beyond all his expectations. As a result of their constant association, the two artists formed a bond which became ever tighter, and was broken only by death. [Not quite correct.] Vogl supplied his young friend with well-meaning advice from his rich store of experience and cared for his wants like a father, whenever the income from Schubert's compositions was inadequate.

This Sheridan-Garrick bond was beneficent to both.

Vogl proved indeed to be a superb interpreter. And he and Schubert set out, giving exciting performances not only in the houses of educated Viennese but in nearby Austrian towns. Vogl had been born in Steyr and took Schubert there (probably July 1818) to show him the beauty of Upper Austria. "The country around Steyr is inconceivably lovely," wrote Schubert to his brother Ferdinand. The little town is situated at the conflux of the rivers Steyr and Enns, about ninety miles west of Vienna. It is one of Austria's most enchanting towns, with an excellently preserved central square and some houses which date back to the fifteenth century. From Steyr Vogl and Schubert went to Linz. Of course Vogl traveled in style, as befitted his fame. Through fields and woods the private carriage with its well-fed horses made its way, the two passengers inhaling the perfume of new-mown hay, the wetness of cool forests, the odor of sawed planks. They listened to the sound of the postilion, who blew his horn as the carriage entered the city portals and the paving stones rattled. When they reached one of the famous abbeys (Stift), the Benedictine Molk, the Augustinian St. Florian, they were welcomed and entertained, Vogl being known everywhere. When they came to the steep hills near Amstetten, they descended from the carriage and even pushed a little as they walked along, to the right the flats of the Danube, to the left gardens and villages, and summer everywhere. It was one of the happiest intervals in Schubert's life, free of worries and enabling him to hear his own work presented to sympathetic listeners, and be often rewarded by the tears of understanding.

To be sure, Vogl sometimes changed Schubert's melodies, to add "operatic" high-low skips and furbelows and roulades. Once when he sang one of Schubert's songs, to which Vogl had added as much rouge as to the face of an old woman, Schubert inquired: "A good song. Who wrote it?" The sarcasm was obvious, but not to Vogl.

The vanity of the operatic star had to be taken in one's stride. No matter; Vogl, twenty-nine years older than Schubert, acted as a father to the younger man, deriving in turn filial benefits. More than a practical and more than an artistic relationship bound the two men, so different in age and constitution. A real affection existed, of the sort Schubert so often evoked. Vogl wrote in his diary:

Nothing proves the need for a good school for singing more clearly than Schubert's songs. How else can we interpret his truly divine inspirations, his musical clairvoyance, and all of which the German language is capable? Many of us could learn, perhaps for the first time, that his world consists of poetry in sound, words in notes, thoughts clothed in music. We could learn that the poems of our greatest poets, transmuted into his musical idiom, become even greater.

5
Twenty

JANUARY 31, 1817, OUT OF THE TEEN AGE; SCHUBERT WAS TWENTY. However calmly the date slipped by—and birthdays were then more often ignored than celebrated—it was a signpost.

The rate at which talent matures varies as much as the speed of a man's stride. At twenty Beethoven had not yet produced anything very memorable, save perhaps his *Cantata on the Death of Joseph II*, from which he took a melody into *Fidelio*'s last scene as Leonore frees Florestan from his chains. Mozart at twenty had behind him some thirty-odd symphonies, no end of serenades (including the "Haffner," K.250), divertimentos, quartets, dances, masses, a half-dozen operas, concertos, some solo arias with orchestra. Haydn had not begun to study music seriously, but he did produce in his twentieth year a little comic opera entitled *The Crooked Devil* (*Der krumme Teufel*). Tchaikovsky had dabbled a little but as yet wasn't at all sure that he would devote his life to music. Schumann was sure: he wanted to be a piano virtuoso, and at twenty he invented a contrivance to stretch the space beteen the fingers (which was later to injure his hands, ending his career as a virtuoso); at the age of twenty, as well, he composed a set of Piano Variations, his Opus 1.

Schubert at twenty continued to wander deeper into the landscape most congenial to him, the region of songs. That year he composed some sixty; by no means all are good, but the best are astonishing, fantastically astonishing, no matter what the age of the author was; they include, in addition to some already mentioned—"To Music," "The Trout"— "Ganymed," Goethe's hymn to Nature on a spring morning of blazing sunshine, in which he basks in "eternal warmth" and marvels at "endless beauty." It is set by Schubert in a double melody, a joyous mood which dissolves into a tribute to the "all-loving Father." The song has the lift of the last movement of Beethoven's *Pastoral* Symphony; nobody had ever heard anything like it before.

Often, however, in contrast to "Ganymed," and even at an age when optimism seems the expected disposition, the clouds hovered over Schubert. To his friends they may have been invisible, but to him they were present, now near, now far, presaging death when his life had hardly begun. Those thoughts emerge in his choice of texts—"Bei dem Grab meines Vaters" ("At the Grave of My Father," by Claudius), "Am Grabe Anselmos" ("At Anselm's Grave," by Claudius), "Der Jüngling an den Tod" ("The Youth Speaks to Death," by Spaun)—and the famous "Death and the Maiden" (by Claudius), a dialogue built on chords in which Death whispers to the maiden that he is a friend, that he is not coming to punish her but to soothe her, so that "in his arms she may gently sleep." Schubert used the melody of the song for the second movement of his D-Minor String Quartet (No. 14), composed in 1824; it is without doubt the most consistently inspired and moving quartet he wrote.

Equally veiled in obscurity, but more cruel, is the song "Gruppe aus dem Tartarus," the poem by Schiller. (The title can be loosely translated "A Group in Hades.") Schubert tried to compose it the previous year, was dissatisfied, and began anew in 1817. Over deep murmuring of the piano the shades of the condemned ask, "How long will our suffering last?"; they are answered with one word, "Eternity." The song ends as it began, with the "dying fall" of the obbligato suggesting "always and forever." Brahms was so impressed by the song that he scored it for full orchestra.

The romantics were preoccupied with Death, who appeared to them no longer as the grinning skeleton of medieval sculpture, nor as the admonitory figure at the side of Dürer's Knight, but as a youth carrying a torch. Dirges sound in romantic music, in Beethoven, Chopin, Berlioz—achieving an ultimate expression in Tristan's death wish. Obviously Schubert was influenced by the Zeitgeist, a *Zeit* during which the suicide rate climbed alarmingly. Schubert's relationship to death, present when he was twenty, struck deeper than fashion. It was the anxiety of a man who feels that whatever he does, whatever he accomplishes, he has not time enough. Too soon will the youth with the torch call on him. This feeling not only rises to the surface in much of his music but can be descried in some of the few letters and diary entries which have been preserved.

The *Unfinished* Symphony is by no means Schubert's only unfinished work. In addition to the superb *Quartettsatz*, a short masterpiece for which he intended to write at least a second movement (he sketched forty bars of it)—what a loss that he didn't!—two other fragments of string quartets are extant, plus nine unfinished piano sonatas and at least one other symphony. (Obviously we have no idea what he threw away or what got lost.) The reason for his breaking off does not lie in a temporary drying up of ideas or in fatigue—just the contrary: it lies in the fullness of ideas which were crowding in. Too much to work out, too many poems to turn into songs, too many instrumental possibilities with which to play. And the sand in the upper part of the hourglass was thinning. He did *not* want the sand to run out, he did not seek solace or refuge in death; as long as he was in good health, the disappointments of his life did not drive him deeper into the dark than they would any man. But the thought that he would have to mark another "Unfinished" on his work, that thought agonized him. One example among several is his oratorio *Lazarus* of 1820. In spite of some beautiful passages, the work is lukewarm, and suddenly Schubert broke off in the middle of a sentence, leaving the thing unfinished. He was a man haunted, plagued, pushed by his talent. "I compose one piece," he said, "and when I have finished one I immediately begin another." Not always did he finish one piece before he began another.

That is not to say that Schubert sat weeping by the brook.

Some seven years after he composed "Death and the Maiden,"* in other words when Schubert was turning twenty-seven, he brought forth the D-Minor Quartet, which has come to be known popularly as the *Death and the Maiden* Quartet, because the variations of the slow movement use quotations from the song. This was his fourteenth string quartet, and the distance from his preceding accomplishments in quartet-writing seems as great as the distance between Mozart's *La Finta Giardiniera* and *Don Giovanni*, or between *Two Gentlemen of Verona* and *Othello*, or for that matter between Schubert's *Unfinished* Symphony and the one of the year before. A gradual climb toward its largeness of panorama and depth of feeling is not observable. It seems to have happened all at

---

*Andreas Schubert, Franz's stepbrother, took the manuscript of the song and cut it into eleven pieces. He distributed these as souvenirs. The Gesellschaft der Musikfreunde in Vienna possesses six of them.

once. How? Why? One can only theorize that the theme inspired him and that an opportunity presented itself. He had met Ignaz Schuppanzigh, leader of the great quartets of Beethoven. For the use of that fine musician, worthily partnered, Schubert composed the gentle and fragrant A-Minor Quartet (published in 1825 as op. 29) and a few months later the D-Minor. How "modern" this music sounds today. Not only the variations of the second movement, but the scherzo which isn't funny at all, and the death-defying finale, the presto! Nineteenth-century critics used to construct an elaborate program for this work. There is no need for such spelling out, though one need not deny all connection with the thought of death.

The romantics did not listen only to funeral songs. Aware as they were of the theme of death, they were equally sentient of a new attitude toward life. Rousseau had implanted the seed; it had grown slowly, taking almost a century for its development. Now it was in bloom. That attitude was the urge to discover one's true self and to express it creatively. The individual became all-important; his passions and impulses were now to be spoken of openly, in language which broke the contained design of the classic tradition. Novalis wrote that genius must be absolved from moral and social obligations; it was "a force above the law." And "romanticizing is nothing but the enhancement of potentiality." In *Childe Harold's Pilgrimage* Byron defined the new poetry:

> For what is Poesy but to create
> From overfeeling, Good and Ill, and aim
> At an external life beyond our fate,
> And be the new Prometheus of a new man,
> Bestowing fire from heaven, and then, too late,
> Finding the pleasure given repaid with pain.

Goethe in *Werther* and *Wilhelm Meister* was the great guide to the romantic vision. In England, in addition to Byron, Shelley (*Prometheus Unbound*), the early Coleridge, and Blake spoke, while in Poland Adam Mickiewicz followed Byron's lead; in Scotland, Scott's *The Lady of the Lake* appeared in 1805, *Ivanhoe* in 1819; in France, Lamartine, Lamennais, and later Victor Hugo (*Hernani* in 1830, *Notre Dame de Paris* in 1831).

This consciousness of the individual—what in German literature was called the *Ich-Roman*—can be traced in Schubert as well. The charming "An eine Quelle" ("To a Source," 1817, by Claudius) or "An die Nachtigall" ("To a Nightingale," 1816, by Claudius) or "Trost im Liede" ("Consolation in Song," 1817, by Schober) or "Freiwilliges Versinken" ("Sunset," 1817, by Mayrhofer) or that famous lullaby "Schlafe, schlafe" (1817, author unknown), to which Richard Strauss paid a compliment by including the tune in his *Ariadne auf Naxos*—these, all composed when Schubert was about twenty, belong to the lighter part of the romantic spirit as surely as does Constable's *The Hay Wain* or Caspar Friedrich's *Man on the Mountain Top*.

A figure who symbolized the romantics is Prometheus, the Titan of Greek myth who serves as the spokesman for Man, man in his strength defying the inimical gods and possessing the courage both to weep and to laugh. From Aeschylus on he has inspired poets. In 1819 Schubert set Goethe's scornful poem to music which tears conventions to pieces in its blazing intensity. "Not until Wagner's *Tristan*," writes Fischer-Dieskau, "do we meet another composition with such daring harmonies and fascinating progressions." It is an *Ich-Roman* which influenced future vocal music. And this paradigm of the romantic movement was produced by a little schoolteacher, still in his early youth.

In August 1817 Schober's brother, Axel, returned from France, and Schober had to ask Schubert to vacate his room. That was awkward, Schubert at that time being poor. Where was he to turn? He asked his father, who once more welcomed him home—but once more exacted what was to the son a harsh condition: Franz was to resume his teaching post. Once more he would have to arise at dawn, make believe that he believed in discipline, look sternly at little boys through his glasses, spend his day in pre-fixed portions of classroom drill, retire early in the evening to dream of music he had no time to compose. In October he did begin work on a Sixth Symphony, but he had to lay it aside and did not complete it till February of the following year; at that, "The Little C-Major" is not a convincing work. At the end of the year Father Schubert was promoted to a new, larger, and more modern school in the Rossau, another suburb. One assumes that his income increased. Son Franz followed to the new school and remained in what he considered slavery until the middle of the following year.

Early in 1818 Schubert experienced the satisfaction of having a song published, the first. It was "Am Erlafsee," a poem by Mayrhofer, tucked into a little guidebook elaborately titled *Picturesque Pocket Book for Friends of Remarkable Localities, Points of Interest of Nature and Art in the Austrian Monarchy*, illustrated, paperbound, and costing six florins, a price which would hinder a large sale. Anyway, there it was, and a month later, on March 1, "an entirely new Overture by Herr Franz Schubert" was performed at a concert at the hall of the hotel The Roman Emperor. To be sure, the Overture was presented in a two-piano arrangement, no orchestra being present, but it did attract some notices, the *Theaterzeitung* of March 14 writing that it was a "wondrously lovely" piece by "a young composer, a pupil of our much-venerated Salieri, who has learned already how to touch and convulse all hearts."

Something more consequential was to follow. Karl Unger, father of Caroline Unger, an adorable girl who charmed Beethoven and sang in the first performance of the Ninth, was an acquaintance of Count Johann Esterházy, a distant relative of Haydn's Esterházys. His wife, Rose (she called herself Heidenröslein after Goethe's poem), and he had two daughters, Maria (born 1802) and Caroline (born 1805), and a son, Albert. The Ungers admired Schubert, and when the Count happened to mention that he was looking for a piano teacher for his daughters they recommended Franz. Both daughters loved music and had pretty voices, though Maria was more intelligent and more talented than her younger sister. Caroline was withdrawn and even years later, when she was thirty, she used to trundle her hoop in the streets of Vienna, all alone. If one wonders why the Count, who could afford the best, would choose somebody who had no experience as a piano teacher, the answer is first that Schubert was available, second that he was young, respectable, and sympathetic, and third that he was willing to serve for very little money (seventy-five florins, A. C., monthly). The Count was parsimonious. Schubert accepted; he was glad to get away from the school and he felt that the sinecure in summer surroundings would leave him leisure to compose.

At the beginning of July Schubert traveled to the Esterházy estate, a castle called Zseliz located near the river Gran (then belonging to Hungary, now part of Czechoslovakia). Zseliz lies about a hundred miles east of Vienna, near where the Danube bends gracefully to flow toward Budapest. It took Schubert fourteen stages, traveling by public coach, to get there, a slow, hot journey. When he arrived, he found that he was to lodge not in the castle but in the servants' building and to take his meals with the staff. That was a shock for the son of a school principal. At least the music room, where he spent most of his time, was beautiful and sunny, the furniture in the best eighteenth-century French style, the paintings pleasant, the piano first class. An excellent little collection of Vienna porcelain was displayed in the corner, and the windows opened onto sun-drenched fields. His first reports were enthusiastic:

Zseliz, 3rd August 1818

Best and dearest friends,

How could I forget you, you who mean everything to me? How are you, Spaun, Schober, Mayrhofer, Senn? Are you well? I am quite well. I live and compose like a god, as though that were as it should be.

Mayrhofer's "Solitude" [*Einsamkeit*] is ready, and I believe it to be the best I have done, for I was without a care. I hope that you are all merry and in the best of health, as I am. Thank God I live at last, and it was high time, otherwise I should have become nothing but a thwarted musician. Schober had better pay my respects to Herr Vogl, to whom I will soon take the liberty of writing . . .[DQ].

("Solitude" is by no means "the best" he had done. He was just being euphoric.)

Yet as quickly as three weeks later a small tone of longing sounded in his letter to Ferdinand:

August 24, 1818

Dear Brother Ferdinand:

It is half-past eleven at night, and your German Requiem is finished. It made me sad, believe me, for I sang it from the depth of my soul. Add what is missing, i.e. write in the words below the music and the signs above it. If you wish to make a number of repeats, do so, without writing to Zseliz to ask me about it. Things are not well with you: I wish I might change with you, so that you might be happy for once. You would then find all heavy burdens cast off your shoulders. I could wish this for you with all my heart, dear brother. —My foot is going to sleep, much to my annoyance. If the dolt could write it could not go to sleep. . . . Good morning, dear little Brother. I have now slept together with my foot and continue my letter at 8 A.M. on the 25th. In exchange for your request I have another: love to my dear parents, brothers and sisters, friends and acquaintances, not forgetting Karl in particular. Did he not remember me in his letter? . . . Kick my city friends mightily, or have them kicked, to make them write to me. Tell Mother [his stepmother] that my laundry is very well looked after, and that her motherly care greatly touches me. (But if I could have more apparel, I should be extremely glad if you were to send me an extra supply of handkerchiefs, scarves and stockings. Also I am much in need of two pairs of—cashmere trousers, for which Hart [a tailor] may take the measure where he will. I should send the money for them at once.) . . . Well and happy as I am here, and kind as the people are, I look forward with immense pleasure to the moment at which the word will be "To Vienna, to Vienna!" Indeed, beloved Vienna, thou holdest all that is most dear and cherished in thy narrow space, and nothing but the sight of this, the heavenly sight, will appease my yearning. Requesting once again the fulfillment of the wishes mentioned above,

> I remain, with true affection for you all,
> Your sincerely faithful Franz.
> A thousand greetings to your good wife
> and your dear Resi [Ferdinand's
> youngest child].

(The *German Requiem* was a composition Schubert wrote for Ferdinand to help him show his ability in music and prove his all-round capability as a teacher. Ferdinand performed the work that year, giving it out as his own. In 1826 Diabelli published it under the name of Ferdinand Schubert. A century later it was republished as a work by Schubert. It is of small value.)

In September in a letter to his friends the note of longing swelled:

8th September 1818

Dear Schober, dear Spaun, dear Mayrhofer, dear Senn, dear Streinsberg, dear Waiss, dear Weidlich,

How infinitely the letters from you, all and sundry, delighted me is not to be expressed! I was just attending a deal in oxen and cows when your nice, portly letter was handed to me. As I broke it open, loud cries of joy burst from me on beholding the name of Schober. I read it in a neighbouring room, with continual laughter and childish pleasure. It was as though I were laying my hands on my dear friends themselves. . . .

In Zseliz I am obliged to rely wholly on myself. I have to be composer, author, audience, and goodness knows what else. Not a soul here has any feeling for true art, or at most the countess now and again (unless I am wrong). So I am alone with my beloved [music] and have to hide her in my room, in my pianoforte and in my bosom. Although this often makes me sad, on the other hand it elevates me the more. Have no fear, then, that I shall stay longer than is absolutely necessary. Several songs have materialized these days—very good ones, I hope.

That the Greek bird [Vogl] flutters about in Upper Austria does not surprise me, since it is his native country and he is on holiday. I wish I were with him, then I should certainly make the most of my time. . . .

Now a description for everybody:

Our castle is not one of the largest, but very neatly built. It is surrounded by a most beautiful garden. I live at the inspectorate. It is fairly quiet, save for some forty geese, which at times cackle so lustily together that one cannot hear oneself speak. Good people around me, all of them. It must be rare for a count's retinue to fit so well together as these do. . . . The inspector, a Slavonian, is a good fellow, and has a great opinion of his former musical talents. He still blows two German dances in ¾ time on the lute, with great virtuosity. His son studies philosophy, is here on holiday just now, and I hope I shall take to him. His wife is a woman like all women who want to be ladies. The steward fits his office perfectly: a man with an extraordinary insight into his pockets and bags. The doctor, who is really accomplished, ails like an old lady at the age of 24. Very unnatural. The surgeon, whom I like best, is a venerable old man of 75, always cheerful and happy. May God give every one so happy an old age! The magistrate is an unassuming, excellent man. A companion of the count, a merry old fellow and a capable musician, often keeps me company. The cook, the lady's maid, the chambermaid, the nurse, the manager, etc. and two grooms are all good folk. The cook rather a rake; the lady's maid 30 years of age; the chambermaid very pretty and often my companion; the nurse a good old thing; the manager my rival. The two grooms are more fit for traffic with horses than with human beings. The count is rather rough, the countess haughty but more sensitive; the little countesses are nice children. So far I have been spared dining with the family. Now I cannot think of any more; I hardly need tell you, who know me, that with my natural candour I hit it off quite well with all these people. . . .

And now, dear friends, the very best to you all. Only write to me very soon. My favourite and most valued entertainment is to read over your letters a dozen times.

Greetings to my dear parents, whom please tell that I long for a letter from them [DQ].

The next month he did get a letter from Ignaz, his intellectual hunchback brother, who wrote:

[*Vienna*] *October 12* [*1818*]

Dear Brother,

At last, at long last, as you will think, one sets eyes on a few lines. But indeed, I believe you would have seen nothing even now, had not the welcome vacations arrived in the end, much to my relief, and given me leisure enough to write a decent letter, undisturbed and without any irksome thoughts.

You happy creature! How enviable is your lot! You live in sweet, golden freedom, can give free rein to your musical genius, may let your thoughts stray where they will; you are loved, admired and idolized, while the likes of us wretched scholastic beasts of burden are abandoned to all the roughnesses of wild youngsters and exposed to a host of abuses, not to mention that we are further humiliatingly subjected to an ungrateful public and a lot of dunderheaded bigwigs. You will be surprised when I tell you that it has got to such a pitch in our house that they no longer even dare to laugh when I tell them a funny yarn about superstition in the Scripture class. You may thus easily imagine that in these circumstances I am often seized by a secret anger, and that I am acquainted with liberty only by name. You see, you are now free of all these things, you are delivered, you see and hear nothing of all these goings on, much less of our pundits. . . .

Your Brother Ignaz

If you should wish to write to Papa and me at the same time, do not touch upon any religious matters [DQ].

The letter is significant since it indicates what his brothers thought of Franz. "Happy creature . . . enviable . . . musical genius . . . loved, admired and idolized." The "happy creature" not only gave musical instruction to more or less responsive young ladies, but played dinner and dance music for the occasional evenings at Zseliz castle. This was a throwback to Haydn's days, minus the peruke, as if the promotion of the musician's social status, inaugurated by Beethoven, had never happened. And the longer Schubert remained at Zseliz among the haystacks, the stables, the cattle auctions, and the cackling geese, the less comfortable did he feel. The chambermaid notwithstanding, in October he wrote Ferdinand: "My longing for Vienna grows daily."

He returned in the middle of November to the city of his dreams. Better inhaling dust and getting a glimpse of St. Stephen's Cathedral than breathing good air and seeing plowshares.

2.

Vienna that year was taken captive by the bubbling melodies of "Signor Crescendo," the one and only Gioacchino Antonio Rossini. His *Tancredi* had been given in 1816 and the big "hit" of that opera, "Di tanti palpiti," was being whistled by high and low. His *L'Italiana in Algeri* had its Viennese premiere when Schubert was twenty, and *The Barber*, though not yet performed there, was already well known. When five years later Rossini visited Vienna, people followed him whenever he appeared on the streets, strangers stopped him to express their admiration, mothers lifted their little children to point him out, crowds filled the square in front of his hotel, forcing him to appear on the balcony and to sing—his face lit by an all-embracing smile—"Figaro qua, Figaro là" at 2 A.M. Beethoven, though he scolded Vienna for its infatuation, admired him, and so did Schubert, who liked *The Barber* especially, as well as *Tancredi* and the last act of *Otello*. Schubert's two overtures "in the Italian style" (so named by his brother Ferdinand) are obviously influenced by Rossini, though the first, the one in D major, is certainly more Schubert than Rossini and contains a beautiful lyric section, while the second, in C, does evoke the Italian, his wit and brio, crashes and crescendos.

Returned to Vienna, Schubert decided that under no circumstances, come what might, would he continue teaching. It was the second parting from the work he hated, and this time there was no *auf Wiedersehen*. He left his father's house, left the Rossau, and moved in with Johann Mayrhofer, the young poet. Mayrhofer lived in the inner city, in the Wipplingerstrasse (now No. 2), sharing his one room with Schubert. Their landlady, Anna Sanssouci, a tobacconist, treated the two young men kindly. Schubert remained there from 1818 till the end of 1820.

In the summer of 1819 Vogl took him on a tour where he poured Schubert songs into willing ears; slowly his fame increased, not only through Vogl's advocacy but through such knowledgeable men as Ignaz Sonnleithner, in whose house a Schubert cantata, *Prometheus* (*not* to words by Goethe but by Philipp Dräxler), had its second performance in 1819. Ignaz's son Leopold described the impression the cantata made on him:

> The work, full of expression and emotion and brilliantly orchestrated, nevertheless did not receive a public performance. I proposed it repeatedly for performance at the concerts of the *Musikverein*, but nobody would risk presenting the work of a young, as yet unrecognized composer. Alas, the work has taken its own revenge for this insult: it is lost.

It was never found, in spite of much effort. Tradition has it that it contained an impassioned appeal for liberty; perhaps that was the real reason why it was not publicly performed.

This was the year, too, in which Steyr's eminent patron of music, Sylvester Paumgartner, a wealthy bachelor, commissioned Schubert to compose the *Trout* Quintet. Paumgartner loved the song and was equally delighted with the Quintet, on which Schubert expended much care. Water in motion, light in motion, fish and frog and butterfly in motion—the joy of free movement, which you find at its happiest in the famous *Trout* Quintet. Music itself is motion if it is anything, and that is the feeling we get from this work. "Gems of earth and sky begotten," as George Eliot wrote. Let's for once connect the composer with the composition, because we know that Schubert composed it in a blissful mood during that beneficent summer he spent in Steyr with Vogl and other friends. At least such was his mood when he began the work and it was strong enough to last till the autumn of 1819, when he finished it. He lingered over it and the sun seems to have shone on the music paper. It is one tune after another. There are five movements, the most famous being the fourth, the andantino, a set of variations on the song itself. The fifth variation is a wonderful meditation for the cello; in the last, piano and violin state the song in a gay finale.

After 1819 the composition disappeared and nobody heard of it until ten years later. Ferdinand Schubert then sold it to Josef Czerny, the Viennese publisher, who published it in May 1829. Czerny announced that "musical connoisseurs" had declared it "a masterpiece . . . by the unforgettable composer." That praise came too late.

Fortunately other praise came sooner. Leopold Sonnleithner asked him why his songs, by this time quite well known, had not been published. Schubert answered that no publisher was interested and he didn't have the money to publish them himself. Whereupon Leopold rallied a few friends, raised some money, and paid the publisher Diabelli to have a small collection of them printed in an edition of a hundred copies. At one of the get-togethers in Sonnleithner's home, Leopold "laid the bundle on the table and announced that if anyone wanted to possess these songs, he could buy them." To attest that these copies were the true first edition, Leopold marked the back of each with "Sch" or "Schbt." Another version of the story says that it was Schubert himself who marked the copies. They cost one florin, thirty kreuzer, a reasonable price, and they were quickly snapped up. Shortly after, "Gretchen am Spinnrade" was engraved and published in two editions, selling 500 copies. The mixed Goethe songs (op. 3) sold 400 copies in two printings. As to the "Erl-könig" (op. 1), that proved to be the most popular, as expected: three editions were published, selling about 600 copies. When Diabelli published the song at two florins, the advertisement in the *Wiener Zeitung* read:

At the House of Cappi and Diabelli, Graben, No. 1133, is
newly published and to be had:
ERLKING
Ballad by Goethe, set to music and reverentially dedicated to
the Hon. Herr Herr [sic]
Moritz, Count von Dietrichstein
by
Franz Schubert.
Price . . . . 2 florins, V.C.

The value of this composition has already been so favourably and advan-
tageously expressed in the ingenious young composer's honour by the public
verdict at the concert given in the I. & R. Court Opera theatre last Ash
Wednesday, where, delivered by our celebrated Court Opera singer, Herr
Vogl, its repetition was unanimously demanded, as well as by several public
journals, that my further recommendation should be as superfluous as its
appearance in print and its possession by every connoisseur and lover of
song at home and abroad should be welcomed [April 2, 1821].

These publications earned Schubert about 2,000 florins, V.C. Little
enough, but it buttered some parsnips.

Two years previously Josef Hüttenbrenner, writing to his brother Heinrich, had prophesied: "Schubert will actually shine as a new Orion in
the musical heavens."

The mention of Antonio Diabelli (1781–1858), of Beethoven's thirty-
three Variations fame, seems the right moment to say a word about the
music-publishing business in Schubert's time. Music publishers ran retail
shops and there offered for sale products of composers with whom they
had entered into agreements. Later they engraved and printed these works.
Most of the publishers were sincerely interested in music's welfare, though
of course they were businessmen, their first consideration being the necessity to make money. They chose "saleable" stuff, meaning things
people could play or sing. "Don't, don't make it too difficult," was a
constant plea. Several of the publishers, Diabelli among them, began as
composers themselves, but couldn't make the creative grade. On the other
hand, Carl Czerny (1791–1857) was not only an indefatigable composer
but a successful teacher (how children used to hate those piano exercises!)
and a fine theoretician; he ventured into publishing to augment his already
sizable income.

[74]

At one time Schubert entered into a relationship with Ignaz Sauer and Josef Leidesdorf, the first a failed musician, the second an insignificant composer, and both wretched businessmen, never having enough capital to carry on any orderly trade. Schubert had to return to Cappi and Diabelli, a firm he hated.

Partnerships changed, firms combined, the push to make money accelerated. Publishers paid the artist as little as they could—until he became famous. Then—well, Rossini or Beethoven reversed the pressure. That old disagreement, artistry versus commerce, is still with us: "My book didn't sell because the publisher didn't promote it sufficiently."

But the matter is not entirely one-sided. Some publishers took chances, some were forward-looking, some dared to experiment. In the main the publishers treated Schubert shabbily, but it is quite untrue that *nothing* by Schubert was published during his lifetime. His output was so large that no one publisher could handle it. As usual, there is a bit of truth on both sides. About half of Schubert's major works were published during his life. For them he was paid a shameful pittance. But until his last two years he did not dare to ask for more. He knew the worth of his work musically, not its commercial value. As a businessman, he must be written off.

6

The "Young Intellectuals"

EVERY ARTIST IS A PLANET, MINOR OR MAJOR, AROUND WHICH SEVERAL
moons circle. He, the artist, holds these moons in orbit by the force of
his personality; his genius sheds a glow on those who would like to be
artists but are *not*, or on those who are curious to explore the world of
art—headier than their own world—or on those who merely derive
vicarious excitement from knowing "a celebrity." Schubert attracted many
moons, he had many friends, astonishingly many, and it was they who
gave him connection with the world, provided practical help, lavished
admiration, offered warmth and affection, and shared with him their
hopes and thoughts during those late evenings at Vienna's coffeehouses,
thick with smoke and thin with light wine, evenings which have been
misinterpreted as orgies-at-the-inn. His friends were Schubert's real family. It was a giving, understanding family. Conversely, their lives were
made exciting and some of them were rescued from oblivion because
they knew Schubert.

What kind of men were they? With all the differences in education,
disposition, endowment, wealth, we can make some general observations.
Most of them were young and unmarried when the friendships were
formed. Most of the friends acquired early (Spaun, Hüttenbrenner, Schober)
remained steadfast and loyal to Schubert, remarkably so. Schubert hardly
lost a single friend through indifference or a quarrel. They were artistically
inclined, enthusiastically appreciative of poetry and music. With one
exception none of them possessed a strong creative talent. They dabbled
in the arts and were at best pleasant dilettantes. One feeling they held

unanimously: they all shared a hatred of the prevailing political conditions, they all longed for change.

Schubert participated in this longing. His friends and he were at one in the belief that "things couldn't remain as they were." The famous *Schubertiaden,* the get-togethers when they read Goethe and Herder and Schiller, were as well meetings in which political ideas were bandied about. Between the jokes and the sociability came serious ideas. Schubert belonged to these "revolutionaries," who, to be sure, did not mount barricades or issue hot pamphlets but merely grumbled and talked long hours. Nevertheless they were the forerunners of the March uprising of 1830 and the European revolutions of 1848, undermining in their loathing the Metternich system.

There was plenty to loathe. Austria was veering more and more toward a police state. Even Grillparzer, Austria's national poet, suffered under a censorship which grew ever stricter. His drama *King Ottokar's Fortune and End* lay for years in a drawer of the Censorship Bureau; nobody could find anything objectionable in it, but everybody was afraid of a story depicting a king's downfall until the Empress read it, liked it, and insisted on its being performed. Schiller's *Maria Stuart* could not be given, and as to his *Wilhelm Tell,* there was no question that this incendiary call for revolution was to remain permanently on the Index. If a "villain" was to appear in a play, he could not be a minister, a general, a priest, a chancellor, but only a person of low degree, to show that nothing could be wrong with the government. All manuscripts—essays, novels, plays, songs, even inscriptions on gravestones—had to be submitted to the Censorship Bureau, legibly written, with wide margins for comments. The Bureau decided that a manuscript was *admittitur* (admitted), or *transeat* (admitted with reservations, such as that it was prohibited from being announced in the newspapers), or *absque loco impressionis* (place of publishing could not be mentioned), or *omissis deletis* (can be printed if changed according to instruction by the censor), or finally *damnatur* (altogether forbidden).

Schubert experienced one or two set-tos with the censorship. In 1817 (probably) he composed a song called "To Death," text by Friedrich Schubart. It is a wretched poem and the song doesn't amount to much, but one of the verses speaks of "Death avoiding the golden palace of the sovereign ... till he has had enough of vainglory." According to the censorship law of 1810, paragraph 10, "all writings tending to loosen the relationship between sovereign and subject are forbidden." The song was promptly forbidden.*

Early in 1829 Czerny planned to publish, among other Schubert compositions, his song "Der Kampf" ("The Battle," by Schiller). It received a *damnatur*. What was offensive about it? Czerny pointed out that the poem could be bought in any bookstore. No matter—it took till March before the song received a *transeat*.

Metternich employed an army of private police whom the Viennese called *Spitzel* (spies) or *Naderer* (informers). "Now the Assembly is working on a law"—wrote a friend in Beethoven's Conversation Book—"which prescribes how high the birds are permitted to fly and how fast the rabbits may run." Things got worse after 1819, when Metternich used the Kotzebue assassination as a reason for appointing "monitors" to supervise teaching in the universities. The universities were to have no contact with exterior institutions, and the establishment of the Austrian Academy of Science, attempted several times, was several times postponed (until 1847). Swimming and other communal gymnastics were frowned upon because they gave young people an excuse to congregate.

Vienna being Vienna, one learned to walk slyly around the law. A visitor from Germany reported that to his astonishment he found that "everybody was freely talking politics, constantly launching bonmots against crown and the purple; one finds *forbidden* books in all houses; they subscribe to *forbidden* periodicals, they smoke *forbidden* tobacco even where smoking is prohibited, they buy *forbidden* goods which would have cost more had they not arrived in Vienna by *forbidden* means, they drink *forbidden* wines, and find wherever they want *forbidden* girls" (Adolph Glassbrenner, *Impressions and Dreams from Vienna*, 1836).

Of course life was not all grim, especially if you were young. The beauty of the city remained untouched. The coffee remained excellent, the wine comforting, the forbidden tobacco—which Schubert *had* to have—easily obtainable. Yet, and not in Austria alone, "The spirit of unrest, which was the spirit of the first half of the nineteenth century, was seething in every country. It was not the lees of 1789; it was the ferment of a new and no less inebriating vintage. It was not the rise of the internal and external proletariat; it was the rise of the internal and external bourgeoisie, the revolt of the young intellectuals" (Harold Nicolson, *The Congress of Vienna*).

*The document prohibiting the song was burned in the fire of the Vienna Palace of Justice in 1927. The story of the song was researched by Walter Dürr.

Schubert in 1825—a highly idealized watercolor by Wilhelm
Rieder. (Schubert Museum, Vienna)

Schubert's birthplace—it was not a hovel.

Schubert's father—a portrait by an unknown artist. Was he really as dour as that? No reasonable portrait of his mother nor of his stepmother exists. (Schubert Museum, Vienna)

Ferdinand—a photograph taken of Schubert's favorite brother in his old age.

Franz Schubert. A drawing by Joseph Teltscher (1801–1837), a popular portraitist and a friend of Schubert. This drawing, from 1825 or 1826, has never before been published. (Courtesy of the Historic Museum of the City of Vienna.)

Johann Michael Vogl, the famous singer who combined his later
career with Schubert's.

Early and lifelong friend Josef
Spaun. Portrait by Kupel-
wieser.

Moritz Schwind, the talented
illustrator of German legends
and fairy tales, idolized Schubert. (Lithograph, Vienna
State Library)

Franz Bruchmann, Schubert's
friend. Pencil drawing circa
1821. (Historic Museum of
Vienna)

Karl Mayrhofer—Schubert set
several of his poems to music.
Mayrhofer committed suicide.
Pencil drawing by Schwind.
(Innsbruck Library)

Franz Schober, the brilliant
"Mephistophelian"
character of the Schubert
circle. The Napoleonic
gesture is characteristic.
(Schubert Museum,
Vienna)

Johann Michael Senn, the
Tyrolean poet, who was
condemned and banished.
Schubert never forgot him
or his fate. (National
Library, Vienna)

The extraordinary collaboration: Vogl and Schubert. Sketch by Schwind. (Schubert Museum, Vienna)

"Vogl and Schubert set out to do battle and win." This caricature first appeared in Dresden.

Schubert's friends, and Schubert himself, belonged to the rising bourgeoisie. The "spirit of unrest" can be felt in what they wrote and how they acted, and in several of the texts which Schubert formed into songs.* Not all of his friends, of course, were firebrands. They ranged from the conservative and conciliatory—for example, Josef Spaun—to the advocates of revolt, such as Bauernfeld, who dared to exclaim early, "In the name of hell, *when* are we going to abolish censorship?"

Let us now look more closely at some of Schubert's friends and their roles in his life.

Josef von Spaun (1788–1865) was Schubert's first good friend. The two met at the Seminary, where Spaun, very musical, played in the school orchestra. He was nine years older than Schubert and had almost completed his study of law under Professor Heinrich Watteroth, a liberal and understanding teacher, the same man for whom Schubert composed a cantata—on the subject of Prometheus—"for money for the first time." (The work is lost.) Spaun was the son of well-to-do parents. His background and education inclined him to view the world tolerantly, however faulty he found it. He believed in traditional government, and realizing that he did not, with all his love for music, have enough talent to become a professional, he set out on a government career. He recognized Schubert's talent when as yet it was but an indication, and from then on, as long as Schubert lived, he was tireless in promoting his friend's cause. He introduced Schubert to his fellow law students Mayrhofer, Schober, and Witteczek, who formed the nucleus of the Schubert circle. All of them liked Spaun, though they differed with him politically. Spaun was investigated by official functionaries—the documents addressed to Emperor Francis are extant—and received high marks for reliability, character, and behavior. He "could be trusted." Consequently his career was successful; he became an important Austrian official and Director of the Government Lottery, and as such had to absent himself from Vienna several times, in 1821 for five years. He returned and the friendship was resumed as if the two had seen each other yesterday.

It was Spaun who made it possible for Schubert to receive the hospitality of Watteroth when he left his parents' home in 1816. It was Spaun who in that same year gathered a bundle of the Schubert-Goethe songs and sent them to the Olympian at Weimar with a letter which began with:

* Examples: "Der Vatermörder"; "Der zürnende Barde"; "Die gefangenen Sänger"; "Orest"; "Irlicht." And of course *Prometheus*.

April 17, 1816

Your Excellency:

The undersigned ventures to rob Your Excellency of a moment of your valuable time with these lines, and only the hope that the enclosed collection of songs might be a not altogether unpleasant gift can excuse him for taking so great a liberty. The works in the enclosed book are by a 19-year-old composer named Franz Schubert, whom Nature has endowed from his earliest years with the most remarkable talent for composition, which Salieri, the Nestor among composers, has brought to maturity, by means of his selfless devotion to his Art . . .

and after much verbiage came to the point:

The artist wishes humbly to dedicate this collection to Your Excellency to whose so magnificent poetry he is indebted, not only for the origin of a large part of them, but essentially also for his own maturing as a German composer. Yet, as he is too modest to consider his works worthy of the great honour of confronting a name so celebrated wherever the German language is spoken, he has not the courage to request this great favour of Your Excellency. I, therefore, one of his friends, and permeated with his music, venture to ask Your Excellency for this favour on his behalf; care will be taken to prepare an edition worthy of this favour.

Goethe probably did not even open this package but returned it wordlessly. A second group of songs, sent by Spaun, was not even returned. Hindsight has censured Goethe for his shortsightedness. No doubt the famous man acted neither courteously nor kindly; but we must remember that the poet, growing old and withdrawing from the world, was inundated with petitions, requests to read this or that, tributes and flattery. He could not decipher a musical score and was musically dependent on the opinions of Carl Zelter, one of his good friends and one of the very few who addressed him by the familiar *du*. Zelter, director of the Berlin Singakademie and teacher of Mendelssohn, was an archconservative and would have disapproved of Schubert's "Gretchen am Spinnrade."*

Spaun wrote several reminiscences of Schubert, loving and modest. The last of his manuscripts ends with, "I thank him for the benison of beautifying the lives of his friends." I have said that I believe these reminiscences to be accurate. Yet one or two sentimental bits of fiction have

---

* Zelter composed an "Erlkönig"; it was one of about seventy settings of that poem and was promptly forgotten.

been stuffed into them, to be repeated in later biographies. For example, Spaun tells us that he came on Schubert "all aglow reading the 'Erlkönig' aloud," pacing up and down in his room. Suddenly he sat down and "in no time at all" the ballad was done. They ran to the Seminary, "as Schubert had no piano" (definitely wrong) and "the Erlkönig was sung and wildly acclaimed." Maurice Brown has pointed out that it would be impossible—even for Schubert—to write out the piano part "in no time at all." Brown (and Brahms) also doubted the claim that Spaun supplied Schubert with music paper; the Seminary had plenty of it, as proved by the paper on which his early scores are written. These are minor faults; what is important is that Spaun's love and admiration glow through the many pages he wrote about his friend.

Franz von Schober (1796–1882), was the sharp contrast to Spaun! He shone as Schubert's circle's fiery star. A character out of Dumas, he was daring, politically radical, endowed with a brilliant mind, but unanchored, rushing from one enthusiasm to the next. The son of a Viennese mother and a Swedish father, he was wealthy enough not to have to worry about earning a penny—and he didn't. Having heard some of Schubert's songs, he sought him out without waiting for an introduction, and found him in the schoolroom correcting papers. At once Schober remonstrated with Schubert: he was wasting his life, he must summon the courage to throw over schoolmastering and devote himself to music. Schober himself, one year older than Schubert, never found a firm vocation, trying the law, writing, acting, producing plays, publishing, lithography. Personally this "Count of Monte Cristo" was irresistible, an indefatigable womanizer of rakish looks with the typical little moustache. As a friend said of him, he "despised women and knew only two kinds, the worthwhile ones who went to bed with him and the unworthy ones who could not rise to this opportunity" (letter by Josef Kenner to F. Luib, May 22, 1888). Schober constructed a philosophical system for himself to serve his own justification, proclaiming "an aesthetic oracle as obtuse to himself as it was to his disciples, but which served his hedonism." As he grew older he saw himself "not only as a prophet but as a deity, permitting no other God." Yet this misogynist loved, loved selflessly, Bruchmann's sister, Justina, who died early in childbirth. (More about Bruchmann in a moment.) He, like Spaun, helped Schubert selflessly; three times they shared lodgings, with Schober paying. Schubert called him "a divine fellow," admired his insouciance, his elegance, his nonchalant attitude. The other friends were jealous of Schober. His influence on Schubert was both beneficial and baneful. He inaugurated the "reading evenings" which Schubert loved, and organized many a country excursion.* However, he suggested other, less healthful excursions as well, those to the rooms of Viennese doxies.

He wrote for Schubert the texts of many poems, of which Schubert chose a dozen. One, "An die Musik," is one of the most touching of Schubert's songs. Who can fail to be moved when music and text, perfectly unified, speak of "gray hours" of discouragement, pay tribute to music for its power to lift us to "a better world," and end with an exclamation of gratitude to that *holde Kunst,* that "lovable art"?

For his part in this collaboration Schober earned immortality. One of the autograph copies in Schubert's handwriting (he made several) is in the Paris Conservatoire, enclosed in an envelope marked *manuscrit très précieux.*†

The playwright Eduard Bauernfeld summed up Schober: "He is intellectually superior to all of us, most certainly in his conversation. Yet, because much in him is artificial, his best abilities end in a void."

Johann Mayrhofer (1787–1836) wrote:

> My friendship with Schubert began after one of his friends [Spaun] had given him my poem *Am See* to set to music. Schubert came with this friend into the room which we were to share five years later. It is in the Wipplingerstrasse. Both the house and the room had felt the weight of the years, the ceiling had sunk somewhat, the light was blocked by a large building opposite—there was a much used piano and a tiny bookcase. The room and the hours spent in it will never be erased from my memory (Mayrhofer, *Reminiscences,* 1829).

Ten years older than Schubert, he longed to be a poet, a great poet like Goethe, whom he idolized, but he didn't possess genius, just a certain skill with words—manipulating the standard vocabulary and sentiments

---

*Meetings of Schubert's friends were held in Atzenbrugg from 1817 to 1822. It was a beautiful village, about twenty miles from Vienna, surrounded by fields where one could picnic and play games.

†If the reader will pardon an autobiographical note: One of the wonderful recollections of my long concert-going career was Lotte Lehmann's singing of "An die Musik." She sang it as a last encore in her farewell recital (February 16, 1951) and broke down in the middle of it, overcome by tears.

of romanticism, "longing," "moon," "secret," "farewell," "violets of night." Schubert set forty-eight of these poems to music, but Mayrhofer knew the poems weren't good enough. He certainly could not make a living as a poet—he was poor—and so became, of all things, a book censor! Spaun wrote of him:

> Mayrhofer was renowned above all for his profound knowledge of Latin, Greek and the classical authors. He was often very badly off, but, apart from his pipe, he had few wants. Since his superior literary background was well known in certain circles, he was given a minor, though reasonably well-paid post in the office of the book censor, and was later promoted to the post of Book Censor. Since he had extreme liberal, indeed democratic sentiments, and was keenly in favor of a free press, only necessity could have driven him into the office of the book censor. What is surprising, when one considers his views, is that he was feared by all booksellers, because of his strictness.

He was a man, then, who loved liberty and served repression. This deepened the moroseness of a nature inclined to melancholy. Taciturn and withdrawn—his favorite book was Young's *Night Thoughts*—he was unpopular with the other friends, but Schubert remained loyal to him. After Schubert's death he sank into deeper shadows. One day in 1836 he took a pinch of snuff and threw himself out of the window of his office. He died after two days.

The Hüttenbrenners, Anselm (1794–1868) and Josef (1796–1882), were brothers. Anselm was a friend since Schubert's school days. He met Schubert through Salieri, from whom Anselm took lessons and who formed him into a technically competent composer—technically competent, nothing more. There was a third brother, Heinrich, and all three knew Beethoven. Anselm was present when Beethoven died. The brothers were well-to-do and lived in Graz. Anselm was head of the Styrian Musical Society, Josef became an assistant in the Ministry of the Interior. Though Schubert enjoyed their hospitality, their greatest importance lay in the collection and preservation of much which concerned Schubert: Anselm possessed the manuscript of the B-Minor Symphony (the *Unfinished*). The story is well known that this manuscript was forgotten until Josef told Johann Herbeck, a conductor, that his brother had a number of Schubert memorabilia in his possession. This was thirty-seven years after Schubert's death. Herbeck went to the old, emaciated Anselm and asked diplomatically whether Anselm had any of his own compositions

Herbeck could perform. Of course he did, certainly. Herbeck dutifully chose two overtures. Did Anselm still have some things by Schubert? They would be useful in filling out an all-Viennese program. "Help yourself," said Anselm. "There are a lot of papers in that old chest." Herbeck began to search. After much rummaging and much getting his hands dirty, he found the symphony. It had its premiere the same year.

Josef called himself to A. W. Thayer "Schubert's prophet, singer, friend and pupil." More likely he was Anselm's prophet in later years. Both he and Anselm wrote copious reminiscences of Schubert, enthusiastic but inaccurate.

Schubert treated Josef rather cavalierly; he was irked by Josef's admiring everything that came from Schubert's pen: "That fellow likes everything by me." Just the same, on February 21, 1818, when Schubert and Anselm were in Vienna and brother Josef in Graz, Schubert wrote Josef:

> Dearest friend:
>
> I am extraordinarily happy that you like my songs. As proof of my most sincere friendship, I am sending you a new one that I have just written here at midnight at Anselm Hüttenbrenner's. I wish that we could become even closer friends over a glass of punch —Just now, as I meant to sprinkle the thing with sand in something of a hurry, I was very drowsy, and, taking up the inkwell instead, calmly poured it all over the manuscript. What a calamity!

A photograph of the manuscript with the big ink blot was made in 1870. The original manuscript is lost.

The new song was "Die Forelle" ("The Trout").

Franz Seraph von Bruchmann (1798–1867), though born to an aristocratic family, stood firmly on the extreme left, and though he was a year younger than Schubert, his attitude toward his friend was that of an older, wiser, more experienced man. He was learned and serious, and his influence on Schubert was important, not only because he guided Schubert to much that was beautiful and stimulating in literature—Bruchmann was an indefatigable reader—but he confirmed Schubert's own hope for a freer breath. Bruchmann was a man of contemplation, not of action. And he was imbued with the spirit of love, a truly religious soul. One feels this reading his poems, his letters, and his autobiography. He opened his house, at first presided over by his pretty wife, Justine, to Schubert at any time, day or night. He was constantly intimidated by the police, and constantly blaming himself for not being braver. He wrote: "We were all too weak [meaning the whole Schubert circle] to carry on the fight against this secular authority, and . . . we deserved to be punished for our exuberances, our fiery opposition, and for our headstrong yet impotent defiance." Yet he secretly went to Erlangen University—Viennese students were forbidden to enroll at foreign universities—where he met the philosopher-poet August Platen, whose work he recommended to Schubert. One of Schubert's gayest songs was the result: "Die Liebe hat gelogen" ("Love Died"). When Bruchmann's wife died in childbirth in 1836, he withdrew into isolation, studied Spinoza, returned to Vienna, where he took holy orders, being barred from any political work. When his youngest sister, Justina, became secretly engaged to Schober—whom Bruchmann disliked—he decided to break with all of Schubert's friends. Yet his friendship with Schubert remained unimpeded. Schubert expressed his friend's creed in the powerful song "Der zürnende Barde" ("The Furious Bard"), the burden of that poem being that the bard fears someone might destroy his lyre.

Moritz von Schwind (1804–1871) is a name familiar to German children for his illustrations of fables and fairy tales. He joined the Schubert group when he was only seventeen. He was as yet unknown to fame, a young man so handsome that when he passed more than one Viennese girl gave him a long glance. He had a high voice and his gestures were soft and feminine. In his work he was a complete romantic in the tradition of his romantic predecessors Caspar David Friedrich and Philipp Otto Runge, though Schwind's talent was not equivalent to either. He was a mediocre painter but an imaginative draftsman, living in the world of Melusine, Rumpelstilzken, Beauty and the Beast. He adored Schubert—Schwind's nature may have contained some homosexual tendencies—to which Schubert responded only lukewarmly. The playwright Bauernfeld described the relationship, possibly with an iota of poetic license:

The relationship between Schubert and Schwind was special and unique. Moritz Schwind, an artist through and through, was as made for music as for painting. The romantic element in his nature was for the first time convincingly and compellingly satisfied by the compositions of his older friend—this was the music that his soul had longed for. And so he moved

[85]

closer to the master with all his youthful passion and gentleness. He loved him dearly, and Schubert, who jokingly called him his beloved, took the young man to his heart. He thought a good deal too of Schwind's understanding of music, and every new song or piano piece was first played to his young friend, to whom it always sounded like a fresh revelation of his own soul.

Schwind to Schober:

Vienna, February 14, 1825

Schubert is well and busy again after a certain stagnation. He has recently come to live next door to me, where the ale-house is, on the second floor, in a very pretty room. We meet daily, and as far as I can I share his whole life with him. . . . The new Variations for 4 hands (Op. 35) are something quite extraordinary. The theme is as grandiose as it is languid, as purely set—don't laugh—as it is free and noble. In eight variations these pages are quite independently and vitally developed, and yet each again seems to reveal the theme. The character of the marches and the unheard-of depth and loveliness of their trios would astonish you. He is now doing songs. . . . "Diana in Anger" and the "Night Piece" have appeared and are dedicated to Frau von Lászny, Fräulein Buchwieser that was. What a woman! If she were not nearly twice as old as I and unhappily always ill, I should have to leave Vienna, for it would be more than I can stand. Schubert has known her a long time, but I met her only recently. She is pleased with my things and with myself, more than anybody else except you; I had quite a shock the first time, the way she spoke to me and went on with me, as though there were nothing about me she didn't know. Immediately afterwards she was taken ill again and spat blood, so that I have not seen her for a long time; but we are to eat there tomorrow. So now I know what a person looks like who is in ill repute all over the city, and what she does.

Years afterward, Schwind produced the famous sepia drawing called "Schubert Evening at Spaun's." It shows Schubert at the piano, Vogl in an imperious pose singing, a host of friends listening, and a bevy of pretty women (including Katherina Lászny) strewing adoring glances about them. It is an imaginative record: several of those shown could not have been present. (The drawing now hangs in Schubert's birthplace in Vienna.)

Eduard von Bauernfeld (1802–1890) was introduced to Schubert by Schwind; they met in the house of Vincentius Weintridt, a professor of theology who was so outspoken a freethinker that his chair was taken from him in 1820. The friendship between Schubert and Bauernfeld began in 1822 and therefore he was one of the last members of the circle. Yet his observations are among the most perspicacious, simply because he was a professional writer. He was in fact one of Vienna's most popular playwrights. His feathery farces, though they were neither as funny as those of Johann Nestroy nor as humane as those of Ferdinand Raimund, were performed almost twelve hundred times at the Burgtheater, and his shafts of wit rescued many a social evening which threatened to become dull. One of his characters, a "Herr Blase" ("bladder"), became a political symbol. That pleased him: in his book *Memoirs from Old Vienna* he said, "My achievement lies less in poetry than in my endeavor to oppose, along with my contemporaries, intellectual enslavement."

His book is replete with references to Schubert, and he tells an anecdote which seems never to have been recorded in detail elsewhere. (Deutsch sketches it briefly.)

Bauernfeld (after discussing Schubert's love for poetry):

He who understand poets as well as he did is himself a poet! And if you are a poet and like to imbibe a glass of wine or two in the company of friends and equals, you are far from a drunkard. This so-called "drunkard" was sober enough to study the most serious literature. Excerpts from historical and philosophic essays, written by him, are extant. His diaries, even his poems, contain some highly original thoughts. His favorite companions were artists and men related to the arts. By contrast he was actually shy with ordinary or prosaic or boring people, the so-called "culture mob." Goethe's saying, "I prefer being crude to suffering tedium," was his motto. . . . In mediocre company he felt lonely, uncomfortable, morose, kept silent for the most part, and was wont to display bad humor, however sedulously people catered to the famous man. Is it any wonder that now and then he tippled a bit, and that now and then he broke out in recusant remarks which shocked his listeners?

I myself witnessed such a scene, one more comic than questionable. It was on a summer afternoon that he and I with Franz Lachner went to Grinzing, to the "Heurigen." Schubert liked that wine, to me it always tasted sour. We sat together in animated conversation, and started homeward at dusk. I wanted to return at once to my lodging, which was in a distant suburb, but Schubert absolutely forced me to accompany him to a restaurant, nor did he spare me the usual *Kaffeehaus* visit with which he used to conclude an evening or rather a late night. It was 1 A.M. and we began a discussion about music, heated by glass after glass of punch. Schubert had fallen into a kind of transport and was talking, more eloquently than usual, of his future plans. At this moment, as ill luck would have it, a group of musicians from the Opera orchestra entered the place. At once Schubert ceased talking, his brow contracted, his looks hardened; nervously he pushed his spectacles up and down his nose. Hardly had the musicians recognized who he was than they rushed over, shook his hand, covered him with compliments and a hundred cries of flattery. It appeared that they wanted him to write a new composition for them, every one saying not to forget a solo part for *his* particular instrument. Surely he would be willing to—

Schubert, it seemed, was not at all willing. He remained silent. They stormed at him again. He replied curtly, "No—for you I'll not write again. Never!"

"And why not?" they asked irritated. "We think we are artists—as good as you! There are no better in Vienna."

"Artists," Schubert cried, quickly swallowed his last glass of punch and got up. "Artists?" The little man jammed his hat on and faced one of the burliest of the fellows. . . . "You are street musicians! Nothing more! One bites his brass mouthpiece, the other blows into his horn. You call that art? It's a trade, a job, a way to make a living. And you call that art? . . . I am an artist, I am Schubert, Franz Schubert, whom the world knows and who has created great and beautiful things, things which the world does not yet understand . . . cantatas, quartets, operas, symphonies. . . . I am not just a composer of Country Dances, as the stupid newspapers write. . . ."

Schubert went on in this tenor. I give his tirade exactly as he threw it at the dumbfounded musicians, who listened open-mouthed. Finally we succeeded in calming him and taking him home. It was 2 A.M. . . .

The next morning I called on him. He was still asleep. I waited till he awoke. "Ah, it's you," he said, adjusted his glasses, and with a friendly gesture extended his hand. . . . I could not help mentioning the scene of the previous night. . . . "Nonsense!" he laughed loudly and jumped out of bed. . . . "Don't you know that these fellows are the worst connivers in the world? But don't worry. I am very sorry. I'll compose those Soli for them, and they'll kiss my hand" (Eduard Bauernfeld, *Errinnerungen aus Alt-Wien*, 1872; my translation).

In addition to his recollections and descriptions of the composer, Bauernfeld played a role in Schubert's life as a translator. He translated four of Dickens's novels—and then turned to Shakespeare. August Wilhelm Schlegel and the Tiecks had translated some of the plays so well that some Germans still believe that the translations are superior to the originals, avoiding the obscure "Let her not walk i' the sun" or "Gennets for germans" of Elizabethan prosody. Now a Viennese publisher wanted to publish a "Viennese Edition" of Shakespeare, and Bauernfeld was commissioned to translate *Antony and Cleopatra* and *Two Gentlemen of Verona*. Both translations limp badly, but Schubert extracted from the first the drinking song "Come Thou Monarch of the Vine" and from the second the enchanting song "An Sylvia." He turned to Schlegel's translation of *Cymbeline* to produce the famous "Ständchen" ("Hark, Hark, the Lark"), beloved as a song and in orchestral transcriptions. Bauernfeld had the nerve to write some additional verses to this song which should be, and usually are, omitted. At any rate, I find Bauernfeld's sketch of Schubert apt, vivid, and truthful.

Of the Sonnleithner family, Ignaz, the father, was one of Vienna's prominent barristers. Leopold (1797–1873) was Schubert's age and collected all the facts he could find about Schubert's life. His uncle Josef was highly respected by Francis I, who commissioned him to travel with the object of collecting books, portraits, and prints for the Imperial Library. When the Court Theater got into artistic and financial troubles, Josef was appointed Secretary. It was he who suggested to Beethoven, a frequent guest in their house, the subject of Leonore and Florestan and conjugal love. Altogether the Sonnleithners were a highly cultured family, passionate amateurs of music, representative of Vienna's intellectual aristocracy at its best. They lived in a spacious and beautiful home—the Gundelhof—known to every Viennese, and there Leopold organized musical performances to which as many as a hundred and twenty guests were invited. These evenings formed the nucleus of the Gesellschaft der Musikfreunde (Vienna's Philharmonic Society), of which the Sonnleithners were cofounders. Leopold had long loved Schubert's music and worked to make it known.

Enough! The examples cited should suffice to show that Schubert was surrounded by men and women who recognized his worth. He was not forlorn and not alone. If he sometimes ate his bread with tears, at least the friends saw to it that he had bread to eat. And wine to drink.

It is significant that Schubert did not seek personal relationships with contemporary composers, such as Weigl, Tomaschek, Lanner, and others,

[89]

of whom Vienna had plenty. He was uninterested in these fellow musicians; Beethoven, of course, represented something special. Schubert preferred the company of poets, painters, and philosophers.

There lived in addition another friend of Schubert's youth who impinged on Schubert's fate in a curious curve. His story must be told in some detail. His name was Johann Chrisostomus Senn.

7

The Senn Episode

JOHANN SENN (1795–1857), TWO YEARS OLDER THAN SCHUBERT, WAS A
fellow pupil at the Seminary. As boys the two formed a friendship. In
due course Senn enrolled in Vienna University to study law, but it soon
transpired that his real interest and talent lay in poetry. Senn was born
in Tyrol, and his early poems, written while he earned his livelihood by
giving lessons, show the craggy and vigorous characteristics of the mountain folk of that region, often harassed and often rebelling: "The Gods
I serve may not exist, but I will not leave the heights to search the abyss."
Yet he had left the heights and had come to Vienna, where he soon
gathered a group of young admirers around him. Aside from Schubert,
whom he loved, Bruchmann was his close friend. Others—Kupelwieser,
the poet Feuchtersleben, Mayrhofer, Josef Streinsberg (another of Schubert's friends from the Seminary), Spaun, Anton Doblhoff (who was already in the bad graces of the police, but much later became an Austrian
minister), Johann Zechenter (later the husband of Schober's sister)—all
serious fellows, joined. They met at various coffeehouses and of course
the conversations turned political. Metternich's right-hand man, Friedrich
Gentz, had expressly forbidden such assemblies, believing that without
such caution it would be "difficult to gauge, judging the future by the
present, to what degree of depravity even this state may come, which so
far has remained so calm and happy in the paternal care of a virtuous
sovereign." The propaganda machine was working overtime. Adolf Bäuerle,
the influential editor of the *Theaterzeitung,* staged a fairy-tale play with

music by a songsmith named Wenzel Müller.* Its title was *Aline, or Vienna in Another Continent*, and it contained a song with the refrain "Ja nur eine Kaiserstadt, ja nur ein Wien" ("Only one Emperor City, only one Vienna"). *Aline* became the *My Fair Lady* of its day; the Viennese rushed to see it and were happy to believe its hit song. Schubert saw it—but the Senn group were not convinced of its truth. Not in the least. The murmurs of political discontent continued, with Senn one of the spokesmen.

Something slipped, somebody talked out of turn. In March 1820 the police entered Senn's lodgings, searched for forbidden books and pamphlets. Schubert was present. Senn was arrested.† The arresting officer handed in this report:

March, 1820

REPORT FROM HIGH COMMISSIONER OF POLICE

Concerning the stubborn and insulting behaviour evinced by Johann Senn, native of Pfunds in the Tyrol, on being arrested as one of the Freshmen Students' Association, on the occasion of the examination and confiscation of his papers carried out by regulation in his lodgings, during which he used the expressions, among others, that he "did not care a hang about the police," and further, that "the Government was too stupid to be able to penetrate into his secrets." It is also said that his friends, who were present, Schubert, the school assistant from the Rossau, and the law-student Streinsberg, as also the students who joined later, the undergraduate Zechenter [sic] from Cilli and the son of the wholesale dealer Bruchmann, law-student in the fourth year, chimed in against the authorized official in the same tone, inveighing against him with insulting and opprobrious language. The High Commissioner of Police reports this officially, in order that the excessive and reprehensible behaviour of the aforesaid may be suitably punished. The Chief Constable observes that this report will be taken into consideration during the proceedings against Senn; moreover, those individuals who have

*Müller (not to be confused with Wilhelm Müller) wrote a number of popular songs. His "Kommt ein Vogel geflogen" is nearly always mistaken for a true folk song.

†Another, even harsher version of the incident exists. It appeared in a huge *Biographic Lexicon* of sixty volumes, published in Vienna from 1856 to 1891 (obviously after Metternich's disappearance), which sketched the lives of "all memorable people living in Vienna between 1750 and 1850." (Dr. Conrad Wurzbach was chief editor.) According to this *Lexicon*, the group discovered "a spy" in their midst, asked him to leave; when he refused, they threw him out. In revenge, the police "dragged all of Senn's friends and colleagues from their beds that very night." Senn was arrested, grilled by a police commission, and found guilty of treason, though one of the commissioners stated, "He is a genius." I prefer the earlier, less flamboyant version.

conducted themselves rudely towards the High Commissioner of Police during their visit to Senn will be called and severely reprimanded, and at the same time the Court Secretary Streinsberg as well as the wholesale dealer Bruchmann will be informed of their sons' conduct.

[Outside:]

Arrest of Johann Senn,

Excessive conduct of the same

as also of the students

Streinsberg

Zehentner [*sic*]

Bruchmann and

the School Assistant Schubert.

In addition, a report by the Austrian Chief of Police, Count Josef Sedlnitzky, sent to the Emperor and entitled "Emulation of German Student Life by Some Students of Vienna University," lists the suspects. The list is lost—but according to one source Schubert is listed as "An assistant schoolteacher, a backward youth [*beachränkter Junge*] of a local middle-class family."

What is extant is a document by Sedlnitzky, dated March 25, 1820, addressed to the "Chief Police Bureau" and couched in typical bureaucratese which demands "a detailed report concerning the character of the justly jailed private student Joh. Senn, his private and personal connections, . . . his moral and political views and actions, the indecent behaviour of the aforementioned subject during his arrest . . . as well as full information concerning the Students Bruchmann and St[r]einsberg and their behaviour as observed during the arrest . . . with the object that after such observations official proceedings can be commenced, the results of which are to be immediately reported to the C.P.B." Schubert is not mentioned.

Senn was sentenced to fourteen months in jail and was banished, shipped off to Tyrol in a closed carriage. His career was ruined. To get some money he took the place of a well-to-do student who was due for military service. Such substitution was perfectly legal. Then he eked out a sparse livelihood by copying law briefs. Finally he became an instructor in a cadet school. He never saw Schubert again. Or Vienna.

Schubert was merely reprimanded. Yet—and this is the point—he was no longer politically clean, no longer *persona grata* to the authorities. A blot had fallen on his record, he was now listed in the police files; and this, not ignorance of his work, may account for some of the obstruction to his fame and may explain some of the timidity which publishers felt in printing his music. The fact that Sedlnitzky does *not* mention Schubert is as significant as if he had done so. Of course he and his staff knew all about Schubert, the friend of the "justly jailed" Senn. But he knew as well something of Schubert the composer, who had written songs reviewed in the Vienna newspapers, a commissioned opera (*The Twins*), the *Trout* Quintet, and was a pupil of the illustrious Salieri. But a loyal subject? He may have been, in the view of the police, a talent; but he was not a good boy. Even so youthful and slight a transgression sufficed for the authorities to look at Schubert with an inquisitorial squint.

Schubert's affection for Senn did not wane. He mentioned him often as he wrote to his other friends, and he said that "no new friend could take the place of the old one." Absence, which usually does not make the heart grow fonder, did not dim the radiance of Senn's personality. The intransigent and idealistic Tyrolean, whose letters sometimes seem like an avalanche during a thaw, exercised a special fascination on Schubert and on Bruchmann.

The editor of Bruchmann's *Autobiography,* Moriz Enziger, believed that the impetus for this biography lay in Bruchmann's correspondence with Senn, for whose "harsh fate Bruchmann felt himself partly guilty." Many letters went back and forth between the two, bitter letters on Senn's part, consoling on Bruchmann's, reminiscences of happier times interspersed with comments on religion, philosophy, music—and Schubert. Bruchmann aided Senn with gifts of money, not once, but regularly. "I consider it your duty," he told Senn, "to let me know every time you are in need, be it through your own fault or your circumstances." Schubert could not help with money; he helped with warmth of feeling.

Bruchmann visited Senn in 1822. He wrote Schober:

> *Innsbruck, July 8, 1822*
> I spoke to Senn yesterday and spent the half-day with him in the mountains. We got on well and had a happy and affectionate meeting. . . . He went on [cursing], even though my visit, undertaken on behalf of all of you and all of us, proved that we were not put off by what had happened. . . . As far as his external circumstances and his present, far from ideal situation and his plans for release from the Austrian claws are concerned, I shall report when I see you, since the expected change in his situation in a few months' time will afford us an opportunity to act, but here, too, there is not much explicit news. You will, I hope, be satisfied with these few lines, since it is

so difficult to write with Senn so near. Farewell. My regards to Schwind and Schubert.

There was no "opportunity to act." Senn was never pardoned.

In his young days Bruchmann was an agnostic and a revolutionary, at least in his views. Later he turned to pantheism. When his beloved wife died, he became deeply religious. He wrote his *Autobiography* after his "conversion." He then felt that the spirit of the young group had been rightly punished by God, that the incident with the police was "a bolt of lightning from God's right hand." Even then he mourned Senn's fate. Why did the lightning strike *him*? Because "his head was held highest . . . because among all of us he was indubitably the best and the noblest, the heart, soul and concentrating ray of our unity."

Bruchmann probably brought some of Senn's poems back to Schubert, who set them to music. One was "Schwanengesang" ("Song of the Swan"), not to be confused with the later cycle; the other, "Selige Welt" ("Blessed World"). Neither is one of Schubert's best songs. Schubert never gave the slightest inkling that he thought his loyalty to Senn had earned him a pejorative reputation with officialdom.

Senn died in 1857 "in deepest poverty." After his death some of his poems became appreciated. His friends paid for a modest monument, erected in Innsbruck; it shows the Tyrolean red eagle holding a lyre in its claws.

8

Schubert's Failure

THE LONG JOURNEY OVER, A STRANGER ARRIVING IN EARLY-NINETEENTH-century Vienna and alighting from the confines of the post chaise would feel a bit confused, a bit elated, and more than a bit weary. If he looked respectable he would be at once approached by a *Fiaker* driver. "Where can I take Your Excellency?" There were no fixed rates for cab fares, and if the stranger asked the price the answer would be, "Whatever you like, Your Excellency." On further inquiry the best answer he could get would be, "We won't need the judge to settle it, Your Excellency." And off they would trot.

Once on the way the driver became guide and host. His first recommendation was: "Of course you are going to the Opera." He would drive past the building and crack his whip at the big lump of stone surmounted by the imperial-royal eagle. There was the Kärntnertor Theater, built in 1764 and designated the Court Theater. Since 1794 it had been used exclusively for the presentation of opera and ballet, and it represented the center where the Viennese could ogle and dream, the hall of the fairy tale. The driver had never been inside it, but he and a hundred Viennese like him knew all about its singers, its directors, its intrigues, its scandals, just as thousands of Parisians who had never been inside the Louvre knew that there was a painting called *Mona Lisa*. The Opera served not only as a Parnassian meeting place for the Viennese but as an embassy for those tourists who could appreciate the "nobler things" of life, said the driver—those nobler things consisting of singing, pretty scenery, startling stage effects, and scantily clad ballet girls, of whom the most famous and the scantiest clad was the wife of ballet master Salvatore Viganò, for whom Beethoven had composed *The Creatures of Prometheus*.

The Kärntnertor Theater was a possession of the crown. It was leased to Court-appointed directors, such as Count Moritz Dietrichstein, who was an able one. Schubert dedicated the "Erlkönig" to him. His deputy, Ignaz von Mosel, attempted a definition of opera entitled "Experiments with the Aesthetics of Dramatic Composition." Aesthetics or not, the choice of directors and singers and composers was influenced by the whims of Emperor and Empress, and the usual skulduggery was rampant. That had been true even in Mozart's day and was part of the reason why Schikaneder could operate three independent suburban theaters, including the Freihaus Theater, where *Die Zauberflöte* was given on September 30, 1791.

Operatic tastes became by and by signs of political dissension: here the Guelphs advocating German opera—produced by such practitioners as Hoffmeister, Weigl, Winter, and best by Weber—there the Ghibellines of Italian opera, Salieri, Spontini, with Rossini conquering all. The limelight war was fought with considerable fervor.

When Schubert was twenty-four, the Court concluded a twelve-year contract with Domenico Barbaja, the impresario from Naples (who had become rich selling matériel to the army), who possessed a showman's flair for spotting talent. Within a year he had succeeded in engaging not only Rossini but the composer's former mistress, now his wife, the celebrated Isabella Colbran, the dark-voiced mezzo-soprano who drove Vienna mad with admiration.

It was evident that a Viennese composer ought to produce a viable opera to win favor and florins. Schubert was well aware of it. Early, when he was seventeen, he had completed a *Zauberoper*—an opera the story of which contained "magic" ingredients—to a libretto of a prolific playwright, August Kotzebue. (Kotzebue was assassinated by a German student five years later, which gave Metternich the excuse to dissolve student societies and tighten censorship, forcing his "Karlsbad Decrees" into law.) Magic plays and operas were much in vogue, not only because they could employ spectacular stage machinery but also because they persuaded the audience that this was the best of worlds, furnished as they invariably were with the beneficent deity who appeared to set things right when the author couldn't think of another solution. Schubert's opera was entitled *Des Teufels Lustschloss* (*The Devil's Plaisance*). The manuscript of the first act alone is 128 pages long. The second act is lost because many years later a servant of Josef Hüttenbrenner, Schubert's good friend, used the script to light a fire. The libretto deals with the standard haunted castle, a huge hand which rises from the earth, a seductive Amazon, floods, rocks that split in two, a near-execution, a thunderstorm, and an end which explains that the whole tumult was but a trial to test the hero's courage. This nonsense was inspired—if that is the word—by *Die Zauberflöte*, which, stripped of Mozart's music, doesn't make much sense either,* though Schikaneder was ten times more adroit then Kotzebue.

This was the first of fifteen perplexities, the first of fifteen failures. In his songs Schubert could be dramatic: "Erlkönig," "Gretchen am Spinnrade," "Der Tod und das Mädchen," "Prometheus," "Die junge Nonne," "Der Doppelgänger" are superbly dramatic. Why did Schubert fail to produce a good opera? A mystery! Indeed, I think *the* mystery of Schubert's work.

Fifteen failures—one says fifteen quickly, but what a waste, what frustration the number represents! In sheer volume operas are his largest body of work. He filled some two thousand pages with these so-often-inert notes. With no more expenditure of effort he could have penned nine more symphonies, ten more quartets. Aside from waste, there were the hurt, the hopes crushed, the necessity of telling his friends that once more nothing good had happened.

To explain the failure by saying that Schubert's judgment in choosing his librettos was plainly awful, while true, does not altogether elucidate the riddle. It *is* significant that he who had read Goethe, Schiller, Homer, Shakespeare chose for the most part nonentities: six of his librettos were written by friends, two more by the secretary of the Kärntnertor Theater (G. E. von Hofmann). Whatever half-cooked stew, with ingredients pulled from stale soil, was submitted to him, he seems to have accepted uncritically. An opera with a poor libretto is usually doomed—and I know the exceptions as well as the next man, the gypsy-camp clatter of *Il Trovatore* ("I mixed those babies up, and not a creature knew it," says Little Buttercup), or *Lucia di Lammermoor*'s mindless gullibility. But *Trovatore* and *Lucia* are rescued by the force of their music. In general, the conclusion of Donald J. Grout's *History of Opera* is true: "The

*I disagree with the opinion that the libretto of *Die Zauberflöte* contains profound hidden truths and possesses recondite meanings, as expounded in the book by Jacques Chailley, *The Magic Flute.*

thought of so much buried beauty is saddening; for it is buried for the most part beyond recall."

Buried beauty lies beyond recall in some of Schubert's operas. To understand why we are never likely to hear these operas performed, we must briefly examine the nature of the beast. Gerald Abraham, analyzing Mozart, that supreme master of opera, wrote:

> What matters above all in the opera house is not the ability to write beautiful music, but the much rarer ability to create characters and dramatic situations in music, just as an ordinary dramatist creates them in words. Observe that they must be created *in* music, not taken ready-made from the librettist and set to music; the librettist can and must provide dramatic possibilities, or at least sketches for the characters, but he cannot create them in opera. Only the musician can do that. No composer can succeed as a musical dramatist simply by supplying a good libretto with appropriate music; he must himself have the gift of visualising dramatic situations, of living in them, above all of thinking himself into the skins and skulls of his characters, no matter how diverse or how different from himself. Verdi, Wagner, Moussorgsky possessed this gift; Puccini had it in a more limited range. . . . Mozart was most richly endowed with it [in H. C. Robbins-Landon and Donald Mitchell, eds., *The Mozart Companion*].

An opera cannot do without good melodies (that is true even of such "unmelodious" works as *Wozzeck, Lulu,* and *Il Prigioniero*), nor can good melodies alone sustain a work. In all of Schubert's operas one hears some melodies which sing at heaven's gate, yet the works, regardless of whether they are unpretentious *Singspiele* or deadly serious romances, are boring. What seem to me the two essential ingredients of opera are missing. First of these is the *alternation* between drama and lyricism. Shout and whisper, clash and contemplation, must spell each other. Take any successful opera, works as diverse as *Tristan* and *Turandot, The Barber* and *Norma,* and you find the alternation. The second essential is *action,* whether that be interior or exterior. Something must happen, and that something must be comprehensible to the audience, or at least interesting. In Schubert's operas plenty happens, but what happens is confused and uninteresting.

The librettos are not alone responsible for the failure. The masters of opera were able to create characters through the music, often in spite of second-rate stories. These characters exist, they move us, they excite us, they please us, they frighten us through the music. Many of them have become so real to us that they are part of our lives, their mere names sufficing to place them vividly before us. Don Giovanni and Leporello, everybody in *Figaro* including even little Barberina, Fiordiligi and Dorabella, Sieglinde and Hans Sachs, Leonore and Florestan (never mind that improbably malicious mastiff Pizarro), Violetta and Rodrigo—they are neighbors of our imaginations. Alas, who remembers a single operatic character by Schubert? So many from the songs—not one from the operas. In Schubert the characters stand around and sing; they do not exist.

Opera is theater and theater is prevailingly drama and drama calls for *tension*. Without the audience caring what will happen next, a yawn spreads through the house. Schubert's operas lack tension, at least over any reasonable distance.

One would hardly call *Fidelio,* a type of the then-popular "rescue opera," a believable libretto. Yet the greatness of Beethoven's music formed its chief protagonists into wonderful characters who *do* exist. And the dungeon scene juxtaposes these characters in a dramatic confrontation of Shakespearean tension. *Fidelio* lies above verisimilitude. But the tension is there in a mighty buildup. Will Leonore succeed in her seemingly hopeless quest against the odds? Will liberation come in time? Can she hold off Pizarro's murderous plan?

Yet Schubert liked opera. He went to the Kärntnertor Theater and his friend the painter Moritz von Schwind recollected (though many years later) that he sold his schoolbooks to go and hear *Fidelio*. He greatly admired *Die Zauberflöte*. He heard with pleasure Anna Milder, the young opera star, sing; she was later to influence his life. But he learned little either from *Fidelio* or from *Die Zauberflöte,* and t' ir successors were either weak or vulgar—or both—imitations. German opera and Viennese productions of operettas had no strong historic base on which he could build. The operas popular in Vienna around 1813, when Schubert began seriously to work on stage projects, were of heterogeneous origin—mostly imports such as Paër's *Leonore,* Gluck's two *Iphegenia*s, Boieldieu's *Jean de Paris,* Spontini's *La Vestale,* Cherubini's *Medea,* all of Rossini. (Weigl's *Schweizerfamilie,* very popular and first performed in 1809, was an exception, a homegrown product; it was one of the first operas Schubert heard.)

If this sounds like an excuse—well, perhaps it is. The fact remains that Schubert was not comfortable in the drafty air of the opera house, as Henry James was unable to write a successful play in spite of many tries. Schubert's choice of *subjects* as well as his choice of partners betrays his uncertainty.

Einstein blames the texts more inclusively than I would:

> Even his literary taste, usually so sure in his choice of texts for his songs, forsook him completely in his operas. The real god of Schubert's lyrics, for all the existence of rival gods, is Goethe. The god of his opera libretti, is August von Kotzebue. It is an ironical twist of chance that this unscrupulous and accomplished corrupter of German taste, that this adversary of every lofty ideal which Herder and Goethe and Schiller had striven after, should have been born in Weimar, the hallowed shrine of German poetry, and it is no less a coincidence that he happened to be living in Vienna when Schubert was born.
>
> Alfred Einstein, *Schubert*

2.

In 1815, the year after *The Devil's Plaisance*, he tried a *Singspiel* to a scenario by Theodor Körner, not a bad poet. It was called *Der vierjährige Posten* (*The Four-Year Sentry*). It concerns Duval, a French soldier, who is inadvertently left behind when his regiment leaves. He remains, marries the daughter of the village judge, and lives happily, until his regiment returns and he is in danger of being accused of desertion. All ends happily, thanks to an understanding French general. The music? A charming overture and nothing much more, by an eighteen-year-old.

Schubert had hardly completed this when he rushed on to another *Singspiel,* this one submitted by Albert Stadler, one of his Seminary friends; it was called *Fernando.* Schubert favored these little "plays with songs" because they were short, they suited popular taste, and they were relieved by much spoken dialogue in verse or prose. In that year, 1815, he attempted no fewer than seven small operas! After *Fernando* came a satirical playlet by Goethe, not a good one, *Claudine von Villa Bella.* That might have been an ingratiating morsel, but of it we possess only the first act because that same terrifying servant of Hüttenbrenner's stuffed acts two and three into the oven.

Schubert next turned to another of his friends, Johann Mayrhofer, who prepared a macédoine of fruits, taken presumably (the full text is lost) from *Così, Twelfth Night* (the heroine's name is Olivia), Calderón, Lope de Vega. The title of this cheerful effort is *Die Freunde von Sala-*

manka; the effort was made in vain, though one or two numbers are attractive, chiefly a tenor aria (No. 2) and a serenade (No. 15). If comedy wouldn't do it, perhaps tragedy would. Fewer than five months after *Salamanka*, he completed the first act of a heroic story called *Die Bürgschaft (The Hostage)*. Set in Syracuse, it dealt with an attempt to overthrow a tyrant and liberate an oppressed people. Even if it had been a masterpiece, it would have had no chance in the imperial city, but as it was, Schubert gave up after the first act, though he had wasted no fewer than sixteen numbers on it. The author of the libretto remains unknown to this day.

Mayrhofer was the perpetrator of another tragedy, one called *Adrast;* seven numbers, then Schubert dropped it. Still another fragment was *Der Spiegelritter (The Looking-Glass Knight)*, furnished by Kotzebue. In connection with this effort Kotzebue himself wrote a preface which indicates how jerry-built was the stuff with which Schubert worked:

> People have often asked me to write an opera in the modern manner, and now at last I have done so. I trust that the reader will find it just as droll, as romantic and silly as its older brothers and sisters on the German stage. Of all an author's works, this kind of opera is the easiest to write. May heaven grant me the same good fortune which it has granted to Herrn (Ferdinand) Eberl and Consorten. In other words, may it present my *Looking-Glass Knight* with music like Dittersdorf's, Mozart's, Martin's, or Reichardt's. Then the fellow will make his way in the world successfully.

With a record of failures behind him, it is the more to be wondered at that in 1820 Schubert should receive a commission to compose more operatic music. Perhaps the commission was just a reflection of his general reputation, which was high by that time. At any rate, he was asked by Georg Hofmann, secretary, scenic designer, and stage-manager of the Theater an der Wien, to compose a spectacular production involving stage magic. Magic was in greater demand than ever since *Die Zauberflöte* had become a favorite. What Schubert produced was *Die Zauberharfe (The Magic Harp)*, premiered on August 19, 1820.

Bauernfeld's diary: "Excellent."

Rosenbaum's diary: "Wretched trash."

Theaterzeitung: "With the best will in the world, nothing very edifying may be said about it."

Eight performances—then the work was dropped. A beautiful women's chorus, "Schlafe, liebliche" ("Sleep, Pretty One"), is all that is still heard from *The Magic Harp*.

The previous year, that is, in 1819, Schubert had used a little farce by Hofmann called *Die Zwillingsbrüder* (*The Twin Brothers*). It was a one-act effort, the story dealing with Brother Franz and Brother Friedrich, look-alikes, and the expected mix-up. Vogl recommended the play, an adaptation from the French (*Les Deux Valentins*), because he wanted to play the double role. How he managed that is a bit of a puzzle, since both brothers are on stage simultaneously at the end. It was undoubtedly he who insisted that Schubert's work be accepted by the Kärntnertor Theater. With some delay it *was* performed, on June 14, 1820. Schubert's friends were there in full force, and so by coincidence was Wolfgang Mozart, Jr., Mozart's youngest son, who happened to be visiting Vienna. He thought the "little operetta . . . contains some pretty things, but is kept a little too serious." Rosenbaum:

> The operetta has nothing to recommend it, yet Schubert's friends made a lot of noise while the opposition hissed—at the close there was a fuss until Vogl appeared and said, "Schubert is not present; I thank you in his name."

Anselm Hüttenbrenner gave a different account: he was sitting with Schubert in the gallery, but Schubert would not appear because he had refused to change his old coat for Anselm's formal tailcoat. He listened to Vogl's curtain speech with a smile. After the performance, he and a few friends went to a wine shop to imbibe a few celebratory pints.

The reviews, quite a few of them, were mixed.

The loveliest number in the inconsequential score is a soprano aria ("My Father Still Calls Me a Child"), for which a singer looking to widen her repertoire ought to be grateful.

The year before the performance, as soon as he had completed the composition of *The Twins*, Schubert in an uncertain and truculent mood gave his excuse for possible failure and delay in the production. He wrote to Anselm Hüttenbrenner:

> In spite of Vogl, it is difficult to outwit such *canaille* as Weigl, Treitschke, etc. That is why instead of my operetta they give garbage, enough to make one's hair stand on end [May 19, 1819].

The artist, but not alone he, sees the world plotting against him.

Working with Schober, Schubert next made an effort to compose a romantic opera, somewhat in the manner of Bellini. This was *Alfonso und Estrella*, and the two friends expected a great success from it. Dramatically it seems interminable; musically it is not Bellini. Schubert sent a copy of the score to Anna Milder. For her reply, see page 119.

His last two tries are no better. Vienna's popular poet Ignaz Castelli gave him a one-act play, *The Conspirators*. The censor jibbed at the title and it was renamed *Der häusliche Krieg* (*The Domestic War*). The plot owes more than a little to *Lysistrata*, but the vigor and wit of Aristophanes have turned flat. Flat, flat—that must be the verdict, as well about his last opera, a romantic-heroic libretto written by Josef Kupelwieser, the brother of the painter, and entitled *Fierabras*. It was composed in 1822, contains a thousand manuscript pages, deals with a braggart, a Baron Munchhausen character; it marks a musical nadir in Schubert's creativity simultaneous with a very zenith of the composer's genius expressed in song, the time of *Die schöne Müllerin*. Time has not eased the paradox.

Fierabras, misshapen, malformed, mistreated—though it was commissioned by the Theater an der Wien, it was never performed—brought further humiliation to the misguided composer. The librettist was paid for his work; Schubert never received a kreuzer. Did he finally realize, did it at last dawn on him, that he could produce only dead flowers for the stage? Not at all. Undeterred, he waxed enthusiastic over a new project suggested by the playwright Bauernfeld, *Der Graf von Gleichen*. That, at last, was to be his triumph, he told Bauernfeld; he talked about it often and said that he would score it brilliantly. Death called a halt.

The ten-year struggle, with only three of his operas reaching performance during his life, ended in oblivion. His fame did not lie where he so ardently desired fame. "I would be quite well, if only this wretched business of the opera were not so mortifying," he wrote in 1822.

Like a gray slack band his stage attempts wind through his life. Is it not significant that the man who was constantly deepening and rendering more astonishing his songs, his symphonies, his chamber music, remained static in his operas? The picture here given is but an overview. A scholar digging through the scores would find here and there a song, a chorus, a twist, a duet to give pleasure. Schubert cannot be a cipher altogether. Yet, practically speaking, few of us will ever hear any of these operas—

some attempts at revivals have been made but they have been unsuccessful—and even recorded excerpts are rare and unsatisfying.

I cannot explain this flatness of the ebullient genius any better than other writers have. All who have studied his work have declared his operatic failure a riddle. That he blinked at the garish stage light is obvious—but why? And why did he so stubbornly, so uselessly, so frequently, persist? What happened to his intelligence and self-critical faculty, both of which he possessed? Was it defiance?

It may be that in Schubert's time opera underwent a change which Schubert did not understand and could not follow. *Die Zauberflöte* had marked a symbol of mysticism. *Der Freischütz* had expressed sylvan poesie. Both were "German," or at least rooted in the German spirit. People became weary of this spirit, tired of allusions, uninterested either in *Singspiele* or profundity. They wanted entertainment. Spectacular melodies were what they wanted to hear, sung more mellifluously than German singers sang. And they wanted grand doings on grand stages, never mind the plot. Rossini's last operas pointed the way—one way to Meyerbeer and Halévy, the other to Bellini, to Donizetti. Lots of high notes, lots of loud notes, lots of love notes. The Italians took over, the tenor in the center. Out of this came the early Verdi. Soon after that came *Rienzi*, which out-Meyerbeered Meyerbeer.

I admit that this is theory, though indicated by history. It is probable that Schubert could not write a good opera under the best of circumstances.

Sadly, we must close the chapter with "Failure."

SCHUBERT'S OPERAS

		Libretto
1813–14	*Des Teufels Lustschloss* (3 acts)	Kotzebue
1815	*Der Vierjährige Posten* (1 act)	Körner
1815	*Fernando* (1 act)	Stadler
	Claudine von Villa Bella (1 act; incomplete?)	Goethe
	Die Freunde von Salamanka (2 acts)	Mayrhofer
	Der Spiegelritter (1 act)	Kotzebue
1815	*Adrast* (unfinished)	Mayrhofer
1816	*Die Bürgschaft* (incomplete)	Unknown
1817	*Das Dörfchen* (revised in 1819)	Bürger

1819	*Die Zwillingsbrüder* (1 act)	Hofmann
1820	*Die Zauberharfe* (3 acts; incidental music)	Hofmann
1821	*Alfonso und Estrella* (3 acts)	Schober
1823	*Der häusliche Krieg* (1 act)	Castelli
	Fierabras (3 acts)	Kupelwieser
	Rosamunde (incidental music)	Chézy
1827	*Der Graf von Gleichen* (sketches only)	Bauernfeld

9
Decline and Renewal

AFTER THE FEW SHORT YEARS DURING WHICH SCHUBERT CREATED A CON-
cord of sound, sweet and sad, which still fills us with wonder, specifically
after the year in which he finished Goethe's song "Prometheus," that
defiant myth in which Schubert's friends saw political countercurrents,
and after the year when he completed the *Trout* Quintet (July 1819), an
ebbing followed. The year 1820 started off pleasantly enough; in February he was working on the *Lazarus* Cantata; he was hoping for operatic
success, for increased income, and he was enjoying the gentle touches of
modest fame. Then, in March, came the episode with Senn. To refer to
this episode once again, Schubert knew that Police Commissioner Fertl
recommended that the fathers of two of the "culprits," Streinsberg and
Bruchmann, be "informed of their sons' conduct." It would have been
disastrous for young Bruchmann had Commissioner Fertl carried out his
threat, but doubly disastrous if Schubert's father, school principal, moralist, and conservative Catholic, had got wind of the affair. That moment
when Schubert stared at the uniforms and watched the policemen ransack
Senn's rooms must have been a shock. His father's career could have
been harmed. That this was not an idle supposition is indicated by a later
document written by Sedlnitzky, dated September 15, 1829.* The subject
was this: It had been proposed to honor Franz the father for his many
years of work in the educational system by awarding him the "Civil Gold
Medal of Honor," a high distinction. Sedlnitzky wrote a long memorandum to Emperor Francis acknowledging the senior Franz Schubert's mer-

*The document has been damaged by fire but is still legible. It seems to have escaped the
ever-watchful eye of Deutsch.

its, but suggesting that His Serene Majesty *not* grant the distinction. He gave no reason, but his word was sufficient. The Emperor decreed that decision be "postponed," his usual procedure for dealing with a problem which bothered him. As late as 1844 the question of the medal arose in another document. By that time, of course, Father Franz was long dead; he never got the medal.

Austria's political condition in 1820, with Emperor Francis practicing his plebeian gestures and wearing his false smiles, put a damper on Schubert's work. An indication of his awareness emerged later—he knew as everybody else did to keep silent—when he wrote to Schober on September 11, 1824. "Sick and decrepit do the people creep," he wrote, and "The times fast bring ruin" and "Youth of the present time, where are you gone?"

The clear failure of the operatic attempts did not further the creative mentality, which holds in regard the least of its accomplishments; the less successful, the more truculently defended. How did he feel when he read in a long review in the *Allgemeine Musikalische Zeitung* of June 17, 1820, that *The Twins* "has much originality and many interesting passages . . . but it is a blot on the work that the sentiments of simple country folk are interpreted much too seriously, not to say heavy-handedly" or read in the *Sammler* (an important publication devoted to the arts) of August 26 that "*The Magic Harp* music is often thin, insipid, and stale"?

A third cause was the failure to get his work published. Publication was to begin the following year. But at the end of 1820 nothing by Schubert, absolutely nothing, could be bought in the music shops.

Another cause may have been—no overt cause at all! As Anthony Storr in *The Dynamics of Creation* has pointed out, Schubert was "incubating." For Mozart and Schubert the period of incubation "must have been unusually short," compared to the other extremes: Beethoven, who pulled seeds this way and that, always correcting, always tightening, or Darwin, "incubating for at least twenty years before *On the Origin of Species by Means of Natural Selection* was published."* Brahms did not complete his first symphony until his forty-third year, yet he showed Clara Schumann sketches for it twenty years previously. Still, even Schubert underwent a periodicity of creation, never as extreme as that of Balzac, who at some periods would work from 1 A.M. to noon, drinking

*I think Dr. Storr is comparing works which cannot be compared, musical vs. didactic. But the point is valid.

innumerable cups of black coffee and eating little, to be followed by periods of total inactivity, when he would drink four bottles of Vouvray at a sitting and gorge himself on oysters. And nor rhyme nor reason determined these periods.

What further troubled Schubert in 1820 was changes in the lives of his friends.

Mayrhofer had to leave Vienna on a professional trip and Schubert, who had lived with him peacefully for the better part of two years, for the first time moved to a place of his own. The place was nearby, corner of Wipplingerstrasse and Tiefer Graben, a good neighborhood. Schubert could now afford it, with the money he had been paid at Zseliz. The painter Schwind sketched the room: it shows his piano heaped with scores and underneath the piano a container for books, a thick book lying on top. He lived there from the end of 1820 for less than a year and he wasn't at all happy, at least not at home, bothering with the milk and the bread. He missed Mayrhofer, who missed him and who wrote in his memoirs: "Quietly and like a riddle he appeared to me, changing often, now dark, now jocund, but always faithful."

A riddle—and not only to Mayrhofer. What the two had in common was their enthusiasm for Goethe and for the world of antique Greece and Egypt, the latter being the source of the song "Memnon," while from Grecian legend came "Fragment from Aeschylus," the two Orestes songs, and the two Heliopolis songs. Mayrhofer interpreted the old legend of the Egyptian statue which sings at sunrise in terms of man's lack of understanding of Nature's greatness. The statue sings sadly and Schubert's song rises from darkness to a soaring plea, both in voice and piano. It is a transfiguration so mighty that Brahms decided to orchestrate it. In somewhat the same unearthly mood is the song "Lied eines Schiffers an die Dioskuren" ("Song of a Sailor to Castor and Pollux"), text by Mayrhofer, which Vogl admired especially, saying that it was almost incomprehensible that such profundity and maturity could emerge from such a young little fellow.

Spaun was transferred to Linz. Anselm Hüttenbrenner moved to Graz. Therese Grob married at the end of 1820.

The next year his life and disposition changed markedly. He came under Schober's influence and was invited to become the family's guest. The house Schober's mother owned was luxurious, and Schubert stayed there from the end of 1821 to the summer of 1823, with occasional interruptions. That was a long stay for a guest, yet he was welcome, and he indulged in the ease and comfort provided—and the good Viennese food. Without half trying, Schober lightened Schubert's mood. Together the two friends would joke and laugh, Schober being a virtuoso at juggling intellectual seriousness with frivolity. He took Schubert to St. Pölten, a village some thirty miles west of Vienna which was dominated by a famous church. Its bishop, a distant relative of Schober's, was a worldly fellow whose hospitality they enjoyed on two visits (January and November 1821). The purpose of the excursion was to work on a new opera project, *Alfonso und Estrella*, text by Schober. Schubert pinned high hopes on this serious three-act work. (As I mentioned, it was refused by Domenico Barbaja, but long after Schubert's death Liszt performed it in Weimar in 1854 in a truncated version—and it promptly dropped into oblivion.)

The opera is a failed attempt to use the then-fashionable Italian style, the libretto reading like one of those hobbling translations from the Italian which used to pervade German opera houses and the music containing the standard Italianate ingredients, such as the "vengeance aria," the "conspirators' chorus," and of course the virtuoso "love duet." Once in a while, as in the overture and a courtship scene, one hears the real Schubert, but on the whole the work gives the impression almost of a caricature. Schubert actually composed such a caricature: Spaun had introduced him to Mathaeus von Collin (he was a brother of Heinrich von Collin, author of *Coriolanus*), who wrote Spaun a jocular letter to Linz accusing him in rhyme of never writing ("Und nimmer schreibst du?"—"And never do you write?"). He suggested that Schubert set the little poem to music. For fun Schubert did precisely that, furnishing it with mock recitative and aria, allegro furioso, fearsome tremolandos, impossible cadenzas, and an aria with the obligatory high C, all guying the Italian operatic style.

During the time of the work on *Alfonso und Estrella*—of which he was never able to hear a performance—Schober, in a letter to Spaun (November 4, 1821), wrote that in St. Pölten they were much occupied "with balls and concerts" but they did work and Schubert "poured forth rich and teeming ideas. . . . In the evening we always compared notes on what we had done during the day, then sent for beer, smoked our pipes and read." They did more: in January there had taken place the first of the parties which came to be known as *Schubertiaden*. These were not, or not often, drinking orgies, though of this first one Schober had made rather a boisterous gathering, inviting fourteen guests, including his sister. Schubert sang "a lot of splendid songs," accompanying himself; then punch was drunk, transporting everybody into a euphoric mood, "so that it was 3 o'clock in the morning before we parted." In November Schober told Spaun of three other *Schubertiaden*, where "a princess, two countesses, and three baronesses were present, all most generously ecstatic." The bishop was there, too.

Schober took Schubert to Atzenbrugg, where his uncle was steward of a sizable property comprising farms and country lanes, some twenty miles west of Vienna. There Schubert's admirers, joined by a new friend, the painter Leopold Kupelwieser, played games indoors and outdoors with the enthusiasm of children on school-free days. Two illustrations help us to visualize the naive amusements: one by Schwind shows a sort of free-for-all ball game, Schubert sitting calmly on the grass in his shirt sleeves, smoking a long pipe. Another, a painting by Kupelwieser, shows a charade game: two syllables, the whole representing "Rhine Falls," first syllable *rein* (pure), the second impersonated as Adam and Eve, the "Fall of Man," elaborate but not very difficult. Schubert is sitting at the piano watching the proceedings. The painting suggests that he furnished the music for the charade. He accompanied as well the dances, often improvising, but composing a few, the "Atzenbrugg Dances."

The Atzenbrugg excursion with carefree companions, in summer weather among green fields and the Danube not far away, with the good local wines, began to lighten Schubert's mood. Though, like most Viennese, he liked his wine, he rarely drank to excess, his drinking never amounting to stupor, an obliteration of sanity. Rather, it was a companionable gesture, going along with his friends whom, when he was yet unknown to a wider circle, he needed badly. They helped him to work himself out of the flatland. Underneath the games and country dances his genius grew.

He did make new friends who did not quite fill the place of a Mayrhofer, a Senn, or a Spaun, as he himself realized. Early in 1821 Leopold Sonnleithner introduced him to the home of the Fröhlich sisters. They were four gifted and good-looking girls, all of whom were musical and sang prettily. Only Barbara got married; Josephine, the oldest, Kathi, and Anna, the youngest, remained single. They taught singing. Kathi was the most beautiful, with eyes "beaming with dazzling rays as of a heavenly light," and Grillparzer was in love with her. She was his "eternal bride," but the poet, bitter, self-enclosed, never did marry her. Perhaps the "constant bachelor" was afraid to bind himself, yet many a love poem did he address to Kathi.

Anna told the story of meeting Schubert:

> Sonnleithner brought us some songs, composed as he said by a young man of some reputation. Kathi at once went to the piano and tried them out. Gymnich, an official who sang well, began to listen and said, "What are you playing? Are you improvising?"—"No."—"But this stuff is glorious, it is exceptional. Let me look." Now the evening was filled with Schubert songs. After a few days Sonnleithner brought Schubert. After that he came frequently. . . .
>
> Whenever the nameday or birthday of [Louise] Gosmer [a pupil of Anna's, later the wife of Leopold Sonnleithner], I used to go to Grillparzer and beg him to do something for the occasion. I did it once again, shortly before her next birthday: "Dear Grillparzer, there's no help for it, you have to write a birthday poem." He replied, "Yes, if I get an idea." I: "You had *better* get an idea." In a few days he handed me the poem "Serenade." Then I said to Schubert: "Compose this." Schubert: "Let me look at it." He leaned on the piano and exclaimed several times, "How beautiful it is, how beautiful." He studied the paper for a while, then said, "It is ready. I have the idea." Three days later he brought me the composition done for four male voices. I said: "No, Schubert, I can't use it that way, it is supposed to be a tribute to Louise by female friends; you have to re-do the thing for female voices." I remember this conversation very well, we were seated in a window-niche. Soon he brought me the work re-written for Josephine's voice and a female chorus. I took all my pupils in three carriages to Louise's home in Döbling, secretly had a piano set up under her garden-window, and invited Schubert. He did not show himself. When I asked why he answered, "Oh, I forgot all about it."

The "birthday" composition was "Gott in der Natur" ("God in Nature"), a relatively unimportant work. Anna kept and treasured the manuscript.

One event of 1821 further enhanced his reputation, though it left his pocket as lean as ever; this was a "Grand Concert with Recitations and Tableaux" on March 7, 1821, given at Vienna's most elegant theater, the Kärntnertor. It was a charity affair, sponsored by the Society of Ladies of the Nobility for the Promotion of the Good and the Useful. Josef Sonnleithner, Ignaz's brother, was its secretary. Josef was a worthy member of that exceptional family;* he helped Beethoven with the *Fidelio* libretto, he collected musicians' portraits, some of which he himself painted, and he now saw to it that Schubert was to be represented in an evening which was attended by the best Viennese society. (It can be suspected that this gala on Ash Wednesday at 7 P.M. served more to display the elegance of Princess Lobkowitz or Princess Odescalchi than to do much for the good and useful.) Vogl sang the inevitable "Erlkönig," and Schubert furnished two numbers especially composed for the occasion. They were "Das Dörfchen" ("The Little Village"), a vocal quartet for male voices, and an octet to a famous Goethe poem, "Gesang der Geister über den Wassern" ("Song of the Spirits above the Waters"). Caroline Unger sang a Mozart song. So did a young singer, Wilhelmine Schröder (later Schröder-Devrient, later Wagner's Senta and Venus). Fanny Elssler, who was to become the world-famous dancer, appeared; she was then ten years old. Vogl had to repeat the "Erlkönig" to great applause. The evening—artistically meretricious as these evenings usually are—was star-filled and indicated that Schubert belonged in the company of stars. He was there merely as a spectator. From that evening on, frequency of publication increased.

During this period Schober played an important if not a Mephistophelian role in Schubert's life. Otto Erich Deutsch wrote: "Both before and after that [time] Schober was represented by intimates as having lured several of his friends, Schubert included, into loose living." I am inclined to discount this statement, because the Schubert circle was extremely jealous of the meteoric Schober and what they said about him should be regarded in that light. No doubt Schober's influence was considerable, yet whatever were his sybaritic proclivities, I do not see him in the role of the tempter: he was too easygoing and too lackadaisical for that. Schober was supposed to have caused a rift in the friendship between Schubert and Vogl, but as to that we have no direct evidence, just a letter from Spaun's brother to his wife:

Steyr, July 20, 1822
. . . Vogl is very much embittered against Schober, for whose sake Schubert behaved most ungratefully towards Vogl and who makes the fullest use of Schubert in order to extricate himself from financial embarrassments and to defray the expenditure which has already exhausted the greater part of his

*Ignaz (1770–1831) was four years younger than Josef (1766–1835). Ignaz had a son, Leopold (1797–1873), who wrote recollections of Schubert.

mother's fortune. I wish very much that somebody were here who would defend Schubert at least in the matter of the most glaring reproaches. Vogl also says Schubert's opera is bad and a perfect failure, and that altogether Schubert is quite on the wrong road [DQ].

At any rate, the break was soon healed.

In the way which life often has of imitating fiction, Schober's path ran downhill. He did spend all of his mother's wealth, indulging himself in such extravagances as Arabian carpets, Persian dressing gowns, Turkish drapes, elaborate furniture. Perhaps he learned that from Liszt, for whom he worked for a time. (He never met Wagner.)

When he was sixty he married a writer, Thekla von Gumpert, who edited a ladies' journal. The marriage proved most unhappy, lasting fewer than eight years, and Schober's cry, "Thekla, I will strangle you!" became a byword for unhappy marriages. However, he did not strangle her; they endured each other. He lived out his life in Dresden in modest circumstances, surrounded by a thousand books—and one slim volume of his own verses. He died in 1882, eighty-six years old, never with all his multiple gifts having accomplished anything.

2.

Like a plant whose leaves have turned yellow, but from which suddenly fresh blossoms spring, did Schubert's genius renew itself. The reasons for Schubert's resurgence are at least partly discoverable in the comfort and admiration which Schober and his family offered him, covering his bed with a blanket of eiderdown, setting a place for him for steady meals, and delighting his eye with the beauty of the patrician house where they lived, the Göttweigerhof (now 1 Spiegelgasse 9), which was built in the seventeenth century, "modernized" in the eighteenth, and now again modernized in the Biedermeier style, with the white, flower-painted porcelain stoves standing as sentinels in the corners of the rooms. The increasing enthusiasm of his other friends helped. So did, if only secondarily, improved world conditions. Not only in Vienna but all over Europe things were happening which looked encouraging: the Greeks began their struggle against the Turks to gain their independence, Napoleon died in May 1821—none too soon for the peace of mind of Austria and its Emperor—a true German opera, Der Freischütz, was performed with genuine success, and a new poet, of the exact same age as Schubert, published his first collection: that was Heine, to whose work Schubert was to become greatly attached.

Perhaps all this counted for little. The creative organism responds not merely to environment but, unaccountably, "by asking questions," as Arthur Koestler wrote in *The Act of Creation:* "The main incentives to its exploratory activities are novelty, surprise, conflict, uncertainty." The poet explores "the emotive and descriptive potentialities of language; the painter is engaged, throughout his life, in learning to see." The musician is engaged, throughout his life, in learning to hear.

All this is not to imply that Schubert's mind lay entirely fallow during 1820. However subconsciously, he was preparing himself to climb to a new level, to grapple with the problems of chamber and symphonic music and the piano sonata, up to then only incompletely solved. The *Quartettsatz,* sketched in December 1820, gives us a hint: it is different from his previous quartets, different from the classic style, different from the Beethoven Opus 18 Quartets or any other work by Beethoven, though up to then the influence of the composer he worshiped is evident. "After Beethoven," Schubert said, "who can achieve anything more?" It appeared that Schubert could. He began a series of experiments with the piano sonata. Alfred Einstein wrote that "these experiments prove that the problem of the piano sonata not only occupied Schubert incessantly, but irritated him profoundly." From that irritation sprang eventually his great sonatas. In short, he retreated, poised to gather new strength. It was an example of *reculer pour mieux sauter.*

The first result was the rewriting of the composition he had done in 1817, "Gesang der Geister über den Wassern." He now set it for four tenors and four basses and an instrumental group of two violas, two cellos, and a double bass. The text is Goethe's philosophic poem in which he compares man's soul to water, man's fate to wind. It can hardly be claimed that music can probe the content of the poem's symbolism, yet Schubert, pondering the meaning, gives us Goethe's contrast of calm and turbulence, of stillness and storm, in his most pliantly beautiful music. It is one of his astonishing works; too bad that it is so infrequently performed!

He then turned to the Schlegel brothers, Friedrich and August Wilhelm, for his next texts. Both were philosophers and poets; together they founded the literary journal *Atheneum.* August Wilhelm became famous as a translator of Shakespeare and was associated with the brilliant and wayward Madame de Staël, while Friedrich, the better poet, married the philosopher Moses Mendelssohn's daughter, Dorothea. Both were highly fashionable in Vienna, where they lectured to enthusiastic audiences. Friedrich furnished the poem "Im Walde" ("In the Forest"), retitled "Waldes-Nacht" ("Forest Night"), one of Schubert's longest songs, a pantheistic hymn of two hundred bars, which travels melodically through changing moods. From August Schlegel he took eleven poems, including one, "Die gefangenen Sänger" ("The Captured Warblers")—dated January 1821—in which caged birds serve as the symbols of the suppression of artistic freedom. The manuscript of that song was not found till 1883— sixty-two years after it was composed. Schubert was incredibly careless with his manuscripts. He gave them away to his friends and later, when he wanted them, he could not remember to whom he had given them. Some he lost, some he sent to publishers who didn't return them. It was a curious contradiction to his systematically dating his compositions.

In Schubert's new phase he turned once again to Goethe, the poet grown older, his *Sturm und Drang* long behind him, his vision calmer and less worldly, yet still replete with that curiosity which characterized him and still capable of being attracted by a pretty woman as he was in the vigor of youth. Schubert's music underwent a similar ripening, extracting from Goethe a richer ichor. In March he composed the song "Grenzen der Menschheit" ("Limits of Humanity"). It is a pendant to "Prometheus" and warns that man "may not measure himself against the gods." Were he to attempt to "touch the stars" he would lose his footing.

> What separates men from gods?
> They dwell as an eternal stream.
> We are tossed by every wave, then to be
> Swallowed and to drown. . . .

Schubert's stern melody seems to come like a message from the gods themselves, the piano suggests an orchestra of Wagnerian proportions, and the whole suggests not how narrow but how wide are the limits of humanity.

He reworked the two Mignon songs in April, intensifying their emotion. Could he ever surpass their sad beauty? It appears that he could— in still another version five years later. And early in 1821 Schubert became familiar with another facet of Goethe's genius, the *West-Östlicher Divan*. Goethe had turned from his Greek phase eastward, to Persian poetry, specifically to Hafiz. A "divan" originally meant a collection of a poet's work in alphabetical order, but Goethe had no intention of being systematic, merely gathering together various love poems. What caused this flood of amatory verse? The sixty-six-year-old poet fell in love with a thirty-year-old demoiselle, Marianne Jung, who shortly after meeting him married the Senator Johann Willemer, who was twenty-four years her senior.

It is a unique autumn-to-spring story. Their first meeting, in a Wiesbaden casino in company with her future husband, disturbs Goethe. Marianne responds. Soon they are in love. He visits her and she spoils him with attention, swathing his head in a turban of delicate muslin and making him a pair of Turkish slippers. Returned to Weimar, he longs for her and begins a series of love poems, calling himself not Hafiz but Hatem, a combination of the names of two Persian poets, Hatem Thai, he "who gives everything," and Hatem Zagrai, he "who lives most fully." He writes to her: "My life, impoverished, only you can render valid." ("Dass ich nun, verarmt mein Leben, nur von dir gewärtig bin.") She calls herself Suleika and answers him with poetry of her own which—unbelievably!—is equivalent to his. Several of the poems of the Suleika section of the *Divan,* the core of the work, are written by Marianne, and they speak as wisely of the nature of love as his own. He publishes them as his own. After a brief interlude in Heidelberg, the lovers part. They never meet again.

A number of the two hundred poems of the *Divan* have been set to music by Schumann, Mendelssohn, Hugo Wolf. Schubert chose four poems and gave them what to him was an almost completely new style, mixing playfulness with thoughtfulness, and warming them in a gentle flame of sexuality. The first song, "Versunken" ("Immersed"), is clearly erotic, as the poet toys with the locks of his girl, loosening them. The music captures the excitement of the love-play. The second, "Geheimes" ("Secrets"), asserts that he alone knows the meaning of her glance; it promises him "the next sweet hour." Schubert invests the song with soft charm both in the vocal and the piano line. He dedicated the song to Schober, a dedication from which some biographers have deduced a covert homosexual attraction. I believe there is no good ground for such a theory.

The poems "Suleika I" and "Suleika II" were written by Marianne, but Schubert could not know this, since the secret was not disclosed till many years after. The music of "Suleika I" is passionate, permeated by "a breath of love" which cools and refreshes, bringing a message from his beloved and encouraging him to hurry to her at sundown. Brahms thought that "Suleika I" was the loveliest song ever written; it inspired his own "Von ewiger Liebe." "Suleika II" is a pastoral, the voice floating above a calm accompaniment. By sheer accident Goethe was told of these songs, Marianne writing to him on April 16, 1825:

> Early in the morning I sent to a music shop and had the splendid song by Beethoven, "Heart, my heart, what will befall thee," fetched, and they sent me at the same time a quite pretty melody on the East Wind [Suleika I] and "Secrets" from the *Divan*.

Marianne did not name the composer. And by that time Goethe had probably become indifferent to the whole affair. "Suleika II" Schubert dedicated to Anna Milder-Hauptmann (no longer "Hauptmann," since the marriage had broken up). She loved it.

Anna Milder to Schubert:

> *Berlin, 8th March 1825*
> ... "Suleika's Second Song" is heavenly and moves me to tears every time. It is indescribable: you have infused it with all the possible magic and longing, as in "Suleika's First Song" and "Secrets." The only regrettable thing is that all this endless beauty cannot be sung to the public, since the crowd wants only treats for the ear. Should the "Moth" ["Nachtschmetterling"] not be suited to the making of somewhat brilliant music for the voice, I would ask you to choose another poem in its place, if possible by Goethe, one which can be sung in a variety of measures, so that several emotions can be represented. Such as, for instance, "Diverse Feelings in One Place" ["Verschiedene Empfindungen in einem Platz"] or a similar one, which I will leave to you, so that there may be a brilliant ending.
>
> However many songs you may want to dedicate to me, this can be only most agreeable and flattering for me. I leave here on 1st June, and if I could have such a desirable song from you for my tour and concerts, it would make me indescribably happy; that is to say, if you will put in some suitable passages and flourishes. ...

"Suitable passages and flourishes"—spoken like a singer.

We have here cause for triple amazement: an aging poet writes poems which in lustiness belong to youth; he inspires a young woman in no way remarkable to reach far beyond herself to play a poet's role and to

tenants. In return you know you are living in a respectable house . . . and your rent will be increased only twice each year.

(Historic Museum of Vienna)

One can understand why Schubert returned occasionally to his father's house in the intervals when for one reason or another he could not stay with the Schobers.

Wherever he was, he worked. His major task was the great Mass in A-flat, his fifth, for which many sketches, many corrections are extant and which he finished in September 1822. It is the most treasurable of his church compositions, not even surpassed by the sixth, the one in E-flat which dates from the last year of his life. Richly scored—Schubert added a trumpet, drums, and three trombones to his usual orchestra—it is not so much an assertion of religious faith, which Schubert did not really feel, as it is a plea for life and its beauty, more of a *gloria* than a *resurrexit*. For the first time now we notice a tone of confidence in Schubert's outlook, as he expresses it in a letter to Spaun in Linz with which he sent along the Goethe *Divan* songs just published by the firm of Cappi and Diabelli:

Vienna, December 7, 1822

Dear Spaun,

I hope to give you some little pleasure by the dedication of these three songs, which indeed you so very much deserve that I really and *ex officio* ought to offer you an enormous one, and should in fact do so if I were able. For the rest you will like their choice, for I selected those which you indicated yourself. Apart from this book two others appear at the same time, one of which is already engraved, so that I enclose a copy of that too; the other is now in the engraver's hands. The first of these contains, as you will see, the three songs of the Harper, the second of which, "Who never ate his bread with tears," is new, and is dedicated to the Bishop of St. Pölten. The other includes, as you won't see, the "Suleika" and "Secrets" ["Geheimes"], and is dedicated to Schober. Apart from these I have composed a Fantasy for pianoforte, two hands, which is also to appear in print, inscribed to a certain wealthy person. Moreover, I have set some new Goethe songs, such as "The Muses' Son" ["Der Musensohn"], "To the Distant One" ["An die Entfernte"], "By the River" ["Am Flusse"], and "Hail and Farewell" ["Willkommen und Abschied"]. —With the opera I did not get on in Vienna. I asked to have it back, and it came. Vogl has really left the theater, too. I shall shortly send it either to Dresden, whence I had a very promising letter from Weber, or to Berlin. —My Mass is finished, and is to be produced

[123]

before long. I still have my old notion of dedicating it to the emperor or the empress, as I think it a success. . . .

I should be pretty well, if only the miserable business of the opera were not so galling. With Vogl I have taken up again, now that he has left the theater and I am no longer embarrassed in that respect. I even think I may come up there [Linz] with him again, or after him, this summer; a thing to which I look forward with pleasure, as I shall then see you and your friends again. —Our companionship in Vienna is quite agreeable now. We hold readings at Schober's three times a week as well as a Schubertiad, at which Bruchmann too makes an appearance. And now, dear Spaun, farewell. Do write to me soon and at length, so as to mitigate somewhat the gaping void your absence will always make for me. . . .

A mass dedicated to the Emperor or the Empress? Ambitious, indeed—and neither took any notice of it. As to the opera—it was refused both by Dresden and by Berlin.

Another major work of the year—Schubert mentions it in his letter to Spaun—is the so-called *Wandererfantasie* for piano (not Schubert's title), C major, op. 15. It is difficult to convey in English the exact meaning of the word *wandern* as the romantics used it. To "ramble," to "meander," to "be a vagabond," to "journey aimlessly"—perhaps to "roam" comes nearest to a definition of the half-joyous, half-melancholy notion of shouldering a knapsack containing not much more than a crust of bread and a piece of cheese, walking through village, woods, and fields, sleeping in the open, getting up with the sun, and walking on, stick in hand, here and there knocking on strange doors while the dogs barked. *Wandern* served both as a symbol of freedom, of not being weighed down by responsibilities, and as a symbol of not belonging, of homelessness. On Schubert the word exercised a spell. The Fantasy uses (in a somewhat altered form) a melody of a song he had composed seven years earlier, "Der Wanderer," to a text by an amateur poet who called himself Schmidt von Lübeck, after his native city. Schubert found the poem in an anthology of poems suitable for "public recitation," where it was called "Der Unglückliche" ("The Unfortunate Man"). Cappi and Diabelli published the song in 1821; in the meantime Schmidt had changed his title to "Der Fremdling" ("The Stranger"). Now Schubert retitled his song "Der Wanderer" and dedicated it to Count Esterházy. With a touch of making fun of himself, Schubert wrote on the frontispiece, "Der Wanderer oder Der Fremdling oder Der Unglückliche."

It was not the only time the word appeared: in 1819 he composed

"Der Wanderer" to a philosophic and difficult poem by Friedrich Schlegel, yet the song itself is a marvel of simplicity and clarity. He composed "Der Wanderer an den Mond" to the text of a Viennese poet, Johann Gabriel Seidl. The first song of the *Die schöne Müllerin* cycle is "Das Wandern," which has become impossibly hackneyed—and of course the most famous fusions of music and text, equal miracles both, are Goethe's "Wanderers Nachtlied I" (composed in 1815) and its companion piece, the song of 1823 ("Wanderers Nachtlied II"), to the eight lines Goethe wrote as a young man on a wall of a mountain hut in Thuringia, and where thirty-three years later he returned, refreshed the inscription—and wept.

To return to the Fantasy, it is in my opinion one of Schubert's entrancing works for the piano, opening to the musical imagination both concepts of "wandering," the joyous aspect and the restless one of the outcast. Not everybody shares this enthusiasm, Alfred Einstein, for example, thinking that the finale (allegro) "contrives to be both brilliant and somewhat ponderous since this fugal development very soon loses its breath." The whole composition "is not quite our favourite Schubert." Maurice J. E. Brown thinks that the variations in the slow movement are excessive, "almost guilty of display." (Oh, Maurice—how could you!) Donald Francis Tovey, on the other hand, thought that the work in its alternation of dramatic passages with quiet lyricism looks back to the concertos of Bach (which Schubert did not know) and in its handling of the remotest possible key relationships looks forward to Wagner. Certainly a pianist who understands the romantic style knows how to link the four movements, all of them deriving from the melody of the song which is clearly stated in the second movement, the adagio. Schumann and Liszt loved the Fantasy; Liszt arranged it for piano and orchestra.

A minor work of the period we owe to Antonio Diabelli, who was not only a publisher but fancied himself a composer. He commissioned a number of composers to write variations on a waltz theme proposed by him. Beethoven, one would have said, would be the last man to be interested in so artificial a compendium, the more so as he thought little of Diabelli's theme, calling it a "cobbler's patch." Nevertheless he was intrigued, and after two years, long after the due date, he completed an independent work, constructing what Bülow called "a microcosm of Beethoven's genius." Schubert was the first to hand in his contribution, in March 1821, a charming trifle. Other contributors were Czerny, Moscheles, Weber, Hummel, Archduke Rudolf, and the ten-year-old Liszt.

All lie forgotten in Beethoven's shadow, but it would be interesting for an experimentally minded pianist to play the best of these, the "other" *Diabelli Variations*.

The very casual "meeting" of Beethoven and Schubert at the piano, due to the enterprising Diabelli, directs our attention to Schubert's piano music, the wealth of compositions small and not-so-small for two and four hands which—apart from and in addition to his sonatas—weave through his creative years. What an Aladdin's cave is here to be discovered! What a thousand-and-one tales! The entrance flies open, invites, is unbarred, since Schubert's piano compositions are influenced by Schubert's songs, and are, with all their elegant turns, guided and steered by melody. They give the impression of a composer who, ranging over a wide field, returns to the mode he loves most. They are poems for the keyboard. One can imagine that Schubert must have played them for his own enjoyment. Several of his friends were good pianists, delighted to play with him. Many of the smaller pieces are relatively easy to play, though difficult to interpret truly, the *Wandererfantasie* and the last impromptu of Opus 142 being the only technically challenging works (always excepting the sonatas). Schubert's piano writing differs from that of Mozart and Beethoven, who were virtuoso pianists.

It is significant that Schubert did not write a single piano concerto—or *any* concerto—as against more than twenty-five piano concertos by Mozart and five by Beethoven. Tovey suggests that Schubert's four-handed piano pieces, the "magnificent quality and enormous quantity" of them, may have served him as a compensation for the "lack of opportunity for hearing his own orchestral works." Possibly.

Quantity—fantastic quantity. Not only quantity, but diversity: *moments musicaux,* variations, *écossaises,* dances*—which include Vienna waltzes, Graz waltzes, *Ländler, deutsche Tänze,* marches, rondos, divertissements, *Klavierstücke,* minuets and trios, fantasies, and most important the impromptus, those wonderfully exciting and beautiful impromptus!

4.

As we glance over the chronicle of the years 1821–22, we get the impression of a man launched toward success and being aware of it.

---

*The autograph of the "Original Dances," op. 9, records that he wrote no fewer than eight of them on a single day in November 1819.

Publication, reviews, comments, flatteries combine in an almost steady line:

The *Theaterzeitung* of May 22, 1821, reviewing some of the Goethe songs:

> Each of these songs has its own character, according to the poet's intention; delightful melodies and a noble simplicity, alternating with original force and elevation, unite them into a glorious wreath of song, which joins worthily on to the earlier excellent achievements of this talented composer.

The *Allgemeine Musikalische Zeitung*, January 19, 1822, welcomes the opportunity

> thoroughly to recommend to the music public not only these, but far more particularly the earlier songs published by the same artistic house and written by a young composer with a rich lyrical gift, and openly to express our respect for his excellent talent. Not often has a composer had so large a share of the gift for making the poet's fancy so profoundly impressive for the receptive listener's heart. This is shown with especial felicity by Goethe's song for Margaret at the spinning-wheel, where the vivid imitation of the sound of a spinning-wheel makes a most characteristic background in a Rembrandtesque chiaroscuro for the description of the profoundest depths of a woman's being, lost now in gloomy visions of the present and the future, now in sweetly melancholy recollection of the past. No feeling heart can follow the changes of the unhappy Margaret's emotions depicted here without being seized by sadness and by the foreboding of the fearful proximity of the evil powers which ensnare her.

In March of that year there appeared in the *Wiener Zeitschrift für Kunst* a five-page-long analysis of Schubert's songs by Friedrich von Hentl, a graduate of the Theresanium, the academy where gifted pupils of the nobility were trained. The style is typically romantic:

> Let the divine spark be buried never so deep under the ashes smouldering upon the altar on which we sacrifice to the idol of sensuality, it will blaze up into the brightest flame of enthusiasm on being fanned by the breath of genius, which we can never describe, but only profoundly feel.

"The divine spark," that had become a commonplace.

Josef Hüttenbrenner, reporting to the publisher Karl Peters in Leipzig in August 1822 (certainly with some exaggeration):

Among the newer local composers Vienna again possesses a talent today which has already attracted general attention and enjoyed the resident public's favor—in short, and without exaggeration, we may speak of a "second Beethoven." Indeed that immortal man says of him: "This one will surpass me."

Bauernfeld had written of Schubert the previous year in his diary:

A splendid fellow! I shall have to make his acquaintance [April 22, 1821].

These tributes were not shouldered lightly by the essentially good-natured and modest composer. For a time—and for a time only—his head was turned. For a time he played the "genius," demanding privileges. Is it any wonder? He had had little enough before this. His friends noticed. That companion of his boyhood days, the kindly and straightforward Anton Holzapfel, wrote to Albert Stadler; he was puzzled, though he excused:

Vienna, 22nd February 1822
. . . Schubert, as they say, made *bruit*, and he will likewise, as they say, make his *sort*. I rarely see him, nor do we hit it off very well, his world being a very different one, as it should be. His somewhat gruff manner stands him in very good stead and will make a strong man and a ripe artist of him; he will be worthy of art.

"Gruff"—a peculiar adjective to apply to gentle Schubert. Similarly, Spaun wrote to Schober:

Linz, 5th March 1822
Winter has gone by . . . and much that is of interest must have happened among you, of which you should not deprive your far-off dear one. I am so very anxious to know all that the poetic-musical-painting triumvirate [Schober, Schubert, Kupelwiesen] has produced. It cuts me to the soul that Schubert has ceased to count for me. A song recently found by Max in the "Modezeitung" entitled "The Flowers' Sorrow" ["Der Blumen Schmerz"] was a veritable feast for me. . . . Where have there been any Schubertiads this winter? How are things at the "Crown," to whose people I send greetings? Does the mechanical clock play Schubert's song already? . . . On the whole I am well content, only nothing can make me forget the happy, sociable hours I spent with you all, and which Schubert so often beautified; I fear they will never return so happily for me [DQ].

The Hungarian Crown was an inn which featured a mechanical clock. These clocks, imitating musical instruments, had been popular since the eighteenth century and were brought to a high degree of perfection by Viennese clockmakers. (One can see some of them in Vienna's Watch Museum.) The particular clock Spaun mentioned played a Schubert song, probably "Heidenröslein." Later some cylinders of Schubert waltzes were added.

Schubert's gruff mood, his ungentle manner, seems to have passed quickly. Soon he returned to his true self, evoking and returning affection. One could, one did, love Schubert.

In August 1821 Schubert had begun to sketch a symphony in E minor or major usually numbered the Seventh. He left it unfinished but it is not *the* unfinished symphony. It is an experiment showing signs of the Italian style Schubert had used in the overtures, and of Haydn-related humor in its finale. Its slow movement, an andante, contains that mysterious mixture of tranquility and melancholy so characteristic of Schubert songs. Schubert completed the full score of the first movement up to the beginning of the second theme and from there sketched the work to the end, merely indicating the melody throughout, with here and there a fragment more fully scored. Too little remains on paper to rescue the work, though two attempts have been made to complete it by an "arrangement," one by the conductor Felix Weingartner. The manuscript of the symphony is considered an important document because, with its imperfections, the work does presage certain turns of the Symphony in C Major, Schubert's last and greatest. This manuscript had some curious adventures long after Schubert's death:

Mendelssohn was the first to recognize the greatness of the C-Major Symphony and the first to perform it, at Leipzig on March 21, 1839, eleven years after Schubert's death. Schumann had discovered the C-Major manuscript when he had called on Ferdinand Schubert while visiting Vienna. He had it copied and sent it to Mendelssohn, who was enthusiastic about it and tried to get it performed as well in London and Paris. In gratitude Ferdinand sent Mendelssohn the sketch of the E-Minor Symphony. This was in March 1845. Mendelssohn wrote Ferdinand:

Dear Professor:

Yesterday I received through Doctor Haertel the symphony sketch by your brother, of which you have made me the possessor. What pleasure you give me through so fine, so precious a gift, how deeply grateful I am to you for this remembrance of the deceased master, how honoured I feel that you present me so significant a specimen of his posthumous remains directly to me—all this you can surely put into words for yourself better than I, but I feel it necessary, although in few words, to express my gratitude to you for your gift. Believe me that I know how to esteem the magnificent gift at its true value, that you could have given it to no one who would have greater joy in it, who would be more sincerely grateful to you for it. In truth, it seems to me as if, through the very incompleteness of the work, the scattered, half-finished indications, that I became at once personally acquainted with your brother more clearly and more intimately than I should have done through a completed piece. It seems as if I saw him there working in his room, and this joy I owe to your unexpectedly great kindness and generosity. Let me hope for an opportunity to meet you in the flesh, be it in Vienna or in this place here, and to make your personal acquaintance and then repeat to you by word of mouth, once again, all my thanks.

With respects
Yours faithfully,
Felix Mendelssohn-Bartholdy.

Frankfurt-am-Main,
22 March 1845

When Mendelssohn died the manuscript was left to his brother Paul. After some years Paul learned that Sir George Grove intended to publish *Grove's Dictionary of Music and Musicians* and to write the articles on Schubert and Mendelssohn himself. So he sent Grove the manuscript as a gift. Apparently William Rockstro, one of the contributors to the *Dictionary,* brought it; Grove met him at the London railroad station and the two men walked to Grove's house together. Suddenly they realized with a shock that the manuscript had been left on the train. They waited in nervous anxiety, and sure enough, the next morning the manuscript was returned. (People were honest in London—then.) When Grove died he left it to the Royal College of Music. It now rests in the British Museum.

From one unfinished to *the* unfinished, the famous one, which isn't unfinished at all, being, rather, "incomplete": for what there is of it, its two movements, are finished down to the tiniest note of the double basses. It is one of the world's most popular symphonic works, outranked in record sales only by Beethoven's Fifth and Ninth and Tchaikovsky's Sixth. Currently seventeen versions are listed in the record catalogue. It is the

Mona Lisa of symphonies, the girl everybody knows, loved by people who have only a most cursory interest in music, but—strangely—it has resisted becoming a cliché, emerging unscathed from repetition and "interpretation."

The difference between the *Unfinished* and Schubert's previous symphonies is evident, however much fine music the previous six contain. Here is a new sureness, a presentation of the creator conveying the reliant promise of "You will understand me," which is characteristic of masterworks. It seems to have been always there, just as it is, a fact of life or a fact of art, but exactly right. Snip away one bar—and you have a gash. Add a chord and you distort the face. The outbursts of the first movement are balanced against its melodic content, a progression which seems inevitable. The second, the andante, has an equally perfect shape, soothing, mysterious, entirely Schubertian, yet carrying the paternal influence of Beethoven. "His greatness became fearful," writes Paul Henry Làng in *Music in Western Civilization*, "if we realize that this wonder of a symphony was written in 1822, in the immediate vicinity of the Ninth Symphony." Here is "a work every tone of which is his own, and which can be placed next to those of Beethoven without paling. Never in the subsequent history of music did this happen again."

Why, then, did Schubert leave the work unfinished? However faulty his judgment of his own works may have been, he must have felt satisfaction in contemplating this score. Why break off? Several theories—guesses—have been suggested. The symphony was begun in a piano sketch in early October 1822. By October 30 he began to score the two movements. He then sketched the beginning of a third movement, of which only the first page is written out. In November, probably late in November, he laid the whole thing aside.

Four months after, on April 10, 1823, Johann Baptist Jenger, one of Schubert's admirers, proposed to the Styrian Music Society of Graz that Schubert be elected to honorary membership. The honor had previously been awarded to Beethoven, Salieri, Diabelli, Moscheles, and others. The committee accepted the proposal at once and wrote Schubert:

Sir,

The services you have so far rendered to the art of music are too well known for the Committee of the Styrian Music Society to have remained unaware of them. The latter, being desirous of offering you a proof of their esteem, have elected you as a non-resident honorary member of the Styrian

Music Society. A diploma to that effect as well as a copy of the Society's Statutes is enclosed herewith.

On behalf of the Committee:
Kalchberg. Jenger.

The diploma of the society was given to Anselm Hüttenbrenner to be sent to his brother Josef in Vienna and handed to Schubert by Josef. Schubert was away that summer; he was in Steyr and Linz with Vogl, the two once again presenting the songs to delighted private audiences.*

Schubert acknowledged the honor awarded him on his return to Vienna:

Gentlemen of the Music Society,

I am very greatly obliged by the diploma of honorary membership you so kindly sent me, and which, owing to my prolonged absence from Vienna, I received only a few days ago.

May it be the reward of my devotion to the art of music to become wholly worthy of such a distinction one day. In order to give musical expression to my sincere gratitude as well, I shall take the liberty before long of presenting your honorable Society with one of my symphonies in full score.

With the highest regards, I remain,
Your honourable Society's most grateful,
devoted and obedient servant,
Franz Schubert.

Vienna, 20th September 1823.

Shortly afterward Schubert gave Josef Hüttenbrenner the manuscript of the *Unfinished*, to be delivered to brother Anselm in Graz. Presumably it was a gift thanking Anselm for his services. Alternatively it could have been a gift to the Styrian Music Society for their library, though this is unlikely. But what it could *not* have been was "one of my symphonies in full score," as mentioned in his thank-you letter. That would have

---

*A reminiscence of one of these performances was given years later in Spaun's memoirs. The hostess was Spaun's mother: "A small party had been invited. After the performance of a few melancholy songs the female part of the audience began to howl, so that the sobs brought Vogl's and Schubert's concert to a premature end. Good coffee and cakes, as well as Schubert's and Vogl's humour, restored order to the company. For both artists, who were particularly honoured by those tears, this day, which ended only after moonrise, remained unforgettable."

been tantamount to sending a wedding gift of a tea-service with two cups missing. Schubert was too punctilious, too appreciative, and too tactful to commit so gross an indiscretion. Yet for years it was stated that this was the symphony "presented to the Musikverein of Graz in return for his election." Almost the only certain fact about the *Unfinished* is that it was *not* the work he had promised them.

Let me repeat this statement: I am convinced that the *Unfinished* was not intended for, or sent to, the Graz society as the gift Schubert had promised, *pace* the statement made in most biographies.

What are the possible reasons for the incompleteness of the Eighth?

First, that Schubert decided the work was complete as it stood. This is extremely doubtful, since he usually adhered to the four-part traditional form of the symphony. It is further negated by his sketch for a third movement.

Second, that Schubert did finish it, but that Josef in transmitting the score to Anselm lost part of it, and never confessed his negligence. Very doubtful, since no sign, not a single scrap of paper of the missing movements, has ever turned up.

Third, that Anselm, who in his opinion—and *only* in his opinion— was a great but unappreciated composer, deliberately destroyed the last two movements, prompted by jealousy. This is too knavish to be believable. However, Anselm can be accused of more than simple neglect and forgetfulness; not only did he not lift a finger to bring the symphony to the attention of music lovers and to have it performed at least in Graz (where he was an official of the society), but he hid the score in a drawer. Quite well did he know the value of this music, of which he made a piano arrangement in 1853. The two brothers played this more than once. The next year he made a catalogue of the Schubert manuscripts he owned; Liszt had asked him to do so. There the work is listed. But it took another six years for Josef to tell the conductor Johann Herbeck:

> [Anselm] possesses a treasure in Schubert's B minor Symphony, which we rank with his great C major Symphony, his instrumental swan-song, and with all the symphonies of Beethoven—only it is unfinished. Schubert gave it to me for Anselm to thank him for having sent the diploma of the Graz Music Society through me . . . [March 8, 1860].

When Kreissle published the first biography of Schubert five years later, he still had not heard the work:

There is an orchestral symphony in B minor, which Schubert in a half-finished state, presented to the Musikverein in Graz, in return for the compliment paid to him of being elected an honorary member of the Society. Josef Hüttenbrenner is my authority for saying that the first and second movements are entirely finished, and the third partly. The fragment, in the possession of Herr Anselm Hüttenbrenner of Graz, is said, the first movement particularly, to be of great beauty. If this be so, Schubert's intimate friend would do well to emancipate the still unknown work of the master he so highly honours, and introduce the symphony to Schubert's admirers.

Herbeck now went to Graz and by a trick "liberated" the score from Anselm's drawer. The symphony was first performed on December 17, 1865, in Vienna. It was the year the first part of the Ringstrasse had been opened. *Tristan und Isolde* was given its premiere in Munich. Lincoln was assassinated. Schubert had been dead for thirty-seven years, longer than he had lived.

The two movements were intact. However indifferently Anselm had acted, he was no out-and-out villain. The indications are that nobody destroyed the third and fourth movements: there were no third and fourth movements. Another reason exists for Schubert to have stopped.

10

Illness

SCHUBERT COMPLETED THE TWO MOVEMENTS OF THE EIGHTH SYMPHONY sometime in December 1823 and began sketching a third movement. At that very point he noticed that something had gone amiss with his health. He who was by no means a hypochondriac began to suffer from headaches and pains in his back. At first he tried to ignore them, being immersed in the composition of the piano Sonata in A Minor (op. 143), an intimate work of three movements only which he seems to have written for his own very personal enjoyment, a song as it were of three contrasting moods to be hummed in a small room. He subjected it to especially careful revision before he was satisfied; it is a twilight resting place between his early sonatas and those to follow. All through February he worked on it, but then he could no longer ignore the protests of his body. Writing to Hofrat Ignaz Mosel, now connected with the opera, Schubert apologized: "Kindly forgive me if I am compelled to incommode you with another letter so soon, the condition of my health still preventing me from leaving the house" (February 13, 1823). Mosel knew Beethoven and his nephew Karl, and told Beethoven (in the Conversation Book): "One praises Schubert, but it is said that he hides himself."

He hid himself no doubt because he already suspected what was wrong with him. Then he consulted his regular physician, Dr. August von Schaeffer, and to make sure he consulted Dr. J. Bernhardt, a known authority. Schubert knew Bernhardt through Matthaeus von Collin, whose father-in-law he was. The diagnosis was not difficult: it was undoubtedly a venereal infection and, because of the severity of the symptoms, probably syphilis, though the positive diagnostic distinction between gonorrhea and syphilis was made possible only later, nine years after Schubert's death, by Dr. Philippe Ricord of Paris. The development of Schubert's disease left little doubt that it *was* syphilis. And at the time that was an incontrovertible death sentence. The sentence was certain, not the time of its execution.

Schubert at first might not have believed it. It was all too horrible. Soon he was forced to accept the fact, forced to acknowledge that he was host to the spirochetes in his body, as a rash appeared and as his hair began to fall out. Whatever hope still remained to him, whatever consolation he dreamed himself into, a consolation aided by his doctors through either ignorance or kindness, it is reasonable to assume that he looked back with longing to the time when he was healthy, and thought with shame and bitterness of the incident when he slept with an infected woman. That incident almost certainly coincides with his work on the Eighth Symphony. He would not, he could not, turn back to it, the composition created at the very time of the inception of the disease. The reminder stung too sharply. Such a victory over himself he could not manage, even if he was aware of the worth of the half-symphony he had composed. He gave it up. And forever.

This is conjecture. It cannot be proved. But is it not the most likely explanation of the fact that the *Unfinished* is unfinished? Is it not probable that while he could go on—and did so, the wish for life being strong in him—he could not return?

He thought of suicide. In May he wrote a poem, "A Prayer." It is wretched verse, but perhaps just because it is wretched it appeals to our pity all the more strongly. Here it is in the English translation by Eric Blom (the original German is no better):

My Prayer

With a holy zeal I yearn
Life in fairer worlds to learn;
    Would this gloomy earth might seem
    Filled with love's almighty dream.

Sorrow's child, almighty Lord
Grant Thy bounty for reward.
    For redemption from above
    Send a ray of endless love.

See, abased in dust and mire,
Scorched by agonizing fire,

I in torture go my way,
Nearing doom's destructive day.

Take my life, my flesh and blood,
Plunge it all in Lethe's flood,
  To a purer, stronger state
  Deign me, Great One, to translate.

Thus, half in sadness, half in revolt, Schubert joined those gifted men who were ravaged by the disease: we know some of them—Heine, Nietzsche, Chatterton, Smetana, Goya, Lenau, Donizetti, Hugo Wolf, Maupassant, Delius, Strindberg, Munch.

The news of Schubert's illness spread among his friends. Kupelwieser to Schober: "I heard yesterday that Schubert is ill." That was on July 16; a month later Schubert himself wrote Schober:

Steyr, 14th August 1823

Dear Schober:

Although I write rather late, I hope that this letter will still find you in Vienna. I correspond busily with Schäffer [sic] and am fairly well. Whether I shall ever quite recover I am inclined to doubt. Here I live very simply in every respect, go for walks regularly, work much at my opera and read Walter Scott.

With Vogl I get on very well. We are at Linz together, where he sang a good deal, and splendidly. Bruchmann, Sturm and Streinsberg came to see us at Steyr a few days ago, and they too were dismissed with a full load of songs.

As I shall hardly see you before your return, I once again wish you the best of good fortune in your enterprise and assure you of my everlasting affection, which will make me miss you most sorely. Wherever you may be give news of yourself from time to time to

Your friend
Franz Schubert.

Kupelwieser, Schwind, Mohn, etc., etc. who have also [illegible] been written to, I all greet heartily.

My address:
City of Steyr, to be delivered at the
Square, at Herr von Vogl's.

The disease took its usual capricious course; there were periods during which he felt severely ill and there were others, periods of remission,

[137]

during which he felt quite well and believed—or half-believed—that he was cured. We know that the mind can make itself believe anything it wants to believe, be that anything completely at variance with facts. Often Schubert imagined he had conquered. That is a particular symptom of diseases of chronic infection. Sometimes when he had the courage to face the whole truth, he cried out in despair, as he did in one letter: "I doubt whether I shall ever be well again." In May 1823 he was sick enough to be hospitalized, but luckily his doctors put him into Vienna's General Hospital (Allgemeines Krankenhaus) rather than into the grim hospital for venereal diseases which Josef II had built. Presumably they treated him with a salve of tincture of mercury, which was about the only medication they knew. He now wore a wig. By the end of the year Schwind was able to tell Schober that Schubert seemed better and that it "will not be long before he goes about with his own hair again." Yet the month before, when a farewell party was given for Kupelwieser, who was going to Rome, Schubert could not participate. He did appear at the usual New Year's Eve celebration; how astonished the company must have been when, after toasting the absent Schober, Kupelwieser, and Senn, Bruchmann went and fetched Schubert and he appeared—with Dr. Bernhardt.

Schubert consulted and followed the best medical advice he could get. He did not stint. His regular doctor, Ernst von Rinna, was Court physician. Dr. Josef Bernhardt, a personal admirer, is favorably mentioned by a couple of Schubert's friends. Dr. Josef Vering wrote a treatise on the use of tincture of mercury for syphilis, which was published as early as 1826. He may or may not have been consulted by Schubert about the specific condition of Schubert's illness. Of course neither he nor anybody else could offer anything but the illusion of temporary relief. (When Dr. Vering died in 1862, Dr. Gerhard Breuning, Beethoven's young worshiper now become a well-known physician, wrote a fourteen-page appreciation of him. The line of excellent Viennese physicians was continuous.) In short, the evidence indicates that Schubert wanted earnestly to get well; he did not neglect himself.

Schubert presumably was dismissed from the hospital in the early summer of 1823. (The record is lost.) He determined to spend the summer away from Vienna in a working vacation. Every Viennese who could afford it left Vienna in the heat and dust of July and August. Schubert joined Vogl again at Steyr. They went to Linz, and Vogl sang Schubert songs, to his evident enjoyment and that of the audiences (see Schubert's letter to Schober of August 14 from Steyr). He was sorely in need of money, what with the fees for the doctors and the travel expenses, and he wrote to his publishers Cappi and Diabelli first on February 21, 1823, requesting to know where he stood financially, and complaining— politely but certainly justifiably—that they didn't carry out their obligation "quite according to arrangements. An adequate remuneration seems to be only indicated." Receiving an unsatisfactory answer, he became furious, quite in the tradition of the artist feeling insulted, neglected, and cheated. Mincing no words, he accused them of having paid for his songs less than they were worth, "for I am now in a position to obtain two hundred florins V.C. per book, and Herr von Steiner has repeatedly conveyed to me an offer to publish my works" (letter of April 10, 1823). He demands an "exact account of copies delivered to me." Yet before he sent off this letter, Schubert had entered into a relationship with a rival, Sauer and Leidesdorf, "Imperial-Royal Privileged Dealers in Art, and Alabaster, and Music Publishers," and had turned over to them three songs. The announcement of publication appeared in the *Wiener Zeitung* on the very day, April 10, Schubert wrote his second letter.

Again this overhasty and not entirely straight action is typical of the artist; one is reminded of Beethoven, who promised the *Missa Solemnis* to seven publishers—and then sold it to an eighth. Here the matter is even more "confused": before he wrote Cappi and Diabelli the first letter in February, he had sold them outright the songs of Opus 1 to 7 and 12 to 14 (first published at his own risk with his friends paying the costs). "Outright" sale, for a sum which was probably no more than eight hundred florins V.C., meant the engravings and the publishing rights. Leopold Sonnleithner had begged Schubert not to make this foolish deal, begged him to be patient and to wait, for his "commercial" strength was growing. Had he, Sonnleithner, not been able to earn 1,000 florins for Schubert through private sales? Wasn't it evident that if he could hold out but for a little time, he would receive terms more favorable? But Schubert would not listen to his friend's advice—and, again, this is typical of the artist, who often cannot distinguish between the true friend and the ax-grinder.

He fared no better with Sauer and Leidesdorf. Herr Leidesdorf was almost as awful a businessman as Schubert, planless, neurotic, balancing himself on the edge of bankruptcy. Eventually Schubert had to return to Cappi and Diabelli, and during his final years he tried his fortune—if that is the right word—with four other publishers.

No doubt the publishers were myopic money-grubbers who could not envision Schubert's future stature. No doubt they were tough traders (as I have indicated), often issuing the scores carelessly edited and cheaply printed. "Hell hounds," Beethoven called them. Schubert said that "the artist shall remain for all time the slave of every miserable peddler." Schubert was never given the benison of a Verdi–Giulio Ricordi relationship. There was no Giulio Ricordi in Vienna. Yet, in fairness, one must trot out a few excuses: songs were difficult to sell; who could keep up with Schubert's output?; he was a failure as an opera composer, and opera scores were the most profitable part of their business. One specific reason for the shabby treatment the Viennese publishers accorded Schubert I have previously suggested: they may have been chary of him knowing that, unlike Hummel, Beethoven, Salieri, et al., he did not bask in governmental favor. Sauer and Leidesdorf, for example, were official "Suppliers to the Court"; they had to watch their step.

Schubert had supplied the circle of friends its center of gravity, Schober had lit its brilliant sparks. Now Schober was far away and Schubert was withdrawn. Gradually the circle lost shape and strength. For a time they kept up their reading sessions, but—wrote Schwind to Schober—"The crowd and the mixture of guests are irksome and I do not feel at home." Soon he became further disenchanted.

> I am on the point of resigning from the readings, for the reading is so stifled by business affairs and pranks that even to gather together undisturbed is impossible. If you or Senn suddenly appeared in our midst, we should be truly ashamed of such company. Schubert will stick to me [December 2, 1823].

Bruchmann, too, noticed the change. Writing to Kupelwieser on the same day, he thought "it was secretly felt that we are no longer as sound at the core as before." Schubert himself observed:

> *Vienna, November 30, 1823*
>
> Dear Schober,
>
> For some time I have been itching to write to you, but I have never managed to do so. You know how it happens.
>
> First of all I must pour out a lament over the condition of our circle as well as all other circumstances; for with the exception of the state of my health, which (thank God) seems to be firmly restored at last, everything

goes miserably. Our circle, as indeed I had expected, has lost its central focus without you. Bruchmann, who has returned from his journey, is no longer the same. He seems to bend to the formalities of the world, and by that alone he loses his halo, which in my opinion was due only to his determined disregard of all worldly affairs. Kupelwieser, as presumably you already know, has gone to Rome. . . . True, as a substitute for you and Kupelwieser, we received four individuals, namely: the Hungarian Mayer, Hönig, Sme-tana*and Steiger, but the majority of such individuals make the society only more insignificant instead of better. What is the good of a lot of quite ordinary students and officials to us? If Bruchmann is not there, or even ill, we go on for hours under the supreme direction of Mohn [a painter] hearing nothing but eternal talk about riding, fencing, horses and hounds. If it is to go on like this, I don't suppose I shall stand it for long among them. . . .

And now let's hear from you. How are you? Have you already appeared before the world's eyes [as an actor in Breslau]?

Please be sure to give some news of yourself very soon, and still my longing for you to some extent at least by letting me know how you live and what you do. . . .

For the rest, I hope to regain my health, and this recovered treasure will let me forget many a sorrow; only you, dear Schober, I shall never forget, for what you meant to me no one else can mean, alas!

And now keep well and do not forget

Your eternally affectionate
friend
Franz Schubert [DQ].

In the space of one letter Schubert says that his health seems to be firmly restored—and that he hopes to regain his health.

The disease would allow him only seven more years of life. In those years he composed his greatest music. His doubts that "I shall ever be well again" increased, while the pressure of ideas, present from early youth, became heavier.

Yet were we to take some of the recollections of his friends at face value, we would get the impression that Schubert lived a wayward life, a *Ulysses in Night Town* existence. Eduard Bauernfeld wrote reams about Schubert: once the year after his death, then in the 1850s, then in a book, *Aus Alt- und Neu Wien (Old and New Vienna)* published in 1875, almost half a century after Schubert's death. These mixtures of facts and fictions are responsible for the impression of Schubert the naive:

*No relative of the composer.

How often did the three of us [Schubert, Schwind, Bauernfeld] mosey around till three o'clock in the morning, till dawn, and then being unable to bear parting, how often did we seek shelter here or there. Friend Moritz [Schwind] used occasionally to sleep on the floor, covered by a leather jacket. Once he carved me a pipe from Schubert's spectacle-case, having forgotten mine. In the matter of possessions we took a communistic view: hats, boots, clothes if they fitted halfways decently as well as certain under garments, were communal property. . . .

From time to time it happened that two of us had no money—and the third not a red penny! Naturally Schubert was the Croesus among us and swam in silver when he sold a few songs or a whole cycle of them—for example the Songs of Walter Scott, for which Artaria paid him 500 gulden WW. Now we lived nobly and extravagantly, until Poor Robin took over. In short, ebb and flood.

Sounds convincing. Or does it? The only trouble is that Bauernfeld did not know Schubert till 1822, the year he became ill, and Schubert could not and did not make nocturnal rounds that year, not often, certainly. Neither Bauernfeld nor Schwind was that poor, the first holding a responsible position in the Lottery Administration, the second being soon successful as an illustrator.

Again, Bauernfeld:

Then came Schubert evenings, known as "Schubertiaden," when the wine flowed in buckets, the excellent Vogl served up wonderful songs and poor Schubert had to accompany him for so long a stretch with his short, fat fingers that they hardly obeyed him. It was worse when we gave a dance— we called them "sausage dances" in those simple days—when pretty women and young girls were present. Our "Bertel," as he was tenderly nicknamed, had to play his latest waltz, and play it again and again, while they formed a cotillion. The corpulent little man, dripping sweat, had to wait until a frugal supper was served before he could relax. No wonder that he sometimes failed us and that more than one Schubertiade took place without Schubert, especially when he was not feeling sociable or didn't like some of the guests.

Schubert played the piano with ease; he would hardly have shed a single drop of perspiration playing a waltz. It is fiction.

What is true is that in May of 1823, the year of the Monroe Doctrine, when James Fenimore Cooper began a series of *Leatherstocking Tales* which captured the fancy of readers all over the world, and when Charles Macintosh invented a waterproof fabric which well-dressed Viennese

soon were wearing, in that year Schubert composed twelve country dances
(Ländler) which remained unpublished for forty-four years. Alfred Einstein has this to say about them:

> It is obvious why Schubert never found a publisher for them. They no longer
> have anything whatever to do with improvisation, and were much too am-
> bitious for potential purchasers and for practical use. The harmonic richness,
> the wealth of melody, the originality of the modulations and the different
> types, are all quite unique. No. 1 is like an introduction, an "Invitation to
> the Dance." No. 3 could well be included as it stands in Schumann's *Car-
> naval,* while No. 8 (in A flat minor) could equally have been written by
> Chopin. No. 5 is one of those dances in which only the middle parts seem
> to be in motion and whose "mute happiness" we shall encounter in a few
> more instances—for example in Schubert's most perfect and most individual
> sonata, the G major, op. 78.

Schubert's state of mind in that first year of illness is by chance clarified
by a letter. He wrote to Leopold Kupelwieser a letter which must be read
in full, since it contains first the honest admission of operatic failure,
second a frank confession of his disease—and third the creative contradiction which speaks of loss of enthusiasm at one moment, only to discuss
in the next more daring plans for the future. This letter, addressed to his
friend in far-off Rome and springing from the core of Schubert's heart,
is the most revealing document of a nature not prone to soliloquies. How
did Kupelwieser feel as he deciphered it in the smoke of the Café Greco
on the Via Condotti, meeting place of artists?

M. Signor Leopoldo
Kupelwieser
pittore tedesco,
recapito al caffé grecco [sic]

31, March, 1824

Dear Kupelwieser,

For a long time I have felt the urge to write to you, but I never knew
where to turn. Now, however, Smirsch [an amateur painter who probably
was going to Rome] offers me an opportunity, and at last I can once again
wholly pour out my soul to someone. For you are so good and honest, you
will be sure to forgive many things which others might take in very bad part
from me. —In a word, I find myself to be the most unhappy and wretched
creature in the world. Imagine a man whose health will never be right again,

[143]

and who in sheer despair over this ever makes things worse and worse, instead of better; imagine a man, I say, whose most brilliant hopes have perished, to whom the felicity of love and friendship have nothing to offer but pain, at best, whom enthusiasm (at least of the stimulating kind) for all things beautiful threatens to forsake, and I ask you, is he not a miserable, unhappy being? —"My peace is gone, my heart is sore, I shall find it never and nevermore" [quotation from *Faust*]. I may well sing every day now, for each night, on retiring to bed, I hope I may not wake again, and each morning but recalls yesterday's grief. Thus, joyless and friendless, I should pass my days, did not Schwind visit me now and again and turn on me a ray of those sweet days of the past. —Our society (reading circle), as you probably know already, has done itself to death owing to a reinforcement of that rough chorus of beer-drinkers and sausage-eaters, for its dissolution is due in a couple of days, though I had hardly visited it myself since your departure. Leidesdorf, with whom I have become quite well acquainted, is in fact a truly thoughtful and good fellow, but so hugely melancholy that I am almost afraid I owe him more than enough in that respect; besides, my affairs and his do badly, so that we never have any money. The opera by your brother (who did not do any too well in leaving the theater) has been declared unusable, and thus no claim has been made on my music. Castelli's opera, "The Conspirators" ["Die Verschworenen"], has been set in Berlin by a local composer and received with acclamation. In this way I seem once again to have composed two operas for nothing. Of songs I have not written many new ones, but I have tried my hand at several instrumental works, for I wrote two Quartets for violins, viola and violoncello and an Octet, and I want to write another quartet, in fact I intend to pave my way towards grand symphony in that manner. —The latest in Vienna is that Beethoven is to give a concert at which he is to produce his new Symphony, three movements from the new Mass and a new Overture. —God willing, I too am thinking of giving a similar concert next year. I will close now, so as not to use too much paper, and kiss you 1,000 times. If you were to write to me about your present enthusiastic mood and about your life in general, nothing could more greatly please

	Your
In that case my address would be	faithful Friend
c/o the Art Establishment of	Frz. Schubert.
Sauer & Leidesdorf,	
as I go to Hungary with Esterházy	Fare well!
at the beginning of May.	Very well!! [DQ]

(The Beethoven concert to which Schubert refers is the famous one of May 7, 1824; the Ninth Symphony was premiered and parts of the *Missa*

Solemnis were given. The concert began with the *Consecration of the House* Overture, which was not new.)

The sad letter marks the low point of Schubert's being. His peace is gone; the old closeness and the joyful union have passed; his friends, or most of them, have dispersed. He is ill. He is lonely. He admits his failure as an opera composer. As he falls asleep at night he hopes not to wake again.

Yet the artist continues his work. He is ready to go on. He wants to "pave" his way to new and bolder attempts, especially symphonically. He may become a stranger to life, to probe music all the more deeply.

At the end of the year Schubert composed another work for the stage, this time only incidental music for a spoken play. Beethoven had composed such incidental music for Goethe's play *Egmont* thirteen years previously, and Mendelssohn was to furnish an appreciably better play with music in 1842. Schubert concerned himself with a play by a minor poetess—"minor" is saying too much—who had concocted the wretched libretto of *Euryanthe* for Weber; she was Helmine von Chézy, a blowsy "intellectual" with ready tear ducts, whom Bauernfeld described as good-natured and a bit ridiculous, "cleanliness not [being] her cardinal virtue." She was in Vienna with her two sons to witness the premiere of *Euryanthe*. Schubert received the commission to deck out her play *Rosamunde*—which had been accepted by the Theater an der Wien—with music sometime in October, and tradition has it that he did so to confer a favor upon his friend Josef Kupelwieser. Josef was in love with an actress, Emilie Neumann, who substituted for a lack of talent considerable sex appeal, enough to obtain for herself some glamorous roles. Frau Chézy, who was better at publicity than at playwriting, had drummed up a deal of excitement for the premiere of *Rosamunde,* which took place on December 20, 1823, as a benefit for Emilie Neumann. The text of the play is lost, but a detailed description of it is extant, from which we can glean such master touches as "Corsairs hide in the palace garden in order to abduct Rosamond, but she happens to have playfully changed her princely robe with Claribella." Rosenbaum's verdict: "Empty, tedious, unnatural. Paid 10 florins for my seat" (diary entry, December 20). Schwind, writing to Schober—who was obviously being informed by friends of artistic events in Vienna—reported of Schubert's music:

Vienna December 22, 1823
... A ballet made no impression, nor did the second and third entr'actes.

Well, people are accustomed to talking immediately the curtain has dropped, and I do not see how they can be expected to notice such serious and lovely things. In the last act was a chorus of shepherds and huntsmen, so beautiful and so natural that I cannot remember ever hearing the like before. It was applauded and repeated, and I believe it will deal the chorus in Weber's *Euryanthe* the sort of blow it deserves. An aria, too, though most atrociously sung by Mme. Vogel, and a little bucolic piece were applauded. A subterranean chorus could not be heard and even the gestures of Herr Rott, who was brewing poison the while, could not make it materialize.

Schubert wrote no overture, using the one he had composed for *Alfonso*, though later, when the score was published, the overture to the melodrama *The Magic Harp* was appended to the incidental music. For the play he supplied ten numbers, as generous and delightful as any of Schubert's optimistic music. Einstein wrote that they "are among his greatest inspirations"—but they have little to do with Chézy's presumably lumpy pudding and could as well serve as incidental music for *As You Like It*. The numbers are:

1. Entr'acte, after Act I
2. Ballet Music, Act II
3. Entr'acte after Act II
4. Romance for Contralto, Act III
5. Chorus of Spirits (Male Voices), Act III
6. Entr'acte after Act III
7. Shepherd's melody for clarinets, horns and bassoons
8. Chorus of Shepherds (Male and Female), Act IV
9. Chorus of Hunters (Male and Female), Act IV
10. Ballet Music, Act IV

Rosamunde was given twice, then put on the shelf. Emilie Neumann threw over Josef Kupelwieser and married an actor. Schubert got nothing out of it except an evening's applause and a few days' praise.

The story of the rediscovery of the score in 1867, forty-four years later, is a well-known anecdote, but needs a little correction. Sir Arthur Sullivan and Sir George Grove journeyed to Vienna to look for forgotten musical manuscripts and were there welcomed and aided by the publisher Karl Spina, who put his storage rooms and a supply of good cigars at the disposal of the two impressive Englishmen. Sullivan and Grove knew of the existence of *Rosamunde* and were most desirous of finding the orchestral parts for numbers 4, 5, 8, and 9 so the work could be performed. Rummaging through parcel after parcel, they did find a few

Schubert manuscripts (including that of the *Tragic* Symphony), but no trace of *Rosamunde*. After working for a week, they called on Spina to bid him farewell before continuing their journey to Prague. They still hoped that somehow or other the manuscript would turn up, since Spina had stored a number of theater scores. Grove told the story to his biographer, C. L. Graves:

> The doctor was civility itself; he again had recourse to the cupboard, and shewed us some treasures which had escaped us before. I again turned the conversation to the *Rosamunde* music; he believed that he had at one time possessed a copy of the sketch of it all. Might I go into the cupboard* and look for myself? Certainly, if I had no objection to being smothered with dust. In I went; and after some search, during which my companion kept the doctor engaged in conversation, I found, at the bottom of the cupboard, and in its farthest corner, a bundle of music books two feet high, carefully tied round, and black with the undisturbed dust of nearly half a century. . . . These were the part books of the whole of the music in *Rosamunde*, tied up after the second performance in December 1823, and probably never disturbed since.

Tense with excitement, Sullivan and Grove copied the scores, working till two o'clock in the morning. Then the two frock-coated and punctiliously cravated gentlemen, both exhausted, played a game of leapfrog.

His finest achievement of 1823, indeed one of the high achievements of all vocal music, Schubert regarded rather casually. "I have composed nothing since the opera," Schubert wrote Schober on November 30, "except a few *Schöne Müllerin* songs." A few? There were twenty. Nothing? Except that cycle dealing with the unhappy love of a man for the pretty "Maid of the Mill" would suffice to earn its creator a laurel wreath from every male lieder-singer, from Fisher-Dieskau back to Vogl. Kreissle, Schubert's first biographer, told the story of Schubert's finding the poem:

> One day Schubert called on the private secretary of Count Seczenyi, Herr Benedikt Randhartinger, with whom he was on friendly terms. He had scarcely entered the room, when the secretary was summoned to the Count. He went out at once, indicating to the composer that he would be back shortly. Franz walked over to the desk, where he found a volume of poems lying. He put the book in his pocket and left, without waiting for Rand-

*One they had not examined, since Spina thought it contained no manuscripts.

hartinger's return. The latter noticed that the volume of poems was missing as soon as he came back, and called on Schubert the following day in order to recover the book. Franz put down his high-handed behavior to the interest which the poems had aroused in him, and to prove that his removal of the book had not been entirely unproductive of results, he presented the astonished secretary with the manuscript of the first "Miller" songs, which he had partially completed during the previous night.

This sounds too pat to be true. At any rate, Schubert worked on the cycle off and on throughout the year, in and out of the hospital, in Steyr and Vienna. Wilhelm Müller was a late romantic poet who died in 1827 at the early age of thirty-two and whose best poetry celebrated the Greek struggle for liberty. He was in love with Louise Hensel, a Catholic poetess whose little verse, "Müde bin ich, geh zu Ruh," small German children whisper (or used to) before falling asleep. Louise did not love him, and the *Müller* lieder are an autobiographical plaint. In a wider sense, so are the Schubert songs expressions of profound rejection and resignation. Tender, loving, simple, the cycle tells a story: it begins with the young man arriving at the mill and its brook and his ceasing to wander, though an inner foreboding warns him. No. 1, "Das Wandern" ("Roaming"), describes his feelings as he hears the ripple of the brook. No. 2, "Wohin?" ("Whither?"), confirms his decision to stay. He falls in love with the girl (No. 3, "Halt," and No. 4, "Danksagung an den Bach"—"Thanks to the Brook"). The cycle then marks the course of his fate: the girl's indifference as she bids good night to all with equal voice (No. 5, "Am Feierabend"—"Evening Rest"), the intense questioning by the young man, doubtful and fearful as he whispers, "Say, brook, does she love me?" (No. 6, "Der Neugierige"—"Curious"), his triumph, the climax of his hope (No. 7, "Ungeduld"—"Impatience," a song so famous that it is now not easy to listen to it). With the next the decline of the young lover's fortune begins. In No. 8 ("Morgengruss"—"Morning Greeting") he asks her, "Does my greeting displease you so?" Tears are now present, first in No. 9 ("Des Müllers Blumen"—"The Miller's Flowers"), then in that strange and ominous song (No. 10, "Tränenregen"—"Rain of Tears"). No. 11 ("Mein"—"Mine") is not entirely successful, but it serves as a prelude to tragedy, of a love turned to bitterness, of the girl's breaking faith. The tension and resolution of this section are constructed with superb skill by the man who could not construct an opera; it begins with a still-hopeful statement in No. 12 ("Pause"—"Interlude") and continues with No. 13 ("Mit dem grünen Lautenbande"—"With a Green Lute Ribbon"). Then the cause appears: it is "Der Jäger" ("The Hunter," No. 14) who has captured the girl's fancy. He is dressed in green. The former lover is discarded: "Go, brook, not a word to her of how sad my fate is." His sorrow mounts in No. 15 ("Eifersucht und Stolz"—"Pride and Jealousy"), No. 16 ("Die liebe Farbe"—"The Good Color"), and No. 17 ("Die böse Farbe"—"The Nasty Color")—this is one of Schubert's magic songs—and continues with No. 18 ("Trockne Blumen"—"Dry Flowers") and is followed by a mysterious dialogue (No. 19, "Der Müller und der Bach"—"The Miller and the Brook"); the brook seems to console the young lover's suffering and to invite him "down below into cool peace." No. 20 ("Des Baches Wiegenlied"—"The Brook's Lullaby") closes the cycle with a gentle quiet lament: "Schlaf aus deine Freude, schlaf aus dein Leid!" ("Sleep away your joy, sleep away your pain!")

Through the whole cycle runs the suggestion of the brook, now evident, now but hinted at, always in motion. Piano and voice work in perfect unity, and the waves seem to adumbrate the moods with extraordinary psychological aptness. The most popular songs, often presented separately, are numbers 1, 2, 6, 7, 8, and 20, but it is of course preferable to give and to hear the cycle as a whole. The question remains whether we can still respond to so innocent and tear-drenched a romance. Its music has not aged; words are more time-bound than notes, and poetry, except the very highest, more subject to change of style and viewpoint than is music. We accept with delight the romantic music of the composers of the early nineteenth century, even that of composers less great than Schubert, but who reads Walter Scott's poetry?

How did Schubert choose his texts? As I have indicated, they range from the commonplace to the profound, yet he knew well what served his purpose, and his decisions were not naive. He looked for poems of consistent mood—be that mood playful as in "Die Männer sind mechant" ("Men Are Wicked," text by the Austrian poet Johann Gabriel Seidl; Elisabeth Schumann and Lotte Lehmann used to sing it enchantingly), tragic as in "Die junge Nonne" ("The Young Nun," text by Craigher), mystic as in "Dass sie hier gewesen" ("She Was Here," text by Friedrich Rückert, a good poet; that song, by the way, is exceptionally astonishing, since it foreshadows *Tristan*). He also searched, if only subconsciously, for language that flowed and ended in a climax of one or two words he could express musically. To the symbols we have already mentioned, "roaming," "open sky," "dark night," etc., we must add "water," which attracted him especially. In the year of the *Müller* songs, he composed "Auf dem Wasser zu singen" ("To Be Sung on the Water," text by Friedrich Stolberg), which unites the beauty of a Schubert lied with the beauty of a Schubert piano sonata.

Having said all that, one must again admit that from his friends especially he was now and then inclined to accept poetry with too high a sugar content.

The disease played a cruel game of hide-and-seek with Schubert. Early in 1824 he was in a gay mood and his friends rejoiced. On New Year's Eve the friends held a tipsy celebration in the usual tradition, as reported by Anton Freiherr von Doblhoff, one of the recent additions to Schubert's circle (then twenty-three years old, later to become Austrian Minister of Commerce), to Schober:

> *Vienna, 7th January 1824*
>
> All are quite well and thought of you with intimate joyousness on the festively celebrated New Year's Eve which, although in many respects inferior to that of last year, far surpassed [it] in free, unrestrained pleasure and harmony of the most resounding joy. We met at Mohn's at 11 o'clock. Bruchmann, Schwind, Schubert, Bernhardt, Honig, Smetana, Kraissl, Dietrich, Eichholzer, Steiger, Kiesewetter, Mayer and I. Six Bruchmannish bottles of Moselle precipitated themselves on us and all our splendid absent friends into the new year, and although a little impetuously, this nevertheless developed no other feeling than that of love and friendship, and so we will hope the best of the year which has come of age. . . . Schubert is almost completely well and in nearly constant communication with Bernhardt and Leidesdorf [DQ].

Schwind confirmed this to Schober about a month later, after the birthday celebration for Schubert on January 31:

> *[Vienna] 2nd February 1824*
>
> Justina [Bruchmann, with whom Schober was secretly in love but who married Rudolf Smetana and died giving birth to her first child] read to me from your letter that you [appeared as an actor] with success, and what you write about me. That was on Schubert's birthday. We had a feast at the "Crown," and though we were all fuddled, I wished you were present, if only for the sake of Schubert's pleasure over your good fortune. In my consummate tipsiness I was able to see them all as they are. They were all more or less idiotic, and Schubert asleep. Bruchmann alone, although [he] remembers

nothing of all this, was like some one filled with enthusiasm. He embraced me passionately, drank Julie's health with me alone, and with Schubert and me wished you good health with a warm, everlasting handshake.

A few days after, Schwind to Schober:

> [*Vienna*] *13th February* [*1824*]
>
> Schubert now keeps a fortnight's fast and confinement. He looks much better and is very bright, very comically hungry and writes quartets and German dances and variations without number.

Again, a few days after, Schwind to Schober: "Schubert is quite well. He has given up his wig and grown the charming locks of a swan" (February 22).

And again, after Schubert had told Schwind that Dr. Bernhardt was trying a new treatment on him:

> [*Vienna, March 6, 1824*]
>
> Schubert is pretty well already. He says that after a few days of the new treatment he felt how his complaint broke up and everything was different. He still lives one day on panada [a dish made of sweetened bread] and the next on cutlets, and lavishly drinks tea, goes bathing a good deal besides and is superhumanly industrious. A new Quartet is to be performed at Schuppanzigh's, who is quite enthusiastic and is said to have rehearsed particularly well. He has now long been at work on an Octet, with the greatest zeal. If you go to see him during the day, he says, "Hullo, how are you?—Good!" and goes on writing, whereupon you depart. Of Muller's poems he has set two very beautifully, and three by Mayrhofer, whose poems have already appeared, "Boating" ["Gondelfahrt" (sic)]; "Evening Star" ["Abend Stern"] and "Victory" ["Sieg"]. The last, indeed, I never knew well, but I always remember it as a rich, teeming, almost fairy-like poem, but now [it] is serious, ponderously Egyptian and yet so warm and round, very grand and genuine. Apart from that some twenty German dances, each finer than the last, courtly, charming, bacchic and fugal. O God! I go to see him nearly every evening, he intends to write to you, but I secretly wish he would not do so, to let you see how disagreeable it is to expect letters; but no, do not write to me, I do not wish it [DQ].

Of course they were fooling themselves. By April 1824 the reports sounded different. "Schubert still complains of pains in his bones" (Doblhoff to Schober, April 2). "Schubert is not very well. He has pains in his left arm, so that he cannot play the pianoforte at all" (Schwind to Schober, April 14). "The good Schubert alone complains to me that he is ill again" (Leopold Kupelwieser to Johanna Lutz, May 8 to 12). Pain one day, quiet the next, but present always the knowledge that he was host to the inexorable malady in his bloodstream.

As an artist he sought new roads, undeterred by disease and dolor. Of the quartets he mentions, one, No. 13 in A Minor, was finished in March 1824. He at once began another, the *Death and the Maiden* Quartet. The third belongs to a later period, to 1826. For the first, the A Minor, he used in the slow movement the theme from *Rosamunde,* which he used once more in the variations of one of his most famous impromptus (op. 142). Not only that movement, but the whole quartet is enchanting and easy, an antithesis to the creator's mood, as happens so often. This contradiction is further confirmed by the ebullient spirits of the Octet, "born," as Maurice Brown said, "from this despairing mind." To be sure, it was a commission, no doubt well compensated. Ferdinand Count Troyer, chief steward of Archduke Rudolf, who was a clarinet player, wanted a work "exactly like Beethoven's Septet," that superpopular piece of the period. Schubert delivered exactly what was wanted: There are six movements as in Beethoven. Where Beethoven has an adagio Schubert, contrary to his usual practice, writes one too; when Beethoven writes an andante with variations, Schubert does likewise. In both compositions the relationship of keys is identical. What is more, both works breathe a happy mood. Obviously Schubert provides plenty of opportunity for the clarinet. Yet in spite of the similarity to Beethoven's piece, the Octet comes out pure Schubert, though not the greatest Schubert.

Schubert, with mortality in his mind and yet not quite believing it, turned from a song composer to an instrumental composer, his way, halted at the *Unfinished,* now directed toward the "grand symphony," as he wrote Kupelwieser. It is allowable to speculate whether a certain change of taste of musical Vienna—or at least its direction—may have influenced Schubert. Instrumental music, from piano to symphony, lay as it were in the air. Vienna had been full of pianists, led by Johann Nepomuk Hummel, who "carried the Viennese school to its height" (Harold Schonberg, *The Great Pianists*), but in addition to such favorites as Moscheles, Hiller, Czerny, etc., a twelve-year-old boy made people sit up: his name was Franz Liszt, and he played in 1822 and again in 1823. Now the one event that excited all in anticipation was the premiere of the Ninth Symphony. It was ten years since Beethoven had offered a new symphony, and rumors of its wonders circulated as headily as the rumors of a royal wedding. What was this work going to be like, for the performance of which so many European cities vied and which, one was told, needed so huge an apparatus, including singers and chorus? Schubert mentioned it some five weeks before the performance on May 7. He was there and witnessed the jubilation of the audience, of which Beethoven, facing the orchestra, heard nothing and of which he was unaware, until somebody plucked him by his sleeve, turned him around, and then he saw the people cheering. Three weeks before "all men become brothers" was heard, Byron died at Missolonghi (April 19, 1824). Delacroix painted his grim reminder of human cruelty, *The Massacre of Chios*. Austria sharpened its spy system.

Two weeks before the historic performance of the Ninth, Schubert's Quartet in A Minor was given its first public performance in the hall of the Red Hedgehog as part of a subscription series by the Schuppanzigh Quartet. That fact alone would weigh heavily against the belief that Schubert was totally ignored or neglected. For Schuppanzigh—to whom the A-Minor Quartet was dedicated—to consent to study and perform it was high testimony. He was Vienna's leading violinist, the Heifetz of his day, friend of Beethoven, who entrusted him with the rehearsals for the strings in the Ninth. Schuppanzigh, Beethoven's "My Lord Falstaff," was as well known a star as Vogl, and when he and his wife (who was almost equally corpulent) waddled down the Graben, the street boys whistled and music lovers stopped to bow and smile. In short, Schuppanzigh could, and did, select anything he wanted to play. The other members of his group were distinguished musicians as well: second violin was Karl Holz, a cultured young man of whom Schindler was violently jealous; the viola was Franz Weiss; the violoncello Josef Linke, who signed himself once "the accursed cello of the great master," who had to endure many a terrible pun from the great master on the word *links* (left), meaning "awkward."

Schubert's new composition could not have been introduced by a more illustrious group.* Schwind reported to Schober:

> Schubert's Quartet has been performed, rather slowly in his opinion, but very purely and tenderly. It is on the whole very delicate [*weich*], but written in such a way that the tune remains in one's mind, as with the songs, all

*Schuppanzigh also played the first violin part in the private performance of the Octet at Count Troyer's residence, Linke the cello.

feeling and thoroughly expressive. It got much applause, especially the minuet, which is extraordinarily tender and natural. A Chinese sitting next to
me thought it affected and devoid of style. I should just like to see Schubert
affected! A single hearing, what can that mean to the likes of us, let alone
to such a gobbler-up of notes? Afterwards we had Beethoven's famous Septet.

Spring came to the Vienna Woods. It comes as if Nature wants to
imitate the opera: Act I, Scene 1, "A desolate forest" (no interval), Act
I, Scene 2, "A flower-filled woods." Overnight the white flowers called
"snowballs" (Schneeglöckchen) pop up, followed by buttercups and daf-
fodils, then the whole ostentatious parade of blossoms enters, all with
April's speed. Schubert received another invitation from Count Esterházy
to come to Zseliz; he didn't exactly long for the country, but it was
spring, Schober, Spaun, and Bruchmann had left Vienna, he needed money
(as usual), and the terms now offered him were more generous than those
of six years previously, not only in money—a hundred gulden a month
instead of seventy-five—but in respect. He was no longer an unknown
musician. He was not relegated to the servants' quarters but was to stay
with the family in the castle proper and in a room of his own.

The welcome he received and the vernal country air did raise his spirits.
The elder Countess, Marie, was about to become engaged, the younger,
Caroline, was now nineteen and pretty, and Schubert felt drawn to her,
mentioning "a certain attractive star" in a letter to Schwind. As to "the
complaisant chambermaid," she too was there, but Schubert could hardly
renew his relationship with her, even had he wanted to, for enough was
known of the disease to realize that it is spread by intimate contact. The
two Countesses had become proficient pianists, and Schubert's duties
comprised playing four hands with one, then the other, as well as furnishing new compositions for the piano. Among these there was a sonata
in C major, a duet (later published as *Grand Duo,* op. 140), another
duet which was published soon after his return to Vienna (op. 35), some
marches (op. 40), and other music which could be written on a summer
eve. The castle was the same, the bucolic life was the same, the birds
twittered and the pigs grunted in the same tones, and Schubert for a time
basked in the Hungarian heat. Yet the knowledge of his misfortune was
always with him. He hid it from his parents; the last thing he needed
was the kind of letter his father wrote him in June. It was a letter such
as those which from time immemorial parents have written their children
and which have made them furious:

Dear Son:

Your letter of the 31st ult. I received on the 3rd inst. We are all heartily glad that you are in good health and have been so well received in the count's household. Endeavor, therefore, to care for and maintain your health, the first among all earthly possessions, and make it your business to deserve the love and respect of all who mean well by you.

You know that, as a teacher of youth, I am always apt to moralize; but believe me it is not from habit, but from a profound conviction that nobody can be truly happy who is not continually in touch with God and keeps steadfastly to His holy will. We may, nay we should even moderately enjoy the innocent joys of life with hearts grateful to God; but we must not let our spirits sink in gloomy circumstances either, for sorrows too are a blessing of God and lead those who manfully endure to the most glorious goal [DQ].

And so on. His father didn't, but his brother did know the truth. Ferdinand wrote Franz a few days later and related that they had once again "begun to play your quartets" and that at the Hungarian Crown he had heard the clock which played his brother's tunes:

I felt so strange at that moment, I hardly knew where I was; it did not cheer me up by any manner of means; rather did it strike my heart and soul with such an anxious pain and longing that at last melancholy threw its veil over me and I involuntarily shed—.

Now, dear Franz, write to me to say how you are (but expressly addressed to me); whether you are quite well, how you are occupied and how you pass your spare time.

He then reported on various musical matters:

Four weeks ago I was visited by Herr von Mohn, to whom I handed copies of the following ten songs:

1. "The Secret" *(Geheimnis),* by Schiller, 1823.
2. "To Spring" *(An den Frühling),* 1817.
3. "Melodies of Life" *(Die Lebensmelodien),* 1816.
4. "In Windy Weather" *(Beim Winde),* by Mayrhofer, 1819.
5. "Cheerfulness" *(Frohsinn),* 1817.
6. "Wayfarer's Night Song" *(Wanderers Nachtlied)* II.
7. "Consolation" *(Trost),* 1817.
8. "Spring Song" *(Frühlingslied),* 1816.
9. "Orestes Abducted" *(Der entführte Orest)* [sic], 1820.
10. "Language of Love" *(Sprache der Liebe),* by Schlegel, 1816.

A few days later I handed Herr von Kupelwieser, at his request and in exchange for your assignment, the score of your new opera.

Apart from these two gentlemen Herr Hugelmann [an amateur musician] came too, asking me to return to him the scores of Mozart's quartets which you had given me to keep. However, as I did not find them after searching three times, I could not satisfy his request. After that he came to me twice more, once in the training college corridor and once at my home, where he gave me not a little annoyance by inveighing so violently against your thoughtlessness, blustering, screaming and using such coarse expressions that I very much cursed the honour of his acquaintance. Be good enough, therefore, to let me know where the music in question might possibly be, so that I may pacify this raging monster [DQ].

Schubert replied to Ferdinand at once—which was unusual for him, a dilatory correspondent:

Zseliz, (16th or 17th to) 18th July 1824

Dearest Brother:

That I really was a little hurt to have received a letter so late, both from home and from you, you may believe word for word. Neither do I hear anything from Leidesdorf, though I wrote to him. Be good enough to keep an eye on him for a bit at his art shop, to get him to send me what I asked for. You might also inquire about the publication of Book III of the "Maid of the Mill" songs, for I see nothing in the paper. About your quartet party I am the more astonished because you were able to rope in Ignaz!!! But it would be better if you stuck to other quartets than mine, for there is nothing about them, except that perhaps they please you, who are pleased with anything of mine. Your thinking of me is what I like best about it, especially as they do not seem to grip you as much as the waltzes at the "Hungarian Crown." Was it only the pain of my absence which made you shed tears, and could you not trust yourself to write the word? Or did you feel, on thinking of my person, oppressed by an ever incomprehensible longing, that its dismal veil was enfolding you too? Or did all the tears come to your mind which you have seen me weep? Be that as it may, I feel more clearly than ever at this moment that you, and you only, are my truest friend, bound to my soul with every fibre! —Not to let these lines mislead you into believing that I am not well or cheerful, I hasten to assure you of the contrary. True, it is no longer that happy time during which each object seems to us to be surrounded by a youthful gloriole, but a period of fateful recognition of a miserable reality, which I endeavor to beautify as far as possible by my imagination (thank God). We fancy that happiness lies in places where once we were happier, whereas actually it is only in ourselves, and so, although I had an unpleasant disappointment by renewing here an experience already undergone at Steyr, I am better able now to find happiness and peace in myself than I was then. —A grand sonata and variations on a theme of my own, both for 4 hands, which I have already written, shall serve you as proof of this. The variations have met with a special success. As regards the songs you handed to Mohn, I comfort myself with the thought that only a few of them seem good to me, e.g. those included with "The Secret," the "Wayfarer's Night Song" and "Orestes absolved," not "abducted," an error that made me laugh very much. Try to get back those I have named, at least.

Did Kupelwieser not mention what he intended to do with the opera? Or where he is sending it??—

The [Mozart] quintets—(not quartets)—belonging to that archdonkey Hugelbeast have accompanied me here by mistake, and, by Heaven! he shall not have them back until he has atoned for his vulgar rudeness by a written or verbal apology. If, moreover, an opportunity occurs to administer a vigorous scrubbing to this unclean pig, I shall not fail to give him a substantial dose. But enough of that wretch!—

That you are quite well gives me the more pleasure because I hope to enjoy that same well-being in myself in the coming winter . . . [DQ].

He still hoped. But Ferdinand was not fooled and wanted Franz to tell him the truth, "expressly addressed to me." The next month Schubert got tired of the country and, as on his previous visit, he longed for Vienna and his friends. To Schwind he wrote:

Dear Schwind:

"At last, a letter from Schubert," you will say, after three months! — True, it is a pretty long time, but as my life here is as uneventful as possible, I have little material for writing to you or the others. And if I were not only too anxious to know how you and the other friends are faring, especially how things are with Schober and Kupelwieser, perhaps—forgive me—I should not have written even now. How does Schober's enterprise prosper? Is Kupelwieser in Vienna or still in Rome? Are the literary meetings still held or have they gone quite to pieces, as I assume? Now, what are you working at??? . . . I am still well, thank goodness, and should be quite comfortable here, if only I had you, Schober and Kupelwieser with me, but as it is I often long damnably for Vienna, in spite of the certain attractive star. By the end of September I hope to see you again. . . . How is Leidesdorf? . . . Above all I lay it on your conscience to scold Leidesdorf *scandaleusement*, for he has neither answered my letter nor sent me what I asked for. What the devil does he mean by it? . . . [DQ].

To Schober, that spirit who had bewitched the whole circle, Schubert wrote in September:

Dear Schober:

I hear you are not happy and have to sleep off the frenzies of your despair. So Schwind writes to me. Although this makes me extraordinarily sad, it does not surprise me in the least, since such is the lot of almost every sensible person in this miserable world. And what ever should we do with happiness, misery being the only stimulant left to us? If only we were together, you, Schwind, Kuppel [Kupelwieser] and I, my misfortune would seem to be but a light matter; but here we are, separated, each in a different corner, and that is what makes my wretchedness. I want to exclaim with Goethe: "Who only will bring me back an hour of that sweet time!" That time when we sat so snugly together and each disclosed the children of his art to the others with motherly shyness, not without dread expecting the judgment to be pronounced by affection and truth; that time when one inspired the other and thus united striving after the highest beauty enlivened us all. Now I sit here alone in the depth of the Hungarian country, whither I unfortunately let myself be enticed a second time, without having a single person with whom I could speak a sensible word. I have written hardly any songs since the time you went away, but tried my hand at several instrumental things. What is to happen to my operas Heaven knows! Notwithstanding that I have now been in good health for five months, my cheerfulness is frequently damped by your absence and Kuppel's, and I often live through days of great misery; in one of those clouded hours, when I particularly keenly felt the idle and insignificant life that characterizes our time, the following verses escaped me which I communicate to you only because I know that you blame even my weaknesses with affection and indulgence: . . .

Then follows a poem of which I quote only the second strophe, freely translated:

> Too strong the pain which at my being gnaws
> And leaves me but a vestige of my strength.
> The jejune times have robbed me of my power
> Which marks the end of great accomplishments.

One hears the voice of desolation, as unfair as his exclamation of having "not a single person with whom I could speak a sensible word." The reason for his depression, in addition to fear and his own kind of "homesickness," appeared in the same letter:

With Leidesdorf things have gone badly so far: he cannot pay, nor does a single soul buy anything, either my things or any others, except wretched fashionable stuff [DQ].

Not altogether true, of course.

Schubert returned to Vienna in the middle of October 1827, being taken there by Baron Karl Schönstein, who had been a guest at Zseliz. Schönstein had a good voice and had taken part in a private performance of a song, "Gebet" ("Prayer"), Schubert had composed for Caroline; it was a vocal quartet; the Esterházys gathered round, Schubert at the piano—and Caroline loved it.* On the return journey in Schönstein's carriage, Schubert managed to break the back window of the coach, and they all nearly froze to death. But Schönstein endured it with a laugh, "for there never was a journey without some small fatality," as he duly reported to his friend Count Esterházy.

Back in Vienna, Schubert temporarily put up at his father's school-house. "Euphoric" is not too strong a word to describe his new mood: the city, his friends, the music-making, he had them all again. "He is rejuvenated," wrote Schwind to Schober. Schwind had returned from Linz, bringing with him two attractive brothers, Fritz and Franz Hartmann, who were to become close friends of Schubert. Castelli, Grillparzer, the Fröhlich sisters, Vogl, Bauernfeld, they were all there and overjoyed to see Schubert. Even the unreliable Leidesdorf had bestirred himself and published a few things. Spaun got several weeks' holiday, came to Vienna, and spent much time with Schubert. Only the most important friend, Schober, was absent. Schubert was still feeling well, perhaps helped by his sojourn in Zseliz.

At the end of the year, Thaddeus Weigl, a good publisher, brought out a collection of "40 New Waltzes" by various composers, Beethoven among them. Schubert offered him the piece he had composed as a piano duet in Zseliz, now rearranged as a solo. Weigl's collection, handsomely bound, was typical of the offering one could buy as a Christmas gift if one had the money: it cost three florins, V.C., quite expensive. Weigl and Schubert having begun a connection led to Weigl's publishing more important works.

Schubert spent Christmastime of 1824 with Schwind's family, which included his three sisters and his brother. Schwind had decorated his

---

*In 1838 Schönstein moved Liszt to tears singing the *Die Schöne Müllerin* cycle.

lodgings with a large Christmas tree, festooned with his own little draw-ings, with quotations from Schubert's songs, and with a copy of Bauern-feld's new translation of *Two Gentlemen of Verona*. Two years later Schubert was to use this translation for the song "An Sylvia" ("Who is Sylvia?"). On Christmas Eve Schwind gave a party. Schubert and Bauern-feld were there. Vienna was having a severe winter, the kind when "birds sit brooding in the snow." The snow was deep. But—"Merriest conviv-iality," Bauernfeld noted in his diary.

11

A Good Year and a Bad Year

NO PHYSICIAN COULD HAVE EXPLAINED AND NO SOOTHSAYER COULD have predicted it, but Schubert's health, which had already shown signs of improvement at the end of the previous year, continued to gain. The infection, silent and unobservable, went underground and left him feeling refreshed and strong. His despair lightened, his mood became hopeful, the final outcome of his condition, of which he could not help being aware, seemed to recede to a far-off day. It was an about-face for the man who wrote Kupelwieser in March 1824 "in sheer despair" that his "most brilliant hopes have perished." Now there was no further thought given to suicide, and Schwind was right when he wrote to Schober (February 14, 1825), "Schubert is well and busy again after a certain stagnation." There were reasons for such improvement other than his health: A remarkable number of his works were published in rapid succession. Performances of his songs and chamber music increased. He made several stimulating new friends. He undertook a long excursion with Vogl in the summer of 1825, of which more later. These four reasons were less important than the change in himself: a new seriousness filled his mind; the drive toward the creation of a "grand symphony" fascinated him, as he strove to free himself from the embrace of Beethoven. Even aside from music his horizon expanded; he learned to *see* as well as hear. By and large it may be said that the year 1825 was the most forward-looking and the most educational in Schubert's life.

The change did not come about at once. At the beginning of 1825 he took lodgings alone in the so-called Früwirth House, a charming place owned by one Johann Frühwirth. It was near the Karlskirche, and from his window Schubert could see the majestic edifice as well as the green fields where the city merged into the suburbs. Best of all, his room was quite near the Moonshine House, where the Schwind family lived. Young Schwind, of a dreamy, sensitive, easily wounded disposition, adored Schubert and was constantly at his beck and call. With Schwind Schubert was still attending an occasional *Schubertiad*—and unpredictably staying away from some at which he was expected—but he was now preferring to relax with one or two friends in one of the cafés, the more intimate, offering little tables in little corners, the better. One of his favorites was the Café Neuner, in what is now the beautiful little Plankengasse, leading off the Neuer Markt, where stands the masterpiece by the sculptor Raphael Donner, a fountain representing the rivers of Austria. (Maria Theresa objected to it because the figures were nude.) Vogl lived above the café, which was later called the Silver Café because its cutlery and its coat hangers were silvered. It became for a time Vienna's literary coffeehouse and featured on the second floor a room where ladies were admitted and smoking was forbidden.

Schober still exerted so powerful an influence over the friends that he divided the circle, enfeebled by Schubert's waning interest, into two magnetic fields. The overt cause of the split was Franz Bruchmann's objection to his sister Justina's secret engagement to Schober. That had become known, and the whole circle took sides. Electricity was in the air, positive and negative: Schubert and Schwind on Schober's side, Bruchmann and his family on the other. He wasn't going to let his sister marry an actor and a man of such unstable character, however brilliant. The gossip bubbled, jealousies emerged. One feels the dissension in a letter which young Johanna Lutz, the bride of Leopold Kupelwieser, wrote him:

Vienna, 7th March, 1825

I really am very curious to know what Franz [von Bruchmann] will write to you about Schober.

It pained me much, because of you, that the whole circle was so delighted. Alas! how grievous is all parting!

Yet it has its advantages. For when you and Schober had left, the whole circle shaped itself differently, if no better, and had to be dissolved altogether. However, the better ones always find each other again, and then not much is lost.

I can only say what I have heard from the Bruchmanns and from Schwind, the two opposing parties, who no doubt both exaggerated a great deal, and draw my conclusions from that.

Rieder [Wilhelm August, historical painter], Dietrich [Anton, sculptor], Schubert and Schwind are as close together, or as far apart, as before—but their attitude toward the Bruchmanns is very different.

Rieder and Bruchmann are not hostile towards each other, but they do not meet. Schubert and Schwind are in open feud with Bruchmann. They both seem to me like children, and indeed they give vent to their hatred childishly. They do not meet any more at all, cut each other dead, and behave like great enemies. It is true, Justina has been weak and vacillating, and Franz [Bruchmann] deliberately acted badly towards Schober, but he was quite aware of all the facts. And of course Schober's bad side was easier to see than the good. But after all it is none of it their business.

If they did not care for him, that is their affair. But their conduct is infantile.

Yet their affection for Schober is nice.

Schubert is now very busy and well-behaved, which pleases me very much.

The Bruchmanns now have a very small circle. . . .

O Leopold, if once you are back here, everything else will adjust itself, and I rejoice infinitely that everything will take new shape about us and our love always remains the same [DQ].

(Kupelwieser was temporarily in Naples, having left Rome. Johanna evidently couldn't wait to tell him what was happening and wrote him to Naples.)

One disagreement begetting another, it was not long before the wind veered and Schwind, not Bruchmann, was the one who felt hurt. Johanna was right: the circle "shaped itself differently." However, Schubert took but little part in these *Kaffeehaus* tempests, being more interested in his new acquaintances, of whom the most beguiling was a young, beautiful, and extraordinarily talented actress at the Burgtheater, Sophie Müller (no relation of the poet). There she played juvenile roles, and the Viennese public adored her. She herself sang the songs interpolated in her roles, and she sang them exquisitely. She lived with her father in the village of Hietzing, a good hour's drive from the city's center, but that did not prevent Schubert and Vogl and one or two other friends from coming and seeing and hearing her. Vogl and Sophie would alternate singing Schubert songs, sometimes for hours—"five to seven-thirty" or "music till half-past nine," she would note in her diary—with Schubert at the piano. How gracious a scene: the huge man with the failing voice and the artistry gained in a lifetime, the blooming and enthusiastic young girl, the little man bent over the keyboard, the three united! Sophie mentioned the songs she loved especially, such as "The Trout," "Fragment from Aeschylus," "Group from Tartarus," etc. In her diary of March 2, 1825, she writes: "After lunch Schubert came; I sang with him until nearly six o'clock, then drove to the theater." Schubert came again the very next day—how greatly he must have been attracted to her to endure the ride to Hietzing in March weather on two successive days—and he brought her a new song, "Die junge Nonne" ("The Young Nun"). The thunder and lightning which course through the wild night are set against the tolling of the convent bell and contrasted with the thoughts of the girl, who has experienced life's storms and now has found peace in her faith. "Halleluja," she whispers at the end. Two worlds are enclosed in this drama, a "tempest of the soul," one of Schubert's immortal creations. A twenty-two-year-old girl sang the song for the first time. Alas, she died in 1830, only twenty-seven years old.

In May Schubert felt well enough to get away from his doctors and to follow Vogl, who had preceded him to Steyr by a week. From there Schubert made a brief visit to his friends the Ottenwalts in Linz—he liked Anton for his seriousness and wide learning, and he liked Anton's wife, Marie, nee Spaun, for her humor—and then, all by himself, went to see the Abbey of St. Florian with its joyous altar painted by Altdorfer and its fine organ. Early in June Vogl rejoined him, and the two went to Gmunden, at the invitation of Ferdinand Traweger, a well-to-do music-loving merchant who knew many of Schubert's songs by heart. Traweger and his wife, Elisabeth, had two daughters and a son five years old. Schubert loved little Eduard, taught him to sing "Guten Morgen, schöne Müllerin," and gave him a silver toothpick as a reward when the boy didn't cry as leeches were applied to bleed him, which was the popular way of treating a fever. (Somehow or other that toothpick was preserved when so many memorabilia were lost.) Eduard survived the leech treatment in good shape and indeed lived on until 1909 and was therefore the last surviving person to have known Schubert.

Gmunden was even then a popular resort, lying where the River Traun flows into Lake Traun, and Traweger's house stood near where the boats crossing the lake landed. The lake itself is one of the deep blue flecks in the patchwork quilt around Salzburg known as the Salzkammergut. With its green dewy fields, the yellow reddish-brown of old houses, and the copper-colored steeples of churches serving as exclamation marks, this landscape is one of the world's most beautiful. It is lyrical rather than dramatic, friendly rather than spectacular, the mountains which encircle it being of reachable heights. However, to Schubert, who now looked at Nature for the first time—looked receptively—the mountains seemed overwhelming. In a letter to his father and stepmother he described his journey and incidentally teased his brother Ferdinand, who was something of a hypochondriac:

July 25, 1825

... he has doubtless been ill 77 times again, and has thought 9 times that he was going to die, as though dying were the worst that can happen to a man! If only he could once see these heavenly mountains and lakes, the sight of which threatens to crush or engulf us, he would not be so attached to puny human life nor regard it as otherwise than good fortune to be confided to earth's indescribable power of creating new life.

Schubert responded to the romantic landscape, his imagination combining images of love with images of nature, as in Walter Scott's poetry:

To the Evening Star

Come to the luxuriant skies
While the landscape's odours rise,
When far-off lowing herds are heard,
And songs when toil is done,
From cottages whose smoke unstirred
Curls yellow in the sun.

Star of love's soft interviews,
Parted lovers on thee muse.

Schubert took the texts of his next songs from Scott's verse epic, *Lady of the Lake*. These songs were either composed or finished near the banks of Lake Traun. The laments of the Earl of Douglas and "Normans Gesang" were obviously written for Vogl's voice. "Bootgesang" ("Boatsong") and the plaint for Duncan, "Caronach," are part songs. The best song of the cycle (in my opinion) is the strong "Lied des gefangenen Jägers" ("Song of the Imprisoned Hunter"). Of Ellen's three songs, the second ("Hunter, Rest!") is almost excessively romantic, but it is of course the third song, Ellen's prayer, the "Ave Maria," which is the most famous. Beautiful and honest though it originally was, that song has become embarrassing in its nougat arrangements, used endlessly for commercial Christmas programs.

That a man like Anton Ottenwalt appreciated the Walter Scott songs at once appears in a letter he wrote to Josef Spaun at the end of July. A remarkably perceptive letter it is:

Of Schubert—I might almost say of our Schubert—there is much I should like to tell you. No doubt, though, his letter will tell you the best of it. Never, perhaps, except in the case of playing the fraternal host, have I yet experienced the joys of hospitality as I did during the days he spent with me, was our guest at lunch, and passed the evening with us at the "Castle". The fact is that he stayed only a few days at S. [Steyregg] (the count was at Ischl), then came to us again for a few days, until Vogl appeared one morning and, after both had eaten with us, took his friend with him to Steyregg once more; in the end both returned on Sunday evening, again were our guests at midday on Monday (25th), together with Stadler and Therese Haas, who appeared by accident, and, departing after the meal, left us with the hope of possibly seeing them once more on their return from Gastein. We heard Vogl three times, and Schubert himself condescended to sing something after breakfast among ourselves, and also played his marches, two- and four-handed variations and an overture on the pianoforte, compositions of such significance that one cannot trust oneself to discuss them. And if I cannot do so worthily with his latest songs on W. Scott, I cannot keep silent about them either. There are five in particular: 1. "Ave Maria," Ellen's evening song and prayer for her father in the wilderness, where they live in hiding. 2. "Soldier, rest," a captivating slumber song of the kind Armida might sing for Rinaldo to her magic harp. 3. "Huntsman, rest," another slumber song, more simple and touching, I feel, in the accompaniment, the tune of horns, I should say, like the echoes of a hunting song in a fair dream. 4. "Lay of the Imprisoned Huntsman": 'My idle greyhound loathes his food. My horse is weary of his stall. And I am sick of captive thrall.' . . . Accompaniment— ah, how shall I describe those angrily thobbing, briefly cut-off chords? I am almost ashamed again of having taken it into my head to write about it. And what of the last, "Norman's Song"? The warrior with his sacrificial torch, the summons at arms, sings as he fares across the country. Hurrying without respite, he thinks of his errand, of the bride he has left at the altar, of the morrow's combat, of victory, of reunion. The tune and the accompaniment you will have to imagine. Schubert himself regards this as the best of the Scott songs. Vogl himself interprets it heavily (a syllable, often a word, to each note), but splendidly. The most generally appealing, by the loveliness of its melody and the rocking horn music, is "Huntsman, rest." My dear fellow, how we wished each time that you could hear it! If only we could send those tunes into your dreams, as we ourselves hear them around us deep into the night! . . .

Schubert himself was proud of these songs, as he wrote his parents on July 25, from Steyr:

My new songs from Walter Scott's "Lady of the Lake" especially had much success. They also wondered greatly at my piety, which I expressed in a hymn to the Holy Virgin and which, it appears, grips every soul and turns it to devotion. I think this is due to the fact that I have never forced devotion in myself and never compose hymns or prayers of that kind unless it overcomes me unawares; but then it is usually the right and true devotion.

Indeed, they, the Trawegers, must have "wondered greatly," for they knew Schubert to be anything but pious. In the same letter he related that he had gone back to Linz from Gmunden to find a welcome with Spaun's family—Josef was away in Lemberg, the Galician outpost of the Empire—and from Linz he went to the castle of the Weissenwolffs. Countess Sophie Weissenwolff was one of his admirers. Now she heard his Walter Scott songs and they

made such an excessively good impression on her that she even let it be guessed that the dedication of them would be anything but disagreeable to her. But I intend to use a very different procedure with the publication of these songs from the usual one, which yields so very little, since they bear the celebrated name of Scott at their head and may in that way arouse greater curiosity, and might also make me better known in England by the addition of the English words [DQ].

The songs *were* dedicated to the Countess.

Around this time Schubert received some curious letters from the gentle Schwind. Only one letter is extant, and even that one is not outspoken but only lets one guess as to what might have been the cause of the injury which prompted Schwind to write his friend in such a sorrowing vein:

[Vienna] 2nd July, 1825.

My dear Schubert,

I almost think my last letter must have contained something that was disagreeable to you. Let me be frank and confess to you what it is that still rankles. You will no doubt remember that you did not come to Hönig's last time. I should be quite idiotic if I took offense, nay if I even allowed it to annoy me, if you do as you please and take no notice of what I happen to want. Still, had you thought of how much affection was awaiting you, you would have come. Little as I shall allow myself to be deterred from meaning to you and doing for you what had so far always been acceptable to you, I am almost afraid of getting as much pleasure from you, seeing how ill I have succeeded all these years in overcoming your mistrust and your fear lest you should not be loved and understood. That may be the reason for some malicious pranks which I was unable to refrain from, much as they hurt me myself. It is no doubt altogether the sort of thing which is responsible for that accursed spirit of mockery. Why should I not say it? Ever since I knew you and Schober I have been accustomed to find myself understood in all things. Then others come, mocking and spying out associations and thoughts of which they have caught some glimpse or other; we let them carry on at first, then take part in it ourselves, and, man not being made of diamond, we lose irreplaceable things for the despicable price of merely tolerable intercourse. If that is too bitter, I was unhappily often too complaisant. I beg you to give me your answer to this, as rude and candid as I am myself, for anything is better than these torturing thoughts, of which I cannot rid myself . . . [DQ].

The most likely explanation is that Schubert had made some slighting remark about Anna Hönig—"Netti" or "Nettl"—daughter of the barrister Dr. Franz Hönig. She was called "sweet Anne Page" by the friends and was a devout Catholic. Schwind was very much in love with her, became engaged to her, but broke the engagement in 1829. Schwind said, "I can stand a good deal in the matter of Catholicism as a rule, but too much is too much." In his lost reply to Schwind Schubert mentioned an incident at the Hönigs' and in turn Schwind was sure that "Netti" was innocent:

1st August 1825

Dearest Schubert,

I must have written a fair packet of nonsense, as I gather from that farrago of "diamond and glimpse," in which I cannot find any connection at all. But be that as it may, I did hear something that could not have come to me in my wildest dreams—that somebody insulted you at Hönig's. I do not believe it of Netti, and neither do you, I hope, and it would surprise me very much in the others. If only you had told me at once, the whole thing would have been different, or I should not for a moment have expected you to go there; also, you will believe that I myself should no longer have any desire for company of this sort. In the meantime I shall, in the deuce's name, turn the house upside down to see if there is anything resembling your accusation or a definite withdrawal of it. But I can assure you by all the saints that I cannot imagine anything of the kind.

I asked Netti in a roundabout way, but as explicitly as possible, and the very thought was so far from her that I warrant you there was nothing queer, much less equivocal in her behavior. I hope you will not think of the matter any more on your return . . . [DQ].

Schwind confirmed this in a later letter:

Netti Hönig, the only one whom you doubt, shows her endless devotion to you and your cause so frequently and naturally that, if I deserve some credence, I can answer for it that you could not easily live and sing before any one who thinks more highly of you or is capable of feeling more sincere sympathy or deeper pleasure.

The incident would be unimportant were it not for the fact that it shows a certain touchiness in Schubert's character, a certain resentment when he thought that the respect due him was not rendered to him. Notwithstanding all his modesty.

To take up again the chronicle of the 1825 summer, Schubert and Vogl set out for Gastein, traveling by way of Salzburg. As they neared the famous bath, famous since Roman times for its healing waters, the scenery changed from pleasant to awesome, the snowcapped mountains all around it supplying a wild brook which spat and fumed and fell through the center of the village. Vogl went there to seek relief from his gout. But Schubert did not take the waters. There and in Gmunden he was supposed to have composed a symphony which was later called the *Gmunden-Gastein* Symphony. Not a bar of it has been found, and the evidence that it ever existed is weak, based on casual fragments, such as Ottenwalt's letter to Spaun of July 19, 1825—"By the way, he had worked at a symphony at Gmunden"—or Schwind's writing to Schubert on August 14, 1825, "About your symphony we may be quite hopeful." After Schubert's death, Spaun and Bauernfeld spoke of a "Gastein symphony"; Ferdinand didn't, though he knew more of Schubert's unpublished manuscripts than the friends. Maurice Brown, who made a study of the puzzle, concluded that, while Schubert may have made a sketch for such a symphony, he never completed it. The symphony was never lost; Schubert never composed it.*

He did write a detailed description of his journey for his brother Ferdinand. Schubert was usually *schreibfaul,* a lazy correspondent, but he loved Ferdinand enough to want to share his experiences with him. The letter, long though it is, is worth quoting, since it shows not only that Schubert observed alertly but that he could write well when he wanted to:

Gmunden, 12th September 1825.

Dear Brother,

According to your challenge I should certainly like to give you a detailed description of our journey to Salzburg and Gastein, but you know how little gifted I am for narratives and descriptions; yet as I should in any case have to tell you on my return to Vienna, I prefer after all to sketch in writing now, rather than verbally later, a feeble picture of all those extraordinary beauties, since I may hope to do the former better than the latter, all the same.

We left Steyr, then, about the middle of August and went by way of Kremsmünster, which indeed I had often seen before, but can never bear to miss on account of its beautiful situation. For there is a view over a very lovely valley, interrupted by a few small and gentle hills, to the right of which rises a not inconsiderable mountain; on its summit the extensive monastery offers the most magnificent view even from the high road, which leads across a brook opposite, a view enhanced especially by the "mathematical" tower. Here, where we have been known for some time, particularly Herr von Vogl, who studied here, we were very kindly received; we did not stay, however, but continued our journey, which does not call for special mention, as far as Vöcklabruck, where we arrived in the evening: a sorry hole. The next morning we went by way of Strasswalchen and Frankenmarkt to Neumarkt, where we lunched. These places, which lie already in the county

*However, a letter from Schubert to the Austrian Music Society (also known as the Philharmonic Society, located in Vienna and not to be confused with the Graz Society) written in October 1826 stated that he dedicated to them "this, my Symphony." What symphony could this have been? He composed none around this time and it is not probable that he would have sent any of his youthful symphonies, nor the one in E major or the one in B minor (the *Unfinished*), both incomplete. No symphony which could be attributed to 1826 or thereabouts turned up in the Society's files. The most likely explanation is that he intended to compose a new symphony but did not carry out his intentions. As a gesture of good will the Society awarded Schubert 100 florins A.C.—"not as a fee, but as a token of the Society's sense of obligation towards you." Nothing was said of a symphony in the Society's letter of October 12, 1826, or in subsequent communications.

of Salzburg, are distinguished by the peculiar architecture of the houses. Nearly everything is of wood. Wooden kitchen utensils stand on wooden trestles fixed on the outside of the houses, round which run wooden galleries. Also, there are shot-up targets hanging on the houses everywhere, kept as trophies of victories won long ages ago; for they often bear the dates of 1600 or 1500. Bavarian money begins to be used here, too. From Neumarkt, which is the last postal stage before Salzburg, summits of mountains in the Salzburg valley may already be seen, just then covered with snow. About an hour out of Neumarkt the country begins to become amazingly beautiful. The Waller Lake, which spreads its bright, blue-green water to the right of the road, animates this delightful landscape most gloriously. The altitude is very high, and thenceforward it drops continually towards Salzburg. The mountains rise higher and higher, and especially the legendary Untersberg rises from amid the others as by magic. The villages show traces of former affluence. At the meanest farmhouses everywhere one finds window-frames and door-posts of marble, and even sometimes stairs of red marble. The sun darkens and heavy clouds run across the black mountains like nebulous spirits; but they do not touch the Untersberg's brow, they creep past it as though terrified of its dreadful interior. The wide valley, looking as if speckled with isolated castles, churches and farmsteads, grows ever more visible to the enchanted eye. Towers and palaces gradually show themselves; at last one drives past the Kapuzinerberg, whose immense rocky wall rises sheer up hard by the road and frowns down fearfully upon the traveller. The Untersberg and its retinue grow gigantic, their size almost crushing us. And now we enter the town itself through some splendid avenues. Fortifications built all of rough-hewn stone surround this famous seat of the former electors. The city gates proclaim by their inscriptions the vanished powers of clericalism. Nothing but houses of four and five stories fill the rather wide steets, and past the curiously decorated house of Theophrastus Paracelsus [famous physician of the sixteenth century], we cross the bridge over the Salzach, which rushes past turbidly, darkly and mightily. The city itself made a rather gloomy impression on me, because dull weather darkened the ancient buildings still more and, moreover, the fortress, situated on the highest summit of the Mönchsberg, sends its ghostly message into every street in the town. As unfortunately it began to rain immediately after our arrival, which is very often the case here, we were able to see very little apart from the many palaces and glorious churches we caught sight of as we drove by. Through Herr Pauernfeind, a merchant well known to Herr von Vogl, we were introduced to Count von Platz, president of the assizes, by whose family we were most kindly received, our names being already known to them. Vogl sang some of my songs, whereupon we were invited for the following evening and requested to produce our odds and ends before a select circle;

and indeed they touched them all very much, special preference being given to the "Ave Maria" already mentioned in my first letter. The manner in which Vogl sings and the way I accompany, as though we were one at such a moment, is something quite new and unheard-of for these people. Having climbed the Mönchsberg the following morning, from which a large part of the city may be surveyed, I could not help being amazed at the number of wonderful buildings, palaces and churches. Yet the inhabitants here are few: many buildings are empty and some are occupied by only one family, or at most two or three. In the squares, of which there are many, grass grows between the pavingstones, so little are they frequented. The cathedral is a heavenly building, after the pattern of St. Peter's Church in Rome, but of course on a smaller scale. The length of the church is in the form of a cross, surrounded by four enormous courtyards, each of which forms a large square. At the entrance stand the Apostles carved in stone, gigantic size. The interior of the church is supported by many marble columns, adorned with portraits of the electors and in truth perfectly beautiful in every detail. The light, falling through the dome, penetrates into every corner. This extraordinary brightness has a divine effect and might be recommended to all churches. In the four squares surrounding the church are large fountains decorated with the most superb and daring figures. From here we went to the monastery of St. Peter, where Michael Haydn [Josef's brother] resided. That church too is most wondrously fine. Here is also to be found, as you know, M. Haydn's monument. It is rather pretty, though not well placed, but put into a remote corner. Also, the slips of paper [actually they were made of stone] littered about look rather childish. His head is kept in the urn. It hovers round me, I thought to myself, thy tranquil, clear spirit, thou good Haydn, and if I cannot myself be so tranquil and clear, there is no one in the world, surely, who reveres thee so deeply as I. (A heavy tear fell from my eye, and we moved on.—) We lunched at Herr Pauernfeind's, and in the afternoon, when the weather allowed us to go out, we climbed the Nonnberg, which is not high, but affords the finest of views, for one overlooks the inner Salzburg valley from there. To describe [to] you the loveliness of that valley is almost impossible. Think of a garden several miles in extent with countless castles and estates in it peeping through the trees; think of a river winding through it in manifold twists and turns; think of meadows and fields like so many carpets of the finest colours, then of the many roads tied round them like ribbons; and lastly avenues of enormous trees to walk in for hours, all enclosed by ranges of the highest mountains as far as the eye can reach, as though they were the guardians of this glorious valley; think of all this, and you will have a faint conception of its inexpressible beauty. The rest of Salzburg's curiosities, which I shall see only on my return journey, I shall leave until then, for I wish my description to be chronological.

Isn't it curious that in describing Salzburg he never mentioned Mozart?
He continued his vivid observations nine days later:

You will see from the date given that between those lines and these several
days have gone by, and we have unfortunately moved from Gmunden to
Steyr. To continue, then, the account of the journey (which I have by now
come to regret, as it goes on too long for me), I follow the following-up as
follows: the following morning, that is to say, was the finest day in the world
and of the world. The Untersberg, or rather the uppermost one, shone and
glittered gloriously, with its squadron and the common detachment of the
other mountains, in or rather next to the sun. We drove through the valley
described above as if through Elysium, except that it has the advantage of
that paradise that we sat in a delightful coach, a convenience denied to Adam
and Eve. Instead of wild beasts we encountered many most charming girls. . . .
It is all wrong, my cracking such miserable jokes in such a beautiful neigh-
bourhood, but I simply cannot be serious to-day. So we pushed comfortably
on, lost in delight at the fine day and the still finer country, in which nothing
arrested our attention except a pretty building, called Month's Castle, which
an elector caused to be built within a month for his fair lady. Everybody
knows this here, but no one is shocked at it. What enchanting tolerance!
This little building too adds to the valley's charms. A few hours later we
reached the curious but extremely dirty and horrid town of Hallein. The
inhabitants all look like ghosts, pale, hollow-eyed and lean enough to catch
fire. The appalling contrast of the sight of such a rat-hole, &c., in this valley
made the most dismal impression on me. It was as though one had fallen
from heaven into a dung-heap or were listening after Mozart's music to a
piece by the immortal A. There was no inducing Vogl to view the Salzberg
with its salt mines, for his great soul, spurred on by gout, urged him on to
Gastein, like a wanderer in a dark night who yearns for a ray of light. So
we drove on through Golling, where the first high, impassable mountains
began to show themselves, whose menacing gorges are traversed by the Lueg
pass. Having crawled slowly up a great mountain, with terrible rockeries in
front of our noses as well as on either side, so that one would think the
world had been nailed up with boards here, suddenly, at the highest point
of the mountain, you look down into a fearful abyss, which at the first
moment threatens fairly to shake your heart. Having recovered somewhat
from the first fright, you look at these incredibly high rocky walls, which
seem to close up at some distance like a blind alley, and you wonder in vain
where an outlet may be. Amid this terrifying nature man has sought to
commemorate his even more dreadful bestiality. For it was here that the
Bavarians on one side and the Tyrolese on the other of the Salzach, which

here makes its tumultuous way far, far below, indulged in that frightful massacre at which the Tyrolese, concealed in the rocky heights, fired down with hellish shouts of triumph on the Bavarians, who endeavoured to gain the pass but were hurled wounded into the depths without ever being able to see whence the shots came. This most infamous act, which went on for several days and weeks, was marked by a chapel on the Bavarian side and a rough cross in the rock on the Tyrolese, partly to commemorate and partly to expiate it by such sacred symbols. Thou glorious Christ, to how many shameful actions must Thou lend Thy image! Thyself the most awful monument to mankind's degradation, Thy image is set up by them as if they said "Behold! we have trampled with impious feet upon Almighty God's most perfect creation; why should it cost us pains to destroy with a light heart the remaining vermin, called Man?"—But let us turn our eyes from such disheartening views and let us rather see to it that we escape from this hole. After a longish descent, during which the two rocky walls came ever closer and the road, together with the river, becomes narrowed to 2 fathom, the road turns here, where you least expect it, below an overhanging rock where the constrained Salzach rages furiously, to the traveller's agreeable surprise. For now your path goes on wider and level, although still enclosed by sky-high mountains. At noon we arrived at Werfen, a market town with an important fortress built by the Salzburg electors and now being improved by the emperor. On our return we climbed it: it is d———d high, but affords a splendid view of the valley, bounded on one side by the immense Werfen mountains, which can be seen from as far as Gastein. Heavens, and the devil and all, the description of a journey is something frightful, and I can no more. As I shall be in Vienna about the early days of October, I shall hand you this screed myself and tell you the rest verbally [DQ].

One need not, indeed one should not, seek too close a connection between the artist's product and his life's experiences, yet it is evident that Schubert's sojourn in Austria's countryside, his contemplation of fields, flowers, and mountains, evoked in him a religious feeling, a pantheistic wonderment, a sense of world-design to which he gave immortal expression in such a song as "Die Allmacht" ("Omnipotence," words by J. L. Pyrker, a priest who became Archbishop of Venice). "Great is Jehovah, the heavens and the earth proclaim his might; you hear it in the fierce tempest, in the wild call of the mountain stream, in the murmur of the forest trees . . . you see it in the glow of flowers, the gold of wheat, the play of the stars." Similarly, such fine songs as "Im Abendrot" ("Sunset") and "Heimweh" ("Longing for Home") show how vividly he connected landscape with the infinite.

Franz Lachner, Schubert, and Eduard Bauernfeld in Grinzing, drinking new wine.

Schubert the year before he died. Oil painting by Mähler.

The final stop of his long summer journey took him to Linz, once more to visit the Spauns. Early in October he and Josef Gahy, a friend both of Schubert's and the Spauns' (Schubert used to play piano duets with him), hired a private one-horse carriage to take them to Vienna. Even if they shared that expense, which is probable, the journey, which took three days, must have cost each a pretty florin. Evidently Schubert had money at the moment.

Back he was in Vienna, and so were most of his friends, though Vogl had gone to Italy and Spaun was still on duty in Lemberg. Schwind, Bauernfeld, Sophie Müller, Grillparzer were there, Kupelwieser had returned from Rome, Mayrhofer put in an appearance, and, best of all, Schober had come back. The friendship was resumed with all warmth, and Schubert moved in with Schober. Thus ended the year in which a composer was born who turned out to be more "Viennese" than his compatriot: that was Johann Strauss, Jr.

2.

If we try to trace Schubert's creative purpose, which developed in and followed after the year of breathing good air, if we want to understand what he had to convey and what he felt after he came down from the mountains, we should assume a summary rather than a detailed view. He himself said that he wanted to turn from a composer of songs to a composer of instrumental and symphonic music, using the piano sonata and the string quartet as stepping stones—which is not to say that he renounced his former love, for he varied his new efforts with some of his most wonderful songs. Though he never expressed it in words, he came to terms with death, death as a singer of a prize song or as a speaker of a comforting homily, as is evident in the variations of the *Death and the Maiden* Quartet—which is not to say that he shortchanged light and lilting music. Obviously he was too great a genius to pluck only one string.

He was calmer than he had been. His was not the calm of pallid despair—he was too warm-blooded, too active, too positive a personality for that—nor did he allow himself to wallow in resignation, with hands folded, pen idle, eyes half-closed. Death was not "the worst that can happen to you," and in the meantime you hoped and you lived. He was not well enough to come to the New Year's Eve celebration of 1826, for which Bauernfeld had written a skit, a harlequinade good-naturedly satirizing the friends; he was really sorry to miss that. But he soon recovered, and at carnival time he was his indefatigable self, playing dance music at Schober's house for a "Sausage Ball" (*Würstelball*). At those balls, the girls served the men quantities of little sausages, called "Vienna sausages" in Frankfurt and "Frankfurters" in Vienna, and still almost as popular there as they are in the United States.

Up and down went his health, late evenings at dances followed by hours of gloom, changed then to hours of work in an aura of well-being. On a Sunday in February Schubert left Schober's house to go with Bauernfeld to two concerts offering enough music to fatigue the most ardent music-lover. At noon they heard the Philharmonic Society play Beethoven's Second Symphony and *Egmont* Overture, as well as the "Hallelujah" Chorus. From 4:30 to 6:30 they listened to Schuppanzigh's group play a quartet by Haydn, one by Beethoven, Mozart's C-Minor Quintet, and a piano sextet by Georges Onslow. Dinner between the concerts, supper afterward.

He worked all morning, composing and correcting, and spent evenings with Schober, Schwind, Bauernfeld, and now with the young Hartmann brothers, Franz and Fritz, law students, whose cheerful disposition and smiling praise attracted him. The Hartmanns liked to go to Bogner's Café, located in the Singerstrasse, and this quickly became the favorite meeting place of the friends. Quite often Schubert would still drive to Hietzing, and Sophie Müller would give him dinner; the girl must have loved him as a man as she valued him as a musician. "Vogl, the singer, marries Rosa," Sophie noted in her diary on June 26, 1826. Nothing more. To her, twenty-three years old, the marriage of the fifty-eight-year-old Vogl seemed a winter wedding. "Rosa" was Kunigunde Rosa, daughter of the first custodian of the Belvedere Gallery. As soon as Vogl returned from a trip to his home in Steyr with his new wife, he called on Sophie. Schubert was there. If he had only met that enchanting girl earlier!

Early in the year Schubert's father had been awarded the freedom of the city of Vienna. That honor,* not unusual but all the same a considerable one, had come about at the instigation of the community of Rossau and was to mark his school service of forty-five years. To be sure, the award cost him twenty-four florins in additional tax. Was the son present at the ceremony? No document is extant, nor any comment from the friends. Later in the year Franz Sr. sold the paternal house (No. 10

---

*Not to be confused with the proposed gold medal mentioned in an earlier chapter.

Himmelpfortgrund), realizing 6,600 florins A.C., of which Franz Jr.'s share amounted to 200 florins. That was not much, but wife, the other children, grandchildren, etc., had equally to be taken care of.

Like Mozart before him, Schubert tried for an official position, specifically that of Vice Musical Director of the Court Chapel. Salieri had been Chief Court Musical Director, in charge of appointments of musicians, judgments of new music, musical programs for official ceremonies, elections of opera managers, supervision of official music schools, etc., in a word, all matters pertaining to music in the Imperial-Royal city. When Salieri was pensioned off in 1824, his post went to Josef Eybler, a good church composer but now getting on in years—he was five years older than Beethoven—while the post of Vice Director had been left open. Schubert now applied for it, couching his application in the bow-to-the-ground wordage which was customary:

Your Majesty, Most Gracious Emperor,

With the profoundest veneration the undersigned ventures to present the most submissive petition for the most gracious bestowal of the vacant post of vice Musical Director to the Court Chapel, and bases this application upon the following grounds:

1. The same is a native of Vienna, son of a schoolmaster, and aged 29.
2. He enjoyed the most gracious privilege of being for 5 years a pupil of the I. and R. Seminary, as a boy chorister of the Court.
3. He received, according to Enclosure A. thorough instruction in composition from the former first Musical Director of this Court Chapel, Herr Anton Salieri, whereby he is rendered capable of filling any chapel-master's post.
4. By his vocal and instrumental compositions his name has become favourably known, not only in Vienna, but throughout Germany, and he also has in readiness
5. five Masses with accompaniments for larger and smaller orchestras, which have already been performed in various Viennese churches.
6. Finally, he has not the advantage of employment and hopes by means of an assured career to attain fully to his intended artistic goal.

To do complete justice to the most gracious assent to his supplication will be the most earnest endeavour of the

Most submissive servant
Franz Schubert
Vienna, 7th April, 1826.

On the bureaucratic principle that if at all possible one must never decide today what can be decided tomorrow, the question was discussed and rediscussed and names were brought forward by one official after another, who between them managed to waste almost a year's time, till in December Count Karl Harrach, who knew musical conditions in Vienna, sent a long memorandum to his superior, Prince Ferdinand Trauttmansdorff-Weinsberg, Imperial-Royal Minister, in which memorandum he listed eight candidates. Schubert was number three; Harrach did little more than mention Schubert's schooling, dismissing him with a cold paragraph:

> Franz Schubert bases his claim on the services rendered by him as I. & R. choir-boy, confirmed by a certificate from the deceased Court Chapel-Master Salieri that he had learned composition under him, and asserts that he has already written five Masses with larger or smaller orchestra, which have been produced in various churches.

Not a syllable about the songs, the quartets, or Schubert's other music, much of it well known by that time. Count Harrach recommended that Josef Weigl, composer of the then-popular opera *Die Schweizerfamilie* (a crisp piece not without merit), who functioned as well as the leading conductor at the Opera, be chosen. He based his choice on the fact that Weigl was already drawing a regular salary, so they could pay him just a little extra for being the Vice Court Director and save money. In January 1827 Weigl was duly appointed and, probably at the Emperor's wish, at full salary. Josef Spaun recollected that Schubert shrugged off his disappointment, saying, "Much as I should have liked to get the appointment, I will make the best of the matter, since it was given to so worthy a man as Weigl." Well, perhaps he *did* say it. In sober fact, Schubert never had a chance: not only was he politically dubious, but he was not a churchgoer, not a good Catholic, the five masses notwithstanding. Taking an objective view, one must say that Harrach was right, that Schubert should *not* have been appointed, that he would not, and could not, have coped with official duties—any more than one can conceive of Beethoven attending a conference while he was struggling with his last two string quartets and a new finale to Opus 130.

During this time, the spring of 1826, Schubert was supposed to have applied as well for the post of assistant conductor at the Kärntnertor Theater. He had composed for the occasion a couple of arias. Schubert conducted a rehearsal of them with the soprano Nanette Schechner as soloist. At the rehearsal he refused to make alterations in the music Schechner wanted made. Schubert was supposed to have told her that her voice had declined and that she couldn't manage even his simple music. Nanette burst out weeping. They quarreled, and Schubert left the theater in a rage. Thus goes the traditional tale. Not a word of it is true, the chief perpetrator of the tale being that inventor of anecdotes Anton Schindler, who years later must have heard some story or other about Nanette and promptly fabricated the whole incident. Nanette was twenty years old at the time of this putative rehearsal. On May 22 she made a successful debut in Weigl's opera. Schober wrote to Bauernfeld in June:

> In matters theatrical I inform you only that Mlle Schechner revolutionizes the town by her wonderful singing. . . . Schubert has heard her and chimes into the hymn of praise. If only he would write an opera for her; perhaps yours may be suitable.

Later that year Nanette sang Leonore in *Fidelio*. In February of the next year Schindler arranged for her to visit the ill Beethoven, when she told him how greatly she adored his music. Before that Schubert visited her with Anselm Hüttenbrenner, who had not a word to say about any rupture but waxed ecstatic over a dish of *Dampfnudeln*, a highly caloric pastry Nanette's mother had cooked. Everything was friendly, no doubt abetted by the *Dampfnudeln*. As to Schubert's taking up conducting, Spaun's word can be trusted: he had no desire to be a conductor.

What he still attempted, wrestling with the stubbornness which failure inspires, was to compose a successful opera. Bauernfeld agreed to propose a libretto for him; he suggested *The Count of Gleichen,* and Schubert hoped that at last something useful could be obtained from the pen of so dexterous and expert a playwright as Bauernfeld was rapidly becoming. Schubert kept urging Bauernfeld to make haste, he couldn't wait to read the libretto. In July Bauernfeld was on a short holiday in the Salzkammergut. "If only I could have your libretto *now,*" Schubert pleaded, "I could submit it [to the opera management] and if they recognized its worth (which I do not doubt) I could make a start, God willing, or send it to Mme. Milder in Berlin." Bauernfeld returned to Vienna by way of the Danube, landing at Nussdorf, where the Danube steamer discharged its passengers. From a nearby café Schwind and Schubert rushed out. "Where is the opera?" shouted Schubert. Bauernfeld "solemnly" handed him *The Count of Gleichen*. Schubert took it home and studied it. He realized, and Bauernfeld should have known, that the censor would never pass an opera the theme of which dealt with bigamy in a sympathetic fashion. No matter, Schubert felt, I want to set this to music just the same and defy censorship. He began to compose. By and by he thought more realistically of the project. Finally, though off and on he sketched a little music for it even in the last year of his life, he gave the whole thing up. Once again—frustration!

His wish for success—what artist is indifferent to it?—induced him to seek publication of his music beyond Vienna. At that very time he sent virtually identical letters to the publishers H. A. Probst and Breitkopf and Härtel in Leipzig. To Probst:

Vienna, 12th August 1826

Sir,

In the hope that my name may not be wholly unknown to you, I most politely inquire whether you would not be disinclined to acquire some of my compositions at reasonable terms, being very desirous of becoming as well known as possible in Germany. You may take your choice among songs with pianoforte accompaniment, string quartets, pianoforte sonatas, 4-handed pieces, &c. &c. I have also written an Octet for two violins, viola, violoncello, double bass, clarinet, bassoon and horn. Esteeming it an honour in any case to have entered into correspondence with you, I remain, in the hope of a speedy reply, with all respect,

Your devoted
Franz Schubert.

Probst answered with infuriating condescension:

Leipzig, 26th August 1826

It was in truth an honour and a pleasure for me to make your acquaintance by your esteemed letter of the 12th inst., and thanking you cordially for your confidence, I am very gladly prepared to contribute towards the dissemination of your artistic reputation so far as it lies in my power. Only I must frankly confess to you that our public does not yet sufficiently and generally understand the peculiar, often ingenious, but perhaps now and then somewhat curious procedures of your mind's creations. Kindly, therefore, bear this in mind on sending me your MSS. Selected songs, not too difficult, pianoforte compositions for 2 and 4 hands, agreeable and easily

comprehensible, would seem to me suitable for the attainment of your purpose and my wishes. Once the path has been cleared, everything will find
access, but to begin with a few concessions must be made to the public. . . . Receive the highest respects of

Your devoted
H. A. Probst [DQ].

When later Schubert sent Probst some manuscripts, he refused them
altogether, being "overburdened with work by the publication of Kalk-
brenner's" complete *oeuvre*. Besides, Schubert's price of eighty florins
A.C. was too high. Breitkopf and Härtel were equally unable to foresee
the future. They responded on September 7, 1826:

> Your kind inclination to consign to us for publication some works composed
> by you we reciprocate with our sincerest thanks and with the assurance that
> it would be very agreeable to us to enter into a pleasant mutual relationship
> of publishing with you. As, however, we are as yet wholly unacquainted
> with the mercantile success of your compositions and are therefore unable
> to meet you with the offer of a fixed pecuniary remuneration (which a
> publisher can determine or concede only according to that success), we must
> leave it to you to decide whether, in order perhaps to bring about a lasting
> relationship by a trial, you will facilitate the matter for us and accept merely
> a number of copies as a return for the first work, or works, which you will
> send us [DQ].

Thirteen years later Breitkopf and Härtel bought the C-Major Symphony and fifty-eight years after the insulting letter the firm began the
publication of the complete edition of Schubert's works—in thirty-nine
volumes—under the patronage of Brahms.

Schubert's condition looked different now in 1826 from that of a year
before. On July 10 he wrote to Bauernfeld, who was in Gmunden, that
he could not join him. No summer journey now—"for I have no money
at all, and altogether things go very badly with me. I do not trouble
about it, and am cheerful."

If Bauernfeld's libretto of *The Count of Gleichen* were "favorably
received," then—ah, then "there would be money, if not reputation as
well." He added the news that Schober had gone into business (a lith-
ographic firm) and that Schwind was having troubles with Netti. It appeared (from another letter) that she had reproached him for his want

of religion and he had told her, "Go, fall in love with the Pope!" But what about Schubert's finances? What happened? Even if the money he earned at Zseliz had been spent and though his share of the sale of the family house was not yet handed over, he had recently received more than 500 florins for the *Lady of the Lake* songs and some piano compositions. Did he need money for medical care? A partial explanation may be hinted at in an entry in Bauernfeld's diary of August: "Schubert ailing (he needs 'young peacocks, like Cellini')." Cellini, it was known, was syphilitic. The flesh of peacocks, in Renaissance lore, was supposed to make you impervious to disease. Bauernfeld would know that arcane legend and it would have been consistent with his literary style to use it, instead of noting plainly that his friend's disease had broken out again.

3.

During this summer of discomfort and discontent, Schubert had recourse to the artist's miracle drug, creation. Through Bauernfeld's* translations he became better acquainted with Shakespeare's plays; he composed three songs, unfortunately only three. Two of the three rank among Schubert's most popular "popular" works, quite on a par with the "Ave Maria": one is "An Sylvia" ("Who Is Sylvia?") from *Two Gentlemen of Verona,* the other "Ständchen" ("Serenade") from *Cymbeline.* For the latter he used Schlegel's translation, superior to Bauernfeld's. Both songs are so familiar that many of us have forgotten who their author was. Schubert was supposed to have composed the "Serenade" while sitting in a beer garden, jotting the notes down on the back of a menu. The fact is that the Shakespeare songs are written in a little booklet on plain paper, the music staves neatly drawn in pencil. But the back-of-the-menu story, told by Schubert's first biographer, is much more interesting, and we'll always have it with us.

Schubert said that now his most intense thought was devoted to instrumental music. He had begun the *Death and the Maiden* Quartet (D Minor) in March 1824 when he wrote the revealing letter to Kupelwieser (quoted on page 143). At that time, in profound depression, he composed

---

*Incidentally, he had met Bauernfeld at the home of Vicentius Weintritt, professor of theology. Einstein points out that Weintritt was "one of the leading victims of Viennese reaction and imperial bigotry. The fact that Schubert frequented his house is further proof that, so far as politics were concerned, he was either not entirely disinterested or he was disarmingly ingenuous. . . ." I do not think that he could have been *that* ingenuous.

as well four songs to texts by Mayrhofer—with whom his personal relationship had become strained—through which weave a longing for a better and a purer world. In the last of these, "Auflösung" ("Dissolution"), he pleads:

> Geh unter, Welt, und störe
> Nimmer die süssen
> Aetherischen Chöre.
> (Perish, World!
> And nevermore disturb
> The sweet ethereal choirs.)

He repeats, "Perish, World!" by a musical ascension which presages Isolde's "Liebestod." Two years later he was still working on the *Death and the Maiden* Quartet (finishing it in January 1826). Something had changed in the meantime. What we have is a work of various moods, the poignant variations of the slow movement as well as the strength and vigor of the finale; what it does not contain is a wish that the world perish. Perhaps it is allowable to theorize that a contributing element to this vigor was the impression Schubert carried away from Beethoven's Ninth. Its first performance in May 1824 was more than the "first" of a new work by the world's leading composer: it was an unfolding of hope expressed in a huge philosophic symphony. The world, at least that part of it which cared, knew its importance and vied for the honor of its premiere. We cannot be sure that Schubert was there, but in all probability he was. Would he have been absent from such an event? Two of his friends, Josef Hüttenbrenner and Fritz Hartmann, were singing in the chorus. They could easily have passed him in.*

The Quartet in G Major—it was the last Schubert wrote—is certainly "symphonic." It is powered by a new drive, typical of first movements of symphonies, an uplifting and life-enhancing spirit, and it is the work of a great composer who has listened to another great composer. (Tune detectives may find a quotation from Beethoven's Fifth in the last movement.) Schubert wrote it in 1826 in ten days, meaning that he put it on paper in ten days, for surely he must have had it "composed" in his head long before. It is the least ingratiating—the least "pretty"—of the quar-

---

*There is no doubt that Schubert heard the Ninth, if not at the premiere then certainly later, on March 15, 1827. Fritz Hartmann reported on a concert where an overture by Abbe Vogler, a trio and chorus from Mozart's *Davidde penitente*—and the Ninth—were given. Schubert went with him.

tets and one of his most astonishing works. Homer Ulrich in *Chamber Music* writes:

> It is in many ways the most orchestral of all his chamber music; tremolos, forceful unisons, and quantities of sound give the impression that the quartet is about to burst its bonds. Except for a few melodic fragments in the adagio and the tuneful trio, there is virtually none of the lyricism of the earlier— and later—Schubert. In place of the songfulness is a harmonic unrest, a ceaseless shift from one key to another. The quartet as a whole offers perhaps the most striking example of Schubert's departure from the lines of true Classicism. The clear part-writing of earlier decades is almost nonexistent here. A preoccupation with the composite sound of the individual chord, or measure, or harmonic progression replaces the concern for linear clarity. The result is a degree of harmonic freedom that Schubert never again attained. The G major quartet points the way to the vertical conceptions of post-Romantic composers; it is generations in advance of Schubert's own time.

In the same year in which he composed his last quartet, the Shakespeare songs, a new version of four of Goethe's *Wilhelm Meister* songs, and more than twenty other songs, he turned his attention to the piano sonata. Since he was eighteen—or younger—Schubert had often sat on the piano bench, and he was interested in many forms of piano music. Many? One can say in all but the concerto. Schubert never wrote a concerto, undoubtedly because he was not a professional pianist, perhaps could not have played with an orchestra, even if such a chance had been given him, and the collaboration of piano and orchestra, which captured Mozart's imagination more than twenty-five times, was not congenial to him. Some of Schubert's piano music is on the lighter side, the *moment musical,* the impromptu, the scherzo, the march, the waltz, the *écossaise,* etc., destined to be sociable and to delight. In his mature sonatas the wellspring of his thinking is melodic, with all the strength and conviction of their thought and form. The sonatas become ever more unified in their themes and the manipulation of the themes; they become ever more profound till in the last three of his last year they reach their highest, but for one and all the initial impulse is furnished by melody. None is "program music," none bears a title such as *Pathétique* or *Les Adieux.** Schubert gives a

*The title "Storms of Life" given to the piano duet, Op. 144, is the publisher's, not Schubert's.

hint how he felt about his A-Minor Sonata, op. 42, which he composed early in 1825 and dedicated to Archduke Rudolf; he wrote his parents from Steyr:

> What pleased especially were the variations in my new Sonata for two hands, which I performed alone and not without merit, since several people assured me that the keys become singing voices under my hands, which, if true, pleases me greatly, since I cannot endure the accursed chopping in which even distinguished pianoforte players indulge and which delights neither the ear or the mind.

"Singing voices"—it was true as well of the Sonata which he completed the year after, op. 78, in G major, which he dedicated to Josef Spaun and which Schumann called enthusiastically, if somewhat ungrammatically, "Schubert's most perfect in form and spirit." Again it is not "program music."

On New Year's Eve of the preceding year Schubert had been ill. Celebrating the end of the year 1826, Schubert was well and in good spirits. His friends gathered and they all went to Schober's house, where Schober's mother had prepared a festive repast. They ate, told stories, smoked, and waited for midnight. At the stroke of twelve glasses were filled with Tokay (according to Franz Hartmann's diary), they toasted each other's health, after which they drank coffee, smoked some more, discussed some more, told more stories, being loath to face the bitter-cold weather. Finally, at 2 A.M., they began to go home—they "waddled off," wrote Franz—all except Schwind, who slept at Schober's that night. Schubert went home with Bauernfeld, of whom he had become fond. Any disagreement between the two of them had long since evaporated. The bad year had a good end.

One other event of the year is worth noting: not only Vogl but Kupelwieser got married. On September 17, 1826, there took place a happy wedding party. Schwind toasted the bride, Johanna Lutz. Schubert played dance music, improvising it, and would not think of letting anybody else come near the piano: it was the least he could offer to the new couple. Johanna remembered all her life one of the waltz tunes he played on the occasion and taught it to her descendants. (She died in 1883, eighty years old.) It became a tradition in the family, and eventually the tune was heard by Richard Strauss. He wrote it down and rearranged it. That was in 1943!

12

Schubert and Beethoven

It was Schubert's bad luck that he was a contemporary of Beethoven. It was Schubert's good luck that he was a contemporary of Beethoven. "This was sometime a paradox, but now the time gives it proof," as Hamlet said.

As to the first—Beethoven was so tall a tower that he cast his shadow on all who lived and created around him. If in the 1820s you had asked a schoolboy who were the three most famous men in Europe, he would have answered, "Napoleon, Goethe, and Beethoven." In Leipzig and Berlin, in London and Moscow, dictionaries were looked up for adjectives to heap on the composer: "divine," "surpassing," "colossal," "immense," "peerless"—these are actual quotations. In Vienna Weber's *Der Freischütz* for a time captured public imagination; the Rossini craze of 1822–23 passed; Beethoven, proud, withdrawn, exigent, remained, becoming more than ever the symbol of greatness, and people made pilgrimages to the city in attempts to meet the sage. One of them was Louis Schlösser, a young violinist who had come to Vienna in the spring of 1822 and became acquainted with Schubert, who, sensing a kindred spirit, took Schlösser to a revival of *Fidelio* on November 3, 1822, in which Wilhelmine Schröder sang Leonore. After the performance Schuert pointed out Beethoven to Schlösser. It was Schlösser's dearest wish to meet the author of *Fidelio,* but he didn't know how to go about it and he used to follow Beethoven on his walks "until darkness set in." Then what Schlösser considered a miracle happened: the ambassador of the Grand Duke of Hessen, who had taken a liking to Schlösser, handed him a letter to be delivered to Beethoven; it contained an affirmative answer to Beethoven's appeal to subscribe to the *Missa Solemnis*. (The letter was just an excuse for a visit, of course; it could perfectly well have been mailed.)

Schlösser's account of the visit is worth reading, not only because he gives a lively description, but obviously because he must have told Schubert all about it. One can conjecture that the recital added to Schubert's hesitancy to confront the lonely man, who was reputed to be "arrogant" and "uncomfortable."

Schubert himself was considered not very approachable or friendly to strangers (according to Kreissle): he was withdrawn "and only when the conversation became animated, when it dealt with music, *but above all with Beethoven,* did his eyes shine and his mien become excited."

Schlösser:

… My visit probably occurred shortly after he had eaten breakfast, for he repeatedly passed the napkin lying beside him across his snow-white teeth, a habit, incidentally, in which I noticed he often indulged. Steeped in my contemplation of him I entirely forgot the unfortunate man's total deafness, and was just about to explain my reason for being there to him when, fortunately, I recalled the uselessness of speaking at the last moment, and instead reverentially handed him the letter with its great seal. After he had carefully opened it and read its contents his features visibly brightened; he pressed my hands gratefully, and after I had given him my visiting-card, expressed his pleasure at my visit and added (I shall use his very language): "These are heartening words which I have read. Your Grand-Duke expresses himself not alone like a princely Mæcenas, but like a thorough musical connoisseur with comprehensive knowledge. It is not only his acceptance of my work which pleases me, but the value he attaches to art in general, and the recognition he concedes my activities." He had seized his ear-trumpet, so I explained the unbounded veneration accorded his genial works, with what enthusiasm they were heard, and what an influence the perfection of his intellectual creations had exercised on the cultural level of the day. Though Beethoven was so impervious to flattery of any kind, my words which came stammering from the depths of my soul, nevertheless seemed to touch him, and this induced me to tell about my nocturnal pursuit of him after the performance of "Fidelio." "But what prevented you from coming to see me in person?" he asked. "I am sure you have been told any amount of contradictory nonsense; that I have been described as being an uncomfortable, capricious and arrogant person, whose music one might indeed enjoy, but who personally was to be avoided. I know these evil, lying tongues, but if the world considers me heartless, because I seldom meet people who understand my thoughts and feelings, and therefore content myself with a few friends, it wrongs me."

In the same year, 1822, Friedrich Rochlitz, editor of the *Leipzig Allgemeine Musikalische Zeitung,* came to visit:

Some two weeks later I was about to go to dinner when I met the young composer Franz Schubert, an enthusiastic admirer of Beethoven. The latter had spoken to Schubert concerning me. "If you wish to see him in a more natural and jovial mood," said Schubert, "then go and eat your dinner this very minute at the inn where he has just gone for the same purpose." He took me with him. Most of the places were taken. Beethoven sat among several acquaintances who were strangers to me. He really seemed to be in good spirits and acknowledged my greeting, but I purposely did not cross over to him. Yet I found a seat from which I could see him and, since he spoke loud enough, also could hear nearly all that he said. It could not be called a conversation, for he spoke in monologue, usually at some length, and more as though by hapchance and at random.

Those about him contributed little, merely laughing or nodding their approval. He philosophized, or one might even say politicized, after his own fashion.

Almost certainly untrue is Schindler's story of a meeting between Schubert and Beethoven. I quote Alexander Wheelock Thayer (Krehbiel edition):

... Schindler's story is to the effect that Schubert, accompanied by Diabelli, went to Beethoven and handed him the variations for pianoforte four hands, which he had dedicated to him; but that Schubert was so overwhelmed at the majestic appearance of Beethoven that his courage oozed away and he was scarcely able to write the answers to the questions which were put to him. At length, when Beethoven pointed out a trifling error in harmony, remarking that it was "not a mortal sin," Schubert lost control of himself completely, regained his composure only after he had left the house, and never again had courage enough to appear in Beethoven's presence. As opposed to this, Heinrich von Kreissle, Schubert's biographer, adduces the testimony of Joseph Hüttenbrenner, a close friend of Schubert's, who had it from the song composer himself that he had gone to Beethoven's house with the variations, but the great man was not at home and the variations were left with the servant. He had neither seen Beethoven nor spoken with him, but learned with delight afterwards that Beethoven had been pleased with the variations and often played them with his nephew Karl.

Knowing Schindler, who later had his visiting cards printed with "L'ami de Beethoven," one must view with skepticism a story of Beethoven's last days as he wrote it in his biography of Beethoven. As usual, Schindler casts himself in a leading role:

> As only a few of Franz Schubert's compositions were known to him and obsequious persons had always been busily engaged in throwing suspicion on his talent, I took advantage of the favorable moment to place before him several of the greater songs, such as "Die junge Nonne," "Die Bürgschaft," "Der Taucher," "Elysium" and the Ossianic songs, acquaintance with which gave the master great pleasure; so much, indeed, that he spoke his judgment in these words: "Truly, the divine spark lives in Schubert," and so forth. At the time, however, only a small number of Schubert's works had appeared in print.

Thayer wrote:

> Here no date is fixed for the incident and a little suspicion was cast upon the story because of the fact that only "Die junge Nonne" of all the songs mentioned had been published at the time of Beethoven's death. Schindler helped himself measurably out of the dilemma by saying in an article published in the "Theaterzeitung" of May 3, 1831, that many of the songs which he laid before Beethoven were in manuscript. He contradicts his statement made in the biography, however, by saying: "What would the master have said had he seen, for instance, the Ossianic songs, 'Die Bürgschaft,' 'Elysium,' 'Der Taucher' and other great ones which have only recently been published?" As usual, Schindler becomes more explicit when he comes to explain one of his utterances. Now he says:

> As the illness to which Beethoven finally succumbed after four months of suffering from the beginning made his ordinary mental activity impossible, a diversion had to be thought of which would fit his mind and inclinations. And so it came about that I placed before him a collection of Schubert's songs, about 60 in number, among them many which were then still in manuscript. This was done not only to provide him with a pleasant entertainment, but also to give him an opportunity to get acquainted with Schubert in his essence in order to get from him a favorable opinion of Schubert's talent, which had been impugned, as had that of others by some of the exalted ones. The great master, who before then had not known five songs of Schubert's, was amazed at their number and refused to believe that up to that time (February, 1827) he had already composed over 500 of them.

But if he was astonished at the number he was filled with the highest admiration as soon as he discovered their contents. For several days he could not separate himself from them, and every day he spent hours with Iphigenia's monologue, "Die Grenzen der Menschheit," "Die Allmacht," "Die junge Nonne," "Viola," the "Müllerlieder," and others. With joyous enthusiasm he cried out repeatedly: "Truly, a divine spark dwells in Schubert; if I had had this poem I would have set it to music"; this in the case of the majority of poems whose material contents and original treatment by Schubert he could not praise sufficiently. Nor could he understand how Schubert had time to "take in hand such long poems, many of which contained ten others," as he expressed it. . . . What would the master have said had he seen, for instance, the Ossianic songs, "Die Bürgschaft," "Elysium," "Der Taucher" and other great ones which have only recently been published? In short, the respect which Beethoven acquired for Schubert's talent was so great that he now wanted to see his operas and pianoforte pieces; but his illness had now become so severe that he could no longer gratify this wish. But he often spoke of Schubert and predicted of him that he "would make a great sensation in the world," and often regretted that he had not learned to know him earlier.

There is an entry in Beethoven's Conversation Book in 1826 by Karl Holz:

Schubert was just with him, and they were reading one of Handel's scores. . . . He [Schubert] was very pleased, and at the same time rendered thanks for the pleasure *milord's* quartets gave him. . . . He has great powers of conception in song. Do you know the "Erl King"?—He always talked very mystically.

"Milord" is of course "My Lord Falstaff," Schuppanzigh. His quartet gave the first performance of Beethoven's B-flat Quartet, op. 130, on March 21, 1826. Holz's entry implies that Schubert heard it, as well as the other performances of the last quartets.

About eight days before Beethoven died in March 1827—so Anselm Hüttenbrenner told Thayer—Schindler, Schubert, and Hüttenbrenner called on the moribund man. Schindler asked whom Beethoven would want to see first. He answered: "Let Schubert come first." So they did meet, a meaningless encounter probably lasting only a few minutes, beside a sickbed.

Why did they remain virtual strangers? Why did they, so near in genius, remain so apart as men? Why did they not exchange thoughts on music, or if music was a subject on which one did not waste words, why did they not discuss the state of the world, both being fond of "politicking," both conscious of the sad state of their times, both desiring that freedom through which men might "become brothers"? They must have passed each other many times in the streets of the inner city, met on the Graben or the Glacis, or seen each other occasionally in music shops, restaurants, and coffeehouses. In the absence of documents, one must guess. Schubert worshiped Beethoven so greatly that he may have been too shy, too reticent to seek his acquaintance. Then, too, Schubert may have wanted to preserve his illusions about his idol: he knew that Beethoven, who could be "amiable," could the next moment turn gruff and grudgeful, the deaf man venting his own unhappiness on visitors. It was well known that he quarreled with those who were devoted to him, with Schuppanzigh, Lichnowsky, Schindler, Zmeskall, with almost everybody. Beethoven could be rude. Schubert avoided quarrels and was rarely rude.

Schubert's early reputation was that of a songwriter. That was the form of music least interesting to Beethoven, though he did compose a number of songs, mostly on commission. It may be that by the time Beethoven realized Schubert's power as a composer of piano music, chamber music, symphony—if he ever did—he was a captive of his own world and unwilling to look into Schubert's. All this is guesswork. All we have is the strange phenomenon of these two, living in the same city at the same time, pursuing the same ideals, divided only by a generation gap, remaining within two circumferences which did not touch.

On the other hand, Schubert was lucky to live in those years, because Beethoven's creations came at him with all their fresh force, as yet undimmed by distance, uncooled in the mold of history. When Schubert worked on the *Unfinished,* Beethoven began the *Missa.* When Schubert composed the *Rosamunde* music and the *Schöne Müllerin* cycle, Beethoven composed the *Diabelli Variations* and finished the Ninth. When Schubert composed the Quartet in G Major, op. 161, Beethoven wrote his two last quartets, opp. 131 and 135. We do have proof that Beethoven's works were important to him, representing the news of the day, as it were, and that he missed few opportunities to go and hear them.

While it might have been natural for Schubert to regret that Beethoven's fame was all-blanketing, Schubert did not speak of the older composer with jealousy, concealed or open. Yes, once—after that Salieri jubilee—he did write something uncomplimentary, but it was a small splutter, penned more in envy of great Caesar than in derogation, and it was wiped away by lifelong admiration.

Schubert's early instrumental works were of course influenced by Beethoven. How could they not be? A truly original artist is not ignorantly "original." Rembrandt is unthinkable without Caravaggio, Dickens is unthinkable without Samuel Richardson, Beethoven is unthinkable without Mozart, Haydn, and Handel, and Schubert is unthinkable without at least three of those four. An analysis of the influences by Beethoven on Schubert's music would stretch beyond the confines of this biography, but just to cite a few random examples we may observe that the first theme of Schubert's Symphony No. 1 bears a relation to Beethoven's *Prometheus* Overture and the second theme an affinity to the *Pathétique* Sonata. In Schubert's Third Symphony occurs one of those typical Beethoven crescendos. In Schubert's early Quartet in G Minor, composed when he was eighteen, one feels the influence of Beethoven's Quartet op. 18, no. 2. The slow movement of that unbelievably beautiful Piano Trio, appositely numbered 100, is a funeral march: it harks back to the *Eroica*.

Schubert listened to Beethoven's voice when he was young and listened again as he turned to the composition of his final songs. "These were all advanced experiments, groping far into the music of the future" (T. C. L. Pritchard). The experiments were certainly fructified by Beethoven's last phase, though Schubert, great and daring as he was, never reached the vertiginous height of Beethoven's final works.

About this matter of "influence"—clearly Schubert never imitated Beethoven, nor are any of his mature works directly "derived" from the older composer. Beethoven spoke a new language, a bolder language, and Schubert understood it, was inspired by it, and with its help developed his own new language. Of course Beethoven was not the only predecessor who inspired Schubert, but he was the one who best helped Schubert to climb to higher levels. What Schubert produced on these higher levels— the special beauty, charm, melodiousness, and strength of his music— was his own; it was Schubertian, not Beethovian. All this is merely describing the *ABC* of the relationship between two artists. We may repeat that Schubert would not have been possible without Beethoven. We may reassert the obvious: Beethoven's genius was so strong that he changed the expressive possibilities of music. Schubert in his early years had to struggle hard to free himself of this creative cascade, this mighty maelstrom. But he did. Schubert became Schubert.

Musically their methods of working differed, as the sketches show. When Schubert jotted down sketches, they were integral melodies, later to be improved but entities already. Beethoven wrote down themes, isolated fragments, building stones as aids to construction, to be greatly changed after much struggle. Hugo Riemann, analyzing Beethoven's working habits, wrote that "the hastily penned sketches of themes evidently served him to recall them until he found the leisure to take them up again and use them." To put it oversimply—Schubert thought in terms of melody, Beethoven in terms of musical architecture.

2.

Now it was too late for any personal concord to be established between the two. On March 26, 1827, during an unusual thunderstorm, Beethoven died. The news spread through Vienna like the news of a defeat. Rosenbaum noted in his diary: "He is no longer! His name lives in fame's illumination." His body lay in state and a stream of curiosity-seekers beleaguered the house, the courtyard, the surrounding streets, attempting to catch a last glimpse of him. One of those was Schubert's friend Franz Hartmann, who came during a lull and described the visit in his diary. Curiously, Thayer does not mention this, but Deutsch does. Hartmann's impression was remarkably vivid and is worth quoting:

28th March 1827: Out to the Schwarzspanierhaus, where I contemplated the body of the divine Beethoven, who died the day before yesterday, at 6 in the evening. Already on entering his room, which is large and somewhat neglected, I was moved by its desolate look. It is scantily furnished, and only the pianoforte, of which the English made him a present, as well as a very fine coffin, struck a note of beauty in it. In some places lay music and several books. No catafalque had as yet been erected, but he still lay on the mattress of his bed. A cover was spread over him, and a venerable old man, whom I would regard rather as a servant than as a watcher, uncovered him for me. There I saw his splendid face, which unhappily I had never been able to see in life. Such a heavenly dignity lay spread over him, in spite of the disfigurement he is said to have suffered, that I could scarcely look my fill. I departed full of emotion; and only when I was downstairs could I have wept for not having begged the good old man to cut me off a few of his hairs. Ferdinand Sauter [a fine poet who died as an alcoholic], whom I had arranged to meet, but whom I missed, ran across me, and I turned back with him, telling him of my plan. The old man showed him to us once more and also uncovered the chest for us, which, like the greatly swollen abdomen, was already quite blue. The smell of corruption was very strong already. We pressed a gratuity into the old man's hand and asked him for hair from Beethoven's head. He shook his head and motioned us to be silent. So we sadly trundled down the stairs, when suddenly the old man softly called us from the banisters upstairs, asking us to wait at the gate until the three fops had departed who were viewing the dead hero, tapping their swagger-canes on their pantaloons. We then reascended the stairs and, issuing from the door and putting his finger-tips to his lips, he gave us the hair in a piece of paper and vanished. We left, sorrowfully happy about it. [DQ]

On the 29th, the day of the funeral, Vienna's schools were closed. A crowd estimated at 15–20,000 followed the funeral procession. It took an hour and a half for the cortege to wend its way from Beethoven's lodging to the Trinity Church, little more than a long city block away. Around the coffin walked an escort of nine priests and thirty-six honorary torchbearers, all in funeral clothes, white roses and lilies tied with crepe to their left arms, and in their right hands carrying wax torches. These were the most prominent members of Vienna's intellectual circles: Castelli, Czerny, Grillparzer, Weigl, Haslinger, Schuppanzigh, Holz, Linke, Hummel, Kreutzer, Seyfried. Schubert was one of them (surely an indication that he was considered one of the city's important men). And he was among those who went out to the cemetery and heard the famous actor Anschütz deliver the funeral oration, written by Grillparzer.

That night Schubert went with Fritz Hartmann, Schwind, and Schober to the Castle of Eisenstadt café. They "talked of nothing but Beethoven." It was 1 A.M. before they went home. The story that Schubert raised his glass to drink to the one among them who was destined to be the first to follow Beethoven to the grave—that oft-told tale is almost certainly fictitious.

3.

It was not the only time during that period that Schubert kept late hours. The Hartmann diaries and the notes of other friends repeat the refrain, "Up till 3 A.M.," "It was morning before we got home," "Returned very late." Schubert relinquished his cautious habits, as if a prudent regimen no longer mattered. He worked intensively the day long, sought the companionship of his friends in the evening, drank more wine than he used to, discussed Mozart, Goethe, told ghost stories, took part in "twaddle about politics," stayed away from his family, sang songs as the night progressed, and went to sleep at Schober's, who had moved with his mother to the house of the Blue Hedgehog, near the Graben, a fashionable neighborhood where two rooms and a "music closet" had been assigned to Schubert—which was more than he ever had before and where he was to remain for most of the rest of his life. He was often plagued by severe headaches—he surely knew their cause though he did not say so—and he endured them stoically.

Early in 1827, he resumed a relationship with Diabelli's firm and entrusted to a new publisher, Tobias Haslinger, his *Valses Nobles* (op. 77), several songs, and the G-Major Sonata (op. 78), to which Haslinger gave the title "Fantastic, Andante, Menuetto and Allegretto," a fulsome superscription which has ever since saddled the work as *Fantasy*. (It is anything but a fantasy.) Not only did publications of his works increase, but reviews multiplied in Vienna, Berlin, Frankfurt, Mainz, including a review of almost two thousand words in the Leipzig *Allgemeine Musikalische Zeitung* devoted to that same *Fantasy*. Not all these accounts were laudatory or perceptive, but they contradict the notion that Schubert was unknown and neglected. It was not exceptional to read, after a performance of a relatively unimportant chorus for two soprano and two alto voices, "Gott in der Natur" ("God in Nature"):

The name "Schubert" has a fair sound and his works, wholly enwrapped in the rosy veil of originality and feeling, stand high in the public favour. This work can only consolidate it further—this sterling composition has been altogether wrested by Schubert from nature and its inseparable companion, beauty.

Similar notices appeared in the *Wiener Zeitung* and in the Dresden *Abendzeitung*.

Early in 1827 he took up again the love he had never lost, the composition of songs. He returned to the poetry of Wilhelm Müller (who died that year). The result was the cycle of *Die Winterreise* (*The Winter Journey*). Schubert set all of Müller's twenty-four poems to music, the first half in February, the second in October. Quiet as it is, the work is a deep expression of grief and loneliness. Nothing more heartbreaking has been pressed into a song. Once more the motive of the "Wanderer" is sounded; the time is winter and the landscape snow-covered, the river frozen and the trees bare. Schubert filled the "landscape" with music of such intensity as to make us sense his personal commitment—an almost autobiographical attitude—and he subjected the cycle to much revision.* Spaun described the scene when at the end of the year Schubert presented the completed cycle to his friends:

> Schubert had been in a gloomy mood for some time and seemed unwell. When I asked him what was wrong, he would only say, "Now, you will all soon hear and understand." One day he said to me, "Come to Schober's today. I shall sing you a cycle of frightening songs. I am curious to see what you will all say to them. They have taken more out of me than was ever the case with other songs." He then sang us the whole *Winterreise* with great emotion. We were taken aback at the dark mood of these songs, and Schober said that he had only liked one song, *Der Lindenbaum.* To that Schubert only said: "I like these songs better than all the others and you will like them too." And he was right; we were soon enthusiastic about the impression made by these melancholy songs which Vogl sang in a masterly way.

Spaun thought that these songs contributed to Schubert's early death; this is naive. No doubt Schubert was "in a gloomy mood." Yet that mood was caused by the increasing manifestations of his disease as the year went on, which made him break appointments several times, fail to appear at gatherings to which he himself had bidden his friends, and say that he was "unfit for company." Illness beset the man, not his work. *Die Winterreise* was composed because the poems struck a chord with the composer and not the other way round, not because the man went around with a hangdog look and wanted to let the world know about it. While composing the *Winterreise* he also composed "Three Songs from Metastasio" for the famous basso Luigi Lablache which are prevailingly gay songs, one almost Rossinian, and immediately after he wrote the B-flat Piano Trio, op. 99 (summer 1827) and the E-flat Piano Trio, op. 100 (November 1827), neither of which is gloomy. Of the first Schumann wrote that one glance at it—"and the troubles of our human existence disappear and all the world is fresh and bright again." Schubert could compose fresh and bright music simultaneously with "Der Lindenbaum."

It is wrong to choose from so integrated a cycle as *Die Winterreise*

---

*Two complete manuscripts of the cycle are extant. The first has so many corrections and additions as to render it almost illegible. The second was given to Schubert late in 1828; he corrected it. That was one of the last tasks he undertook.

this or that song as outstanding. The songs are variations; they belong together and it is a miracle that they never become wearying. The miracle is due to Schubert's genius, which is here able to give, as it were, different answers to the same question. Nevertheless, the songs of a mystic and symbolic character seem to me the most moving: "Irrlicht" ("Will-o'-the-Wisp"), "Einsamkeit" ("Loneliness"), "Die Krähe" ("The Crow"), which could be compared to one of Goya's black paintings, "Im Dorfe" ("In the Village"), and "Der Wegweiser" ("The Signpost"), with its intimation of mortality. Through the cycle rustles "Der Lindenbaum," to me one of the two most wonderful songs ever written (the other being "An die Musik"), and promises consolation:

> Come hither, friend,
> Here shall you find your rest.

The cycle ends with "Der Leiermann" ("The Organ Grinder"). The words may be overly sentimental, but the music, which in the piano suggests the wheezy sound of turning the barrel organ and in the voice suggests a bleak helplessness, is one of Schubert's most daring creations. It closes with a question: "Curious old fellow, shall I go with you? Will you grind your hurdy-gurdy to my songs?" The question remains unanswered.

4.

If a Viennese were forced to admit that life could be possible anywhere in the provinces, he would choose Austria's second-largest city, the old city of Graz, which lies in the south, has better weather than Vienna, is easy in its tempo, and has charming streets conducive to strolling. Its symbol is a baroque clock tower, but most of the inhabitants forget time. They love to listen to music, and Schubert felt grateful for the honor the Graz Music Society had shown him. He had long wanted to visit Graz, but the journey was cumbersome and for him expensive. In the last two years—that is, from 1825 to mid-1827—more than fifty separate publications of Schubert works had been issued, giving him enough of an income to consider the journey seriously. His friend Johann Baptist Jenger, who served as secretary to the Graz (Styrian) Music Society, had several times urged him to go. It was he who first had called the society's attention to Schubert's works.

Schubert was especially desirous to make the acquaintance of a remarkable woman, whose early life had been linked to Beethoven's. She was Marie Koschak. Born in 1794 in Graz, she early showed unusual talent in her playing and compositions. When she was seventeen she was the piano soloist in Beethoven's *Choral Fantasy* and she wanted to become a concert pianist. Anselm Hüttenbrenner declared that she was the most beautiful girl in Graz, that she was called "heaven's daughter," and that she, highly cultured herself, glowed with admiration for Goethe and Schiller, for Mozart, Beethoven, and Schubert. She gave up a professional career in 1816 when she fell in love with, and married, the prominent Graz lawyer Dr. Karl Pachler. Their house became the center of a social circle, she kept up her musical interests in addition to her domestic duties, and the marriage was a happy one. Karl shared his wife's enthusiasm. They had a son whom in Goethe's honor they christened Faust—poor little boy!—and what she wanted most of all was to meet Beethoven. Karl's brother living in Vienna managed it. Marie had never before been in Vienna, Beethoven never in Graz. Sometime late in 1817 they met and a friendship developed. Little is known of it: Schindler's claim that she was Beethoven's "autumnal love" is one of his sentimental simplifications. He even named her a candidate for the "Immortal Beloved." Marie kept two notes from Beethoven, pencil scrawls, one of which is illegible, the other—

> I am delighted that you are sparing us another day. We will make a great deal more music. Surely you will play for me the sonatas in F major and C minor, won't you? I have not yet found anyone who performs my compositions as well as you do, and I am not excluding the great pianists, who often have merely mechanical ability or affectation. You are the true fosterer of my spiritual children.

Hardly a love note! But there is no question that Beethoven was very fond of Marie.

In 1826, when Beethoven was already ill, Jenger visited him and wrote Marie that the composer, now confined to his bed, spoke of her "musical talents with great joy." He regretted never having gone to Graz to see her; perhaps it would still be possible, "perhaps next year."

Marie's admiration for Schubert grew with every work with which she became familiar. Several times during 1826 she invited Schubert to Graz. After Beethoven's death Marie once again urged Jenger to urge Schubert to come. Now Schubert accepted:

Vienna, 12th June 1827

Madam,

Although I cannot imagine in what way I may have deserved so kind an offer as your honour has informed me of by the letter sent to Jenger, nor whether I shall ever be able to offer anything in return, I nevertheless cannot forbear to accept an invitation whereby I shall not only set eyes at last on much-vaunted Graz, but have the privilege, moreover, of making your honour's acquaintance.

I remain,

with all respect,
your honour's
most devoted Frz. Schubert

Jenger enclosed a note of his own in Schubert's:

Vienna, 16th June 1827

... Friend Schubert was quite enchanted by your kind invitation; and his thanks and promise to accept this pleasant invitation is contained in the enclosed slip.

We both look forward very gladly to this excursion into dear Styria, and I also hope that you, dear lady, will be well satisfied with my travelling companion.

We shall then once again well and truly live for music, and Schubert shall weave many a new and endearing flowerlet into our musical chaplet. Friend Dr. Karl too shall be content with us in all respects; for we shall not lack valour where wine and beer flows either. If only the time of departure were here now; however, these 10 weeks too will pass, and that in agreeable hopes of happy days [DQ].

It was two months before Jenger could report that he and Schubert were ready. They left Vienna on Sunday, September 2, at 9:30 in the evening, traveling by "express coach"—expensive, the fare costing more than nine florins—and arrived in Graz about 9 P.M. on Monday. The Pachlers welcomed them with embraces and kisses and loud cries—and good food.

Travel-stained as he was, what impression did Schubert make on them? Was he the shabbily dressed artist heedless of appearance, with fingernails half-clean and rumpled hair, as he has often been described? We have testimony to the contrary which I believe to be reliable. It comes from Heinrich Hoffman von Fallersleben, who was both a famous satirical poet and the author of simple and charming *Songs for Children*. (Humperdinck used his "Ein Männlein steht im Walde.") Unfortunately, he is remembered chiefly, if remembered at all, for the words of the song "Deutschland über alles," and it is ironic that the perpetrator of that arrogant piece of chauvinism was persecuted by his own government. Some two weeks before Schubert set out for Graz, Fallersleben visited Vienna. Like most tourists, he went to Grinzing. He did not know Schubert, or, rather, knew him only by reputation. At Grinzing, he suddenly saw him, sitting with a girl. In his autobiography (published in 1868) Fallersleben described Schubert:

> He seemed to me to have quite a healthy, vigorous nature. He spoke Viennese, wore, like everybody in Vienna, fine linen, a clean coat and a shiny hat, and there was nothing in his face, or in his whole being, that resembled my [conventional picture of] Schubert.

That is how he must have appeared in Graz, and he was proudly shown off by the Pachlers. Karl and Schubert's old friend Anselm Hüttenbrenner bustled about to arrange a charity concert to take place on September 8 in which Schubert would participate and be honored:

From the *Grazer Zeitung*, September 6:

> A commensurate success being assured by reason of the reunion of all the capital's art-lovers, of the kind collaboration on the part of an artistic and greatly celebrated composer from the metropolis, and above all by the honourable public's frequently proved humanity, it is only requested, without any further exhortation to charity, that the subscribers' priority claims on their seats for the day of performance may be presented to the Inspectorate of the County Theatre on the ground floor of the playhouse before 12 o'clock at the latest, where all other orders for stalls will also be accepted, as well as at the box-office until 6 o'clock in the evening at the latest, whereafter all seats not disposed of will be open to the public.

The concert was a big success and had to be repeated. Privately Marie, Jenger, Anselm, and Schubert made music for their own delight, with little Faust, seven years old, listening now and then, and Karl smoking his pipe. When in the mood, Marie could caricature her acquaintances in "musical portraits," which were sufficiently malicious to make everybody laugh. To Faust, more interesting than his mother's piano playing

were the excursions family and friends undertook to the autumn landscape surrounding Graz, among which the most rewarding was a three-
day visit to the castle of Wildbach, managed by an aunt of the Pachlers,
a spot which had all the equipment required to stimulate the romantic
imagination—decaying walls, an old moat, a wild brook (hence the name).
There a twenty-four-year-old Graz girl sang some Schubert songs accompanied by her music teacher, to the composer's complete surprise and
satisfaction. Her name was Maria Masegg, and Schubert thanked her by
improvising a quantity of German dances and galops. In his holiday
happiness he didn't do much serious work, two songs and twelve little
waltzes—the *Graz Waltzes*, op. 91—and a single galop being the result.
But he promised Marie Pachler that he would compose a simple piano
piece which Faust could learn to play. Marie hoped her son would turn
to music. (He didn't; he became a doctor.)

Three weeks and it was time to say farewell. The return journey, begun
at 5 A.M. on a glorious September 20, was made at a leisurely pace,
Schubert and Jenger stopping to see a few acquaintances in Lower Austria
and climbing a hill or two. Almost as soon as Schubert was back in
Vienna, he wrote Marie a letter which reflects the letdown one feels on
returning from a carefree journey. For the first time he was disappointed
in his beloved city:

Vienna, September, 1827

Madam,

Already it becomes clear to me that I was only too happy at Graz, and I
cannot as yet get accustomed to Vienna. True, it is rather large, but then it
is empty of cordiality, candour, genuine thought, reasonable words, and
especially of intelligent deeds. There is so much confused chatter that one
hardly knows whether one is on one's head or one's heels, and one rarely
or never achieves any inward contentment. 'Tis possible, of course, that the
fault is largely my own, since I take a long time to warm up. At Graz I soon
recognized an artless and sincere way of being together, and a longer stay
would have allowed me to take to it even more readily. Above all, I shall
never forget the kindly shelter, where, with its dear hostess and the sturdy
"Pachleros," as well as little Faust, I spent the happiest days I have had for
a long time. Hoping to be yet able to prove my gratitude in an adequate
manner, I remain, with profound respect,

Most devotedly yours,
Frz. Schubert.

"The happiest days I have had for a long time"—at least this benison was given Schubert. Hospitality, understanding, intelligent admiration, affection, these were vouchsafed to him in the Graz days, sunny days which passed all too quickly.

He kept his promise and wrote a little piece for four hands, a "Children's March," to be played by Marie and Faust on Karl's name day. He had to force himself to do it; it took him more than two weeks, and what he produced is hardly memorable. He apologized to Marie:

> *Vienna, October 12, 1827*
> I herewith send your honour the four-handed piece for little Faust. I fear I shall not earn his applause, since I do not feel that I am exactly made for this kind of composition. I hope that your honour is in better health than I, for my usual headaches are already assailing me again. Pray give Dr. Karl my heartiest good wishes for his name-day. . . .

"My usual headaches"—less than a month later Jenger arranged to have Schubert invited to lunch at the house of Josef von Henrikstein. This man was a pillar of Viennese society, by profession a banker, by choice a patron of music. He had been a friend of Mozart's and had helped Beethoven in the negotiation concerning the three quartets Prince Galitzin in St. Petersburg had commissioned. He was now a director of the Vienna Philharmonic Society. Obviously the lunch not only promised to be interesting but a connection with Henrikstein could have been advantageous to Schubert. On the day of the lunch, November 7, Jenger received a note from Schubert: "I am unable to appear for lunch at Henrikstein's; please forgive me."

The gracious interlude in Graz, the welcome and friendship which Marie and her family accorded him, were to constitute the last unclouded days in Schubert's life. Yet his health, now worse, now better, did not keep him from working. As I mentioned, in November he finished the Piano Trio in E-flat, op. 100, the companion of op. 99—of which Schubert himself was fond, and which has become one of the classics of chamber music. It was obviously written for expert interpreters, dedicated to Schuppanzigh and played by his group. He could not have had better interpreters, and ever since musicians have delighted in playing it. (For example, Rubinstein, Szerying, and Fournier.) It is like a poem by Keats, a dialogue by Byron, a cogitation in rhyme by Racine. The first movement changes almost at once from a challenging allegro to a lyrical andante;

it is followed by a hesitant scherzo and a funeral march, while through the finale, which begins gaily, flutter passages which sound like the wings of ghosts. That finale may be somewhat too long, but Schubert could have answered with what Mozart replied to Josef II when he complained that there were "too many notes in *Figaro*": "Exactly as many as necessary, Your Majesty." The finale again quotes the funeral march, which is reminiscent of the *Eroica*; the procedure is unusual with Schubert.

In more ways than one, there was a connection between the great Ludwig and the great Franz.

13
The Heights

PROBST TO SCHUBERT:

PROBST TO SCHUBERT:
. . . I have further taken delight in several four-handed works . . . which convince me more and more that it would be easy to disseminate your name throughout the rest of Germany and the North, in which I will gladly lend a hand, considering talents like yours. Kindly, therefore, send me anything you have finished to your satisfaction. . . .

Leipzig, February 9, 1828:

B. SCHOTT'S SONS TO SCHUBERT:
We now take the liberty to request of you some works for publication. . . . Kindly fix the fee. . . .

Mainz, February 9, 1828:

SCHUBERT TO PROBST:
. . . I can assign to you some works with pleasure, if you are inclined to agree to the reasonable fee of 60 florins, A.C., per sizable book. I need hardly assure you that I shall not send you anything which I do not regard as thoroughly successful, in so far as this is possible for an author and for some select circles [to judge], since, when all is said, it must be above all in my own interest to send good works abroad.

Vienna, April 10, 1828:

SCHUBERT TO SCHOTT:
The arrangements for and performance of my concert, at which all the musical pieces were of my composition, have prevented me so long from replying to your letter. However, I have since had copies made of the desired Trio (which was received at my concert by a tightly packed audience with such extraordinary applause that I have been urged to repeat the concert), the impromptus and the five-part male chorus, and if the said Trio is agree-

able to you for 100 fl. A.C., and the other two works together for 60 fl. coinage, I can send them off at once. All I should request is publication as soon as possible.

Vienna, April 10, 1828:

SCHUBERT TO PROBST:

The opus number of the Trio is 100. I request that the edition should be faultless and look forward to it longingly. This work is to be dedicated to nobody, save those who find pleasure in it. That is the most profitable dedication.

Vienna, August 1, 1828:

How now—where was the diffident, the timid Schubert? A new self-confidence and a new dignity emerge. These have been ascribed to the extraordinary success of the one and only public concert Schubert gave, on March 26, 1828. True, yet a measure antedated the concert and was due to the increasing awareness of his importance and commercial value among publishers, not only those of Vienna—Haslinger, Diabelli, Leidesdorf—but those abroad. What they paid him continued to be scandalously stingy, but at least their interest, however imperfect and niggardly, helped to firm the ground on which Schubert walked. Where before he importuned them to publish his works, now they importuned him. Once they obtained his works they took a maddeningly long time to engrave them.

As to the concert—Schubert had long dreamed of giving one solely consisting of his own compositions, and his friends had long urged him to do so. He needed courage for such an undertaking: if it failed, it would expose him to financial loss, as well as loss in reputation. The theory given in some biographies, that he had a foreboding of an early death and that he therefore might as well chance it, is groundless; his illness did not seem worse in early 1828 than it had been the previous year. On the contrary, in January and February he was especially ambitious and optimistic. In March he applied to the Philharmonic Society for permission to use their hall, the Red Hedgehog, Jenger helping him to word the petition in proper language. Permission was given. Now Schubert showed surprising organizing ability; he got it all together, though he did have to postpone the event by five days, and he enlisted superb participants.

The concert began with the first movement of the Quartet in G Major, which was listed as "new" though it was almost two years old, and was played by Josef Böhm, violinist, later the teacher of Joachim; by Karl Holz, second violin; Franz Weiss, viola; Josef Linke, violoncello—all excellent (Schuppanzigh was ill). Second selection: Four songs, sung by Vogl, accompanied by Schubert. Third selection: "Serenade" by Grill-parzer, sung by Josefine Fröhlich and the female pupils of the Conservatory. Fourth selection: Piano Trio in E-flat, op. 100, with Karl Maria Bocklet playing the piano part, "admirably," said Schubert. Fifth selection: "Auf dem Strome" ("On the River"), a song specially composed for the occasion, voice, piano, and horn. Sixth selection: "Die Allmacht" ("Omnipotence"), sung by Vogl. Seventh selection: "Battle Song," a pompous piece for male chorus, words by Klopstock, to end the evening on a loud note.

Tickets cost three florins V.C., which was expensive (about $25), but not only was the house, seating about five hundred, sold out, but eager latecomers squeezed into every corner, where they stood from 7 P.M. for the duration, which must have been longer than two hours.

Franz Hartmann's diary, March 26: "I shall never forget how glorious that [the concert] was."

Bauernfeld's diary [end of March]: "On the 26th was Schubert's concert. Enormous applause, good receipts."

The net receipts were 800 florins V.C., a sizable sum (about $4,000 in today's purchasing power). Schubert had reason to be satisfied.

And yet he ran into bad luck. Three days after the concert Paganini made his first Vienna appearance on a tour which took him in triumph through Europe. He was forty-five years old, at the height of his powers, and he soon had Vienna under his demonic spell, with his sunken face, his toothless grin, his eyes hidden by black glasses, and his ability to perform feats which positively could not be performed on the violin—double stops with harmonics, impossibly intricate runs without dropping a single note, heartbreaking sobs and angelic adagios. The demand to hear him was so great he gave fourteen concerts in Vienna at very high prices: five florins V.C. for stalls, twice that for the dress circle. Deutsch calculated his receipts from these concerts at 30,000 florins A.C. or 85,000 V.C. The cabdrivers came to call the five-florin note a *Paganinerl*. Schubert went to hear him at least twice, once not only paying for himself but treating Bauernfeld to a five-florin seat.

Paganini would have been a sensation at any time, yet he fitted two tendencies toward which the taste of the times was turning, one being a preoccupation with the macabre—as exemplified by Turner's painting *Ulysses Deriding Polyhemus* or Delacroix's cruel *Sardanapalus* or Victor Hugo's *Notre Dame de Paris* or Berlioz's *Symphonie Fantastique*—the other tendency being a growth in internationalism, which caused Thomas Carlyle in his essay on Goethe to fasten the attention of English readers on German literature, and caused Rossini to choose Schiller's *Wilhelm Tell* for his last major opera.* Romanticism still reigned supreme, indeed was to remain supreme in Schumann, Brahms, Wagner, but it took new and less Biedermeier-ish directions. Paganini was not only sensationally romantic and sensationally macabre, but "international."

The newspapers were so full of Paganini—the Vienna correspondent of the Dresden *Abendzeitung* writing, "There is but one voice within our walls and that cries, 'Hear Paganini!' "—that Schubert's concert was hardly mentioned. The timing was unfortunate. What wretched luck! If Schubert didn't get the printed attention the occasion deserved, at least he could feel gratification from the enthusiasm of the audience, a demonstration shown not only by his friends but by such a distant acquaintance as Marie Pratobevera, a twenty-four-year-old girl, highly cultured, of an aristocratic family, betrothed to Josef Bergmann, who at the time was a teacher in Cilli in Styria, and later was to become an important historian and an authority on antique coins. Marie wrote Josef:

> *March 31, 1828*
>
> I must tell you about fresh and blossoming life, which prevailed at a concert given by Schubert on 26th March. Only compositions by himself were given, and gloriously. Everybody was lost in a frenzy of admiration and rapture. There was as much clapping and stamping as in "King Lear" (does it hurt you, admirer of "Lear," to know that what is due to him alone is vouchsafed to others as well? Yet you would have been delighted, in spite of the Cillian day and night music). . . . The separate pieces I shall not describe to you: in the golden autumn we shall ourselves play them all for you, kind, considerate poet.

While the Vienna newspapers ignored Schubert's concert, one man, who was the editor of a Viennese journal which dealt partly with the arts and mostly with women's fashions, did take notice. He was Johann Schickh. On April 3, 1828, he wrote Schubert a charming letter addressing him as "Celebrated Composer" and telling him that he had long admired him; further, that somebody had sent Schickh an article about the concert; that he thought the article lame and inadequate; and that

---

*All these works were created between 1827 and 1831.

he himself proposed to write an appreciation of the event. Unfortunately, Schickh's article is lost.

The program of the concert—as well as the creative plans Schubert was deliberating—suggest that he was delving into his talent to deal with the larger issues which were exciting thinkers—S. T. Coleridge published *On the Constitution of the Church and State,* James Mill *Analysis of the Phenomena of the Human Mind.* Nothing so crude as writing to fit the times was involved, of course; I merely indicate the possibility of change in the mind of that sensitive artist, a feeling rather than a calculated purpose. It does seem significant that he chose for his concert two "difficult" pieces of late style, the first movement of the G-Major Quartet and the Piano Trio, op. 100. Both might be called music of the future. He did not trot out earlier and easier compositions. He showed where he was going, not where he had been. Whatever the bent of his thinking, it is certain that the works of his last year mark such an astonishing growth in size, depth, and ambition that an explanation of "maturity" does not satisfy. More was involved; what was *not* involved was that he harbored a belief he was soon going to die. Such mystic forebodings are laid on posthumously.

Schubert intended to give another concert the next year.

What happened to the money, the 800 florins? He seems to have been ill in April and he may have had to pay doctors' bills.* But that couldn't account for the fact that as early as May he had almost no money. To recuperate he wanted to revisit Gmunden and his friend Traweger. He asked Traweger how much he would charge for board and lodging; he didn't want to be a burden to anybody, he did not want to come unbidden. Traweger answered:

Gmunden, 19th May, 1828

Dear Friend Schubert,

You really embarrass me; if I did not know you and your open, guileless way of thinking, and if I did not fear that in the end you might not come, I should ask nothing. But in order to get the idea out of your head that you might be a burden to any one, and so that you may stay on without constraint as long as you like, listen: for your room, which you know, including breakfast, lunch and supper, you will pay me 50 kreuzer, VC, per day, and pay

*Ferdinand Schubert's inventory (December 6, 1828) of Schubert's possessions and debts includes an item: "Dr. Wisgrill for consultation 5 Fl" (about $25). Physicians, even consulting experts, weren't highly paid.

extra for what you wish to drink. I must close, else I shall miss the post. Write to me immediately whether my proposal satisfies you.

Fifty kreuzer? It was of course a ridiculously small sum, a joke. But Schubert did not go.

In June Marie Pachler again invited Jenger and Schubert to Graz. Jenger answered:

Vienna, 4th July, 1828

The absence of two officials from my office to take the waters at Baden, and further the not very brilliant financial circumstances of friend Schubert—who sends a great many compliments to you, friend Dr. Karl and little Faust as well as all acquaintances—are the obstacles that prevent us just now from taking advantage of your kind invitation to come to Graz—Schubert had in any case planned to spend part of the summer at Gmunden and its environs—whence he has already received several invitations—from accepting which he has however so far been prevented by the above-mentioned financial embarrassments.

He is still here at present, works diligently at a new Mass and only awaits still—wherever it may come from—the necessary money to take his flight into Upper Austria.

In these circumstances our excursion to Graz may thus take its turn at the beginning of September again, as it did last year. . . . Above all, it is now a matter of patiently awaiting the time which will bring either roses or thorns with it. . . .

But should I really be unable to get away this year, I shall at least send you friend Schubert, who is already—as he told me today—looking forward to being able to spend a few weeks near you.

Schubert never went. He spent the entire summer in Vienna, partly because his florins had disappeared, partly because he was deeper than ever immersed in composition, a continuous flow of ideas demanding expression, partly because he may not have wanted to get away from the doctors he trusted. The headaches came more frequently now, made worse by spells of dizziness. He became careless in his habits, indifferent to proper eating. Bauernfeld told how late one day he came across Schubert wolfing down six croissants (*Kipfel*) with coffee, having had neither breakfast nor lunch. The names of new beerhouses, inns, taverns, coffeehouses appear in the Hartmann and Bauernfeld diaries, with such notations as "All four tipsy, more or less, but Schubert especially" (June

29), or their going to the Oak Tree, an alehouse, "where we were most merry.... Home at 11.50" (August 26). He now looked seedy and became fat, taking on the shapeless corpulence of a sick man. Once again Marie urged him to come to Graz. He considered it—he expected "an improvement in his finances shortly"—but soon he gave up the idea "as money and weather are wholly unfavorable." Other circumstances depressed his mood, though nothing could stem the onrush of music committed to paper.

Early in September Bauernfeld's verse comedy *The Suitors*—which he considered his most important venture—had its premiere at the Burgtheater. Schubert, Schwind, Schober, Grillparzer were there. The play was a failure and was given only four times. Bauernfeld, with a judgment remarkable for its clarity, thought it was all his fault: "I was as though annihilated and from the very first verses recognized the senselessness of writing a long piece in Alexandrines." He was supposed to meet the friends after the performance, but he couldn't bear to face them. He walked the streets of Vienna and ran into Grillparzer. He felt "battered . . . a frightful awakening."

The next morning Schubert, who understood a creator's pain, called on Bauernfeld, accompanied by Schwind, and said to Bauernfeld: "To me the comedy was extraordinarily pleasing. To all of us. And yet we are no donkeys!" To which Bauernfeld replied: "What is the good of that, if I am one?" Soon after Bauernfeld left Vienna.

The Schubert circle began to unravel. Schwind left for Munich, Mayrhofer lost touch, Kupelwieser and Spaun married, the Hartmann brothers went to Linz.

Schubert complained to Dr. Ernst Rinna of nosebleeds. The doctor did not know what to prescribe—or he knew that prescriptions were useless—but he thought that getting him away from the heat and the cobblestones and into clearer air might help him. Accordingly, Schubert left Schober's house on September 1 and moved to a suburb, the Wieden, where brother Ferdinand had just taken up his abode. The district was open, so new that the street where Ferdinand's house stood had not even acquired a name; the house itself smelled of damp mortar. Yet, and though Schubert loved being with his brother, he was restless and troubled. How slowly did any money arrive, how slowly did the publishers do their work! On October 2 he wrote both to Schott and to Probst. They are still polite letters but anger and frustration can be read between the lines. To Schott:

Vienna, October 2, 1828

Sirs:

As it is now such a long time since I last had a letter from you, and I should be very glad to know whether you have received the composition I sent you, viz. 4 impromptus and the five-part male chorus, which I dispatched through Haslinger, I shall be glad if you will kindly let me have a reply on the subject. I am also particularly anxious that the said compositions should appear as soon as possible. The opus number for the Impromptus is 101 and that for the [vocal] quintet 102. In anticipation of a speedy and agreeable reply,

With all respect,
Frz. Schubert [DQ].

To Probst:

Vienna, October 2, 1828

Sir:

I beg to inquire when the Trio is to appear at last. Can it be that you do not know the opus number yet? It is Op. 100. I await its appearance with longing. I have composed, among other things, 3 Sonatas for pianoforte, solo, which I should like to dedicate to Hummel. Moreover, I have set several songs by Heine of Hamburg, which pleased extraordinarily here, and finally turned out a Quintet for 2 violins, 1 viola, and 2 violoncellos. The Sonatas I have played with much success in several places, but the Quintet will be tried out only during the coming days. If perchance any of these compositions would suit you, let me know.

With much respect,
I subscribe myself,
Frz. Schubert [DQ].

What a helpless letter! Probst had dealt cavalierly with the Trio, op. 100, of the great worth of which he must have had some inkling, since it had been performed several times, including the public performance at the concert in March. Yet, though Probst's support was tepid, or at least snail-paced, Schubert offered him his latest works. As it turned out, Probst did publish the Trio, but so late that Schubert never saw a copy of the work. The last three sonatas, which Schubert "played with much success in several places"—was he exaggerating?—were published ten years after Schubert's death, not by Probst first but by Diabelli, and not dedicated to Hummel, who had died, but to Schumann. The Heine songs were later included in the *Swan Song* cycle. The String Quintet—that work of supreme inspiration—remained mute till 1850, when the Josef Hellmesberger Quartet presented it in Vienna; three years later it was published by C. A. Spina, Diabelli's successor.

Probst answered:

Leipzig, 6th October 1828

In reply to your esteemed letters of August 1st and 2nd inst., I beg to apologize for the fact that your Trio, Op. 100, is not yet in your hands. My travels to France and Holland have doubtless had something to do with the delay, and moreover the work is somewhat bulky. However, its engraving is already done, and also corrected as carefully as possible, and it will go to you, spick and span, with my next consignment to Diabelli & Co. Of your new compositions the songs would suit me best, and I would ask you to send them. Please communicate to me also anything easily understandable *à 4 mains* you may be writing, rather like your variations on the miller's song from [Herrold's]"Marie" [DQ].

The Schott firm was worse than Probst:

Mainz, 30th October 1828

Herr Fr. Schubert in Vienna.

Your very much valued letters of 18th May and 2nd October have duly reached us. Our reply to the former was so much delayed because we too waited for an opportunity to send the Impromptus from here to Paris, when they arrived here.

We have received them back from there with the intimation that these works are too difficult for trifles and would find no outlet in France, and we earnestly beg your pardon for this.

The Quintet we shall publish soon; but we are bound to observe that this small opus is too dear at the fee fixed, for the whole occupies but six printed pages in the pianoforte part, and we assume that it is by some error that we are asked to pay 60 fl., A.C., for this.

We offer you 30 fl. for it, and shall at once settle this amount on hearing from you, or you may draw upon us.

The pianoforte work, Op. 101, we certainly do not regard as too expensive, but its impracticability for France vexed us considerably. If at any time you should write something less difficult and yet brilliant in an easier key, please send it to us without more ado.

We remain, respectfully and in friendship,

B. Schott's Sons.

P.S. In order to save any delay, we enclose a draft for 30 fl on Herr von Heylmann's heir, together with a letter of advice. If you do not accept our proposal, return this draft to us. —The 4 Impromptus we shall enclose in our next consignment to Herr Haslinger.

It is a relief to know that Schubert did *not* accept this chiseling attempt to cut his modest fee in half.

To divert Schubert, Ferdinand proposed a walking tour. Perhaps it was Dr. Rinna who suggested it, to get Schubert out of his room and away from his obsession with work. The tour had to have a purpose: they decided to visit Haydn's grave in Eisenstadt, in the gentle Burgenland, where Haydn had spent years in the service of the Esterházys. The distance was more than twenty miles and they walked for three days. No sooner returned, Schubert continued composing songs to texts by Heine, Rellstab, and Seidl. He no longer seemed to be connected with anything in the daily life that was going on around him, his friends, Ferdinand's children, the publication of his own works. He seemed a Jacob wrestling with the angel, trying to force the angel to disclose the secret of the mystery of music. The wrestler had almost ceased being a man. He had as it were resigned from normalcy, to concentrate waking and sleeping on one struggle, one desire.

On October 31 he went to a restaurant, the Red Cross, located near his birthplace. He ordered fish. Suddenly he laid down his fork: the fish tasted poisonous. He felt nausea, disgust, utter weariness. He fled, then pulled himself together. On the morning of November 3 he listened to a requiem composed by Ferdinand and that afternoon took a walk with him. The next day he visited Simon Sechter along with Josef Lanz. Sechter was master of music at the Blind Institute and was considered Vienna's expert on fugal composition. It is doubtful that he could have taught Schubert anything Schubert didn't know;* he went there only once. Lanz was a violinist and a piano teacher.

Day by day he felt weaker. He had to be supported just to take a few steps around the room; presently he gave it up. But he was still correcting the second part of *Die Winterreise*.

On November 11 (according to Spaun and Bauernfeld; Ferdinand thought it was the 14th) Schubert took to his bed. Ferdinand and his wife, Anna, nursed him. He was still taking the medicines Dr. Rinna had

*He didn't take "lessons in counterpoint," as several biographies state. I think it was just a social visit, more or less. And a brief consultation.

prescribed, being very punctilious about the times he was to take them. He hung his watch beside his bed to remind him. On the 12th he wrote Schober what was to be Schubert's last letter:

Dear Schober,

I am ill. I have eaten nothing for eleven days and drunk nothing, and I totter feebly and shakily from my chair to bed and back again. Rinna is treating me. If ever I take anything, I bring it up again at once.

Be so kind, then, as to assist me in this desperate situation by means of literature. Of Cooper's I have read "The Last of the Mohicans", "The Spy," "The Pilot" and "The Pioneers." If by any chance you have anything else of his, I implore you to deposit it with Frau von Bogner at the coffeehouse for me. My brother, who is conscientiousness itself, will most faithfully pass it on to me. Or anything else.

Your friend
Schubert

This letter has often been quoted to "prove" Schubert's low literary taste. Could he think of nothing better to read than a tale where "the prairie wolf, the owl and the rattlesnake all live in one hole"—to cite a speech by Thaddeus Stevens, "The Great Commoner" of the Lincoln years? To derogate Cooper is a twentieth-century fashion; in his time he was considered an important writer. J. B. Priestley in *Literature and Western Man* points out that Cooper

offered the world something essentially and, in its own fashion, deeply and poetically American, just as Twain did when he stopped clowning and remembered the mighty Mississippi. For there came with these Leatherstocking tales, especially to readers on the other side of the Atlantic, a sense of the vastness and mystery of the American scene, of the presence in it, half poetic, half sinister, of these vanishing tribes of red men, of painted shadowy faces in the forest, of fading clouds of dust on the prairie. . . .

At any rate Schubert, who demonstrably was acquainted with Aeschylus's play *Prometheus,* Goethe's *Werther* and *Faust,* Kleist's short stories, Heine's *Travel Letters,* Walter Scott's novels, Homer's epics, etc.—not to mention the quantity of poems he read—could hardly be called unlettered.

Schubert's condition worsened. On November 16 a consultation took place. Rinna was ill and he asked Josef Vering, his friend, to take over

Schubert's care. Vering's father, Gerhard, had been a distinguished physician, surgeon-general to the Emperor, and Josef had published two books dealing with the treatment of syphilis. But his interest in that disease was merely a coincidence in the present case, for he and the other attending doctor, Johann Baptist Wisgrill, diagnosed "typhus" (*Bauchtyphus*). Whether that was their real opinion or whether they knew the facts and gave the cause a veiled name cannot now be determined. Dr. D. Kerner, who made a study of the case,* came to the conclusion that Schubert showed none of the symptoms indicative of typhoid—no fever, no cramps, no diarrhea.

A few of Schubert's friends—Bauernfeld, Spaun, Josef Hüttenbrenner—came to visit him. Schober did not. Schubert's father did not. Bauernfeld recollected that Schubert still spoke of their unwritten opera, *The Count of Gleichen.*

On the 18th he became delirious. With difficulty he was restrained in bed. Two nurses now took care of him, but Ferdinand too watched. Schubert asked, "Why am I confined in this black hole?" Ferdinand tried to console him with the usual lie of "You will soon get well." He fell asleep.

Father Franz now realized his son's desperate condition. He dispatched a note to Ferdinand:

My dear son Ferdinand:

Days of gloom and sorrow weigh heavily upon us. The dangerous illness of our beloved Franz acts painfully on our spirits. Nothing remains for us in these sad days except to seek comfort in God and to bear any afflictions that may fall on us according to God's wise dispensation with resolute submission to His holy will; and what befalls us shall convince us of God's wisdom and goodness, and give us tranquillity.

Therefore take courage and trust implicity in God; he will give you strength, that you may not succumb, and will grant you a glad future by His blessing. See to it, to the best of your ability, that our good Franz is forthwith provided with the Holy Sacraments for the dying, and I shall live in the comforting hope that God will fortify and keep him.

Sorrowfully, but strengthened in confidence in God, your father

19th November 1828 [DQ]. Franz

*"Was wissen wir von Franz Schubert's letzter Krankheit?" ("What do we know about Schubert's final illness?," published in 1969.)

On the morning of the 19th Schubert lay peacefully in his bed. He felt no pain. The day dawned as a typically Viennese November day, dark and raw. At three o'clock in the afternoon he suddenly turned his head toward the wall. He whispered, "Here, here is my end." He died.

At that moment a splendid wedding was being celebrated at the Stephansdom. Justina Bruchmann was being married, and many of the family's relatives as well as Leopold Kupelwieser attended the ceremony. When they got home, they heard the news.

Schubert was thirty-one years and nine months old.

Ferdinand determined that his brother's funeral should be worthily performed. He wrote to Father Franz:

Most cherished father:

Very many are expressing the wish that the body of our good Franz should be buried in the Währing churchyard. Among those many am I too, believing myself to be induced thereto by Franz himself. For on the evening before his death, though only half conscious, he still said to me: "I implore you to transfer me to my room, not to leave me here, in this corner under the earth; do I then deserve no place above the earth?" I answered him: "Dear Franz, rest assured, believe your brother Ferdinand, whom you have always trusted, and who loves you so much. You are in the room in which you have always been so far, and lie in your bed!" —And Franz said: "No, it is not true: Beethoven does not lie here." —Could this be anything but an indication of his inmost wish to repose by the side of Beethoven, whom he so greatly revered?!—

I have therefore spoken to Rieder [teacher, friend of Ferdinand] about it and inquired what outlay this transfer funeral would involve, and it comes to about 70 florins, A.C.—Much! Very much! —Yet surely very little for Franz! —I on my part could in such a case spare 40 fl. for the moment, having cashed 50 yesterday. —Besides, I think we may expect with certainty that all the expenses caused by his illness and his burial, etc., will soon be defrayed by what he has left. Should you thus be of my opinion, dear Father, another great load would be removed from my mind. But you would have to decide at once and to inform me by the bearer of this, so that I may arrange for the arrival of the hearse. Also, you would have to see to it that the priest at Währing is informed before this morning is out. Your

afflicted son
Ferdinand.

21st November, 1828, 6 A.M.

P.S. The women will surely not appear in black mourning? The undertaker thinks he will not have to procure any crepe, as it is not used for the unmarried, and because the bearers have red cloaks and flowers!— [DQ]

Schubert's funeral, on November 21, was of the second class—there were three classes—therefore quite expensive. Schubert was clad in hermit's habit, as was customary, with a laurel wreath on his brow. It was a private funeral, the weather was still inclement; yet there were quite a few mourners. The body was transported from Ferdinand's house to the St. Joseph Church in the Margareten suburb. A choir sang his "Pax Vobiscum," for which Schober had written special words. A second ceremony followed, then the bier was carried to the cemetery of Währing and lowered into the grave. His wish to be near Beethoven was fulfilled.

Bauernfeld's diary, November 22: "Buried our Schubert yesterday . . . What a life is this!"

Schwind to Schober from Munich, November 25:

. . . I have wept for him as for a brother, but now I am glad for him that he has died in his greatness and has done with his sorrows. The more I realize now what he was like, the more I see what he has suffered. . . . The recollection of him will be with us, and all the burdens of the world will not prevent us from wholly feeling for a moment now and again what has now utterly vanished.

Jenger to Marie Pachler, November 30: "I am still unable to conquer my sorrow. . . ."

Schwind to Schober, Munich, Christmas Eve, 1828: "Schubert is dead, and with him all that we had of the brightest and fairest. . . ."
Josef Kenner [one of Schubert's fellow pupils at the Seminary] to Spaun, Linz, January 27, 1829:

. . . And indeed, had I not unmerited pleasure in my wife and children, I would gladly have died for Schubert, and would have done so unhesitatingly. For he would yet have done something unique of its kind, whereas my daily work at the office could be carried on by any mechanical being.

On December 2 the usual sequestration and the inventory of Schubert's possessions began. Schubert left no will. The official record shows that his "estate" amounted to practically nothing, to sixty-three florins A.C., and that included "some old music estimated at 10 florins," against which his father claimed "according to receipts held by him 269 florins, 19 kreuzer for expenses due to illness and death." Deutsch shows that Schubert left more tailcoats, frock coats, trousers than Beethoven (though fewer waistcoats and shirts). "Some old music" probably meant other than Schubert manuscripts. In judging this inventory, we must remember that Schubert most probably left some of his possessions at Schober's house; he thought he would stay at Ferdinand's only temporarily. We must also remember that these reports to the Sequestration Commission were given as low as possible, which is proved by the fact that, while Schubert's assets were listed at a total of sixty-three florins, Ferdinand in a private report to his father, written four days later, noted Schubert's cash as amounting to 118 florins. There was no inheritance tax, but it was prudent to make oneself out poor, lest one be saddled with an "Army Tax." The Commission usually made no difficulty about a little cheating. Anyway, and forgetting sentimentality, it is still true that Schubert died a virtual pauper.

One item in the questionnaire the Commission had to fill out needs comment. It asked: "Whether literature is found among the property and whether a report has been made concerning it to the Imperial Royal Book-Revision Office immediately after the assessment?" Answer: "None present."

None? Not a single book? Even assuming that Schubert had left his books at Schober's, what happened to the volumes of Cooper which Schubert had asked for and which Schober certainly sent over? Something is not right. One cannot escape the suspicion that Ferdinand spirited all books away, thinking that some were politically questionable and wanting to avoid any involvement with the censorship.

Ferdinand was an upright, practical, reasonable man, and he knew something of the value of the brother he had so dearly loved. Even as the long obituary tributes began to appear, and the commemorative concerts and the first biographical essays, he went to work. He gathered what scattered manuscripts he could find, he took possession of those Schubert had left at Schober's, and he began negotiations with various publishers for the unpublished works. As early as December 17 he sold to Haslinger the three last sonatas and the thirteen songs Schubert had planned to issue under the title *Swan Song*, while by November 1829 he had made a good contract with Diabelli. Ten years later, no doubt at the invitation of Schumann, Ferdinand wrote a biographical essay; it appeared in the Leipzig *Neue Zeitschrift für Musik*. Schubert dead was better cared for than Schubert alive. Nevertheless, when Schumann visited Ferdinand in 1838 he was astonished at the number of manuscripts still unpublished. Champion of old and new music, of Chopin, Liszt, Berlioz, Mendelssohn, Schumann conceived an artist's understanding of, and an eloquent enthusiasm for, Schubert's work. In word and deed. Many words!

The middle of the nineteenth century had arrived before Schubert's greater works were widely appreciated. That appreciation grew steadily. In our times, which have witnessed a return to chamber music, his compositions in that field are as loved as those of Mozart, Brahms, and Schumann, surpassed only by Beethoven's.

The question is often asked: "What would he have accomplished had he lived longer?" He was an artist who grew appreciably almost year by year. At thirty-one Beethoven had completed only one symphony, Wagner *The Flying Dutchman,* Tchaikovsky his first string quartet, and Mahler was revising his first symphony, to name at random composers who continued their ascent. Schubert's creation of his thirty-first year—it is an arrival at the summit he was permitted to reach, but it is as well an indication that it was *not* the summit he might have reached. It is both a farewell and an *auf Wiedersehen* in an air still purer had fate been kinder. In that sense Grillparzer's much-criticized epitaph, engraved on Schubert's tombstone, does have meaning:

The Art of Music Here Entombed A Rich Possession
But Even Far Fairer Hopes.

Grillparzer made five sketches for the wording of the inscription and submitted them to various friends. Perhaps his better version might have been: "He bade poetry sing and music speak. Neither is a mistress, neither a servant; the two embrace as sisters over Schubert's grave."

2.

Like a rondo, the productions of Schubert's last year began with songs and returned to songs at the last. In January he wrote the Piano Fantasy in F Minor, op. 103—four movements; he dedicated the endearing work to Countess Esterházy, and evidently it is a rose-colored reminiscence of the Zseliz days, with the boredom forgotten. The final two movements show a new interest in contrapuntal writing, and probably it was this interest which induced him to consult Simon Sechter.

In February he began what he himself felt was his "strivings after the highest in art," the C-Major Symphony. He finished it by the end of March; the brevity of its genesis is unbelievable, all the more considering the length, breadth, and depth of this work. It is the zenith of Schubert's achievement, a mind-stretching structure, and like all great works of art, it gives us something new to contemplate, something that was not there before and about which we ask ourselves, "How was it not?," "How could we have done without it?" As Lawrence Gilman commented: "It gives us the sense of an enchanted familiarity, that sense both of the wonder and the intimacy of the world—the conviction that just beyond the next hill lies some accessible paradise for the pilgrim mind." That is true: not only is the symphony "accessible" because it is now melodious, now rhythmic, now rich with orchestral effects, but because it is a *combination* of two styles of artistic expression to which we easily respond. De Quincey spoke of classicism as "Beauty, sublime and severe, which can be defined only by theory and understood only by Reason." Isaiah Berlin has defined romanticism as the "impulse—to live and act in the light of personal, undictated belief and principles," which could be understood only by the heart. Schubert's symphony unites both, both heart and reason, whether in that arch which spans the opening pages, or in the mysterious oboe tune of the second movement. Wordsworth wrote of such music:

> Sighing I turned away; but ere
> Night fell I heard, or seemed to hear
> Music that sorrow comes not near
> A ritual hymn
> Chaunted in love that casts out fear
> By Seraphim.

The history of the Symphony No. 9 (sometimes called No. 7) is well known. Schubert never heard it. He offered it to the Vienna Philharmonic Society before he died; they shied away from it as being too long and too difficult. Ferdinand preserved the manuscript, and made some fruitless attempts to sell it to a publisher. When Schumann visited him in the winter of 1838–1839 and rummaged through the papers, he discovered the score and at once wrote to Mendelssohn in Leipzig. Schumann's account is famous:

Who knows how long the symphony of which we are speaking might have lain buried in dust and darkness, had I not at once arranged with Ferdinand Schubert to send it to the directorate of the *Gewandhaus* Concerts in Leipzig, or rather, to the conducting artist himself, whose discerning glance never overlooks the most modest beauty, nor the outstanding and dominant one [Mendelssohn]. My hopes were fulfilled. The symphony went to Leipzig, was heard, understood, heard again, and joyously admired by almost everyone.

I must say at once that he who is not yet acquainted with this symphony knows very little about Schubert; and when we consider all that he has given to art, this praise may appear to many exaggerated. Partly, no doubt, because composers have so often been advised, to their chagrin, that it is better for them—after Beethoven—"to abstain from the symphonic form." It is true that of late we have had but few orchestral works of consequence; and those few have interested us rather as illustrations of their composers' progress, than for their art or as creations of decided influence on the general public. Most of the others have merely been pale reflections of Beethoven; not to forget those tiresome manufacturers of symphonies who recall the powder and perukes of Mozart and Haydn, but not the heads that wore them. Berlioz belongs to France and is only occasionally mentioned as an interesting foreigner and a hothead. The hope I had always entertained—and many, no doubt, with me—that Schubert, who had shown himself in his older compositions firm in form, rich in imagination and versatile, would also turn to the symphony and find a mode of treatment certain to impress the public, is here realized in the most glorious manner. Assuredly he never proposed to continue Beethoven's Ninth Symphony, but, an indefatigable artist, he continually drew from his own creative resources symphony after symphony. The only thing that seems to us objectionable in the publication of this Seventh Symphony, or that may lead even to a misunderstanding of the work, is the fact that the world now receives it without first having followed its creator's development of this form in its forerunners. Perhaps, however, these may now be made accessible; the least among them must possess Schubert characteristics; Viennese symphony writers did not have to go so very far in search of the laurel they are so much in need of, for in a suburb of Vienna, in Ferdinand Schubert's study, they might have found sevenfold richer laurels. And here, for once a wreath was to be found! But so is it often! Should the conversation turn to—[Mendelssohn], the Viennese never cease to praise their own Franz Schubert; but when they are among themselves, they do not seem to think much of either. But enough of this! Let us refresh ourselves with the wealth of ideas which flow from this precious work! Vienna, with its Cathedral of St. Stephen, its lovely women, its public pageantry, its Danube that decks it with countless silvery ribbons; this Vienna, spreading over the verdant plain and reaching towards the lofty mountains; Vienna, with its reminiscences of the great German masters, must be a fertile terrain for a musician's imagination. Often when gazing on the city from the heights above I have thought how frequently Beethoven's eyes may have glanced restlessly toward the distant silhouette of the Alps; how Mozart may have dreamily followed the course of the Danube as it disappears into thickets and woods; and how Haydn may have looked up to the spire, shaking his head at its dizzy height. If we put together the cathedral spire, the Danube, and the distant Alps, casting over the whole a soft haze of Catholic incense, we shall have a fair picture of Vienna; and when before us lives this charming landscape, chords will vibrate that never yet have sounded within us. On hearing Schubert's symphony and its bright, flowery, romantic life, the city crystallizes before me, and I realize why such works could be born in these very surroundings. I shall not attempt to give the symphony its proper foil; different ages select different sources for their texts and pictures: whereas the youth of eighteen hears a world event in a musical work, the adult only perceives a national event; the musician himself, however, probably never thought of either but simply gave the best music that he happened to feel within him at that moment. But everyone must acknowledge that the outer world, sparkling today, gloomy tomorrow, often deeply stirs the feeling of the poet or the musician; and all must recognize, while listening to this symphony, that it reveals to us something more than mere beautiful song, mere joy and sorrow, such as music has ever expressed in a hundred ways, leading us into regions which, to our best recollection, we had never before explored. To understand this, one has but to hear this symphony. Here we find, besides the most masterly technicalities of musical composition, life in every vein; coloring down to the finest gradation; meaning everywhere; sharp expression in detail; and in the whole a suffusing romanticism such as other works by Franz Schubert have made known to us.

And then the heavenly length of the symphony, like that of a thick novel in four volumes, perhaps by Jean Paul who also was never able to reach a conclusion, and for the best reason—to permit the reader to think it out for himself. How this refreshes, this feeling of abundance, so contrary to one's experience with others when one always dreads to be disillusioned at the end and is often saddened through disappointment. It would be incomprehensible whence Schubert had all at once acquired this sparkling, easy mastery in the handling of the orchestra, did we not know that this symphony had been preceded by six others, and that it was written in the stage of virile power (on the score is the date, "March, 1828"; Schubert died in the following November). We must grant that he possessed an extraordinary talent in attaining to such idiomatic treatment of the single instruments as well as of the orchestral masses—they often seem to converse like human voices and choruses—although he scarcely heard any of his own instrumental works performed during his lifetime. . . . Another proof of the genuine, mature inspiration of this symphony is its complete independence of the Beethoven symphonies. Here you can see how correct, how prudent in judgment Schubert's genius reveals itself! As if conscious of his own more modest powers, he avoids imitating the grotesque forms, the bold proportions which we find in Beethoven's later works; he gives us a creation of the most graceful form possible, yet full of novel intricacies; he never strays far from the central point and always returns to it. Those who closely study this symphony must receive the same impression. At first, we feel a little embarrassed by the brilliancy and novelty of the instrumentation, the length and breadth of form, the charming variety of vital feeling, the entirely new world that opens before us—just as the first glimpse of anything to which we are unaccustomed confuses us; but a delightful feeling remains, as though we had been listening to a fleeting tale of fairies and enchantment. We feel that the composer has mastered his tale, and that, in time, its connections will all become clear. This assurance is immediately produced by the elaborate romantic introduction, although here everything still appears veiled in secrecy. The passage from this into the allegro is wholly new; the tempo does not seem to change, yet we reach port, we know not how. It would not give us or others any pleasure to analyze the separate movements; for to give an idea of the fictional character that pervades the whole symphony, the entire work should be copied. Yet I cannot without a few words take leave of the second movement, which speaks to us in such touching tones. There is in it a passage where a horn, as though calling from afar, seems to come from another world. The instruments stop to listen, a heavenly spirit is passing through the orchestra.

Is this tribute exaggerated? Does Schumann say too much? Does his enthusiasm run away with his critical judgment? No—no indeed! However much he says, *what* he says is just. Like his words, the symphony pulsates with "life in every vein."

After much demurring by the Gewandhaus Orchestra—the strings especially found the last movement finger-breaking—Mendelssohn gave the premiere on March 21, 1839 (though in a shortened version). It was a sensation. The day after, Breitkopf and Härtel offered to buy the publishing rights, proposing a fee of 180 florins, instead of the 250 florins Ferdinand had asked for. Schumann advised Ferdinand to take it. Mendelssohn sent the manuscript to the London Philharmonic Society. They tried it out at rehearsal—and laughed at it. They didn't play it till after 1844; in that year Prince Albert gave a performance of it with his "domestic orchestra" at Windsor Castle. What could that performance have been like? The Philharmonic Society of New York gave it on January 11, 1851. There is no record of anybody laughing.

The symphony is not easy to perform, and the musicians of Vienna and Leipzig cannot be blamed too severely. I have heard it played by Furtwängler, Walter, Szell, Klemperer, Karajan, Bernstein, Giulini, Mehta, Ormandy, Haitink, Reiner—all good performances, but there is one performance I will never forget. That is the one Toscanini conducted with the Philadelphia Orchestra in November 1941. One can still hear it on a record, though in monaural and anemic sound. Toscanini once said that when he read a score he saw the portrait of the composer on the pages. Here indeed is Schubert! From the first bar one feels that Toscanini knew exactly where he was to arrive at the last chord. Every note is in place, every ingredient, both the classic and the romantic, is justly dealt with, every emotion explored, nothing overdramatized, nothing understated, all within the compass of Schubertian beauty. Especially wonderful is the second movement, the hushed dance in Elysian fields. Spike Hughes, who called the performance "legendary," writes about the finale:

> With the Philadelphia Orchestra the rhythm springs naturally and inevitably from a basic tempo which is always under control. The excitement bubbles out of the music spontaneously instead of being imposed upon it from outside, and one feels that everything is so confident and controlled, so perfectly timed, that like a great tennis player Toscanini always seems to have all the time in the world to make his stroke.
>
> *The Toscanini Legacy*

After the jubilant close of the symphony, Schubert wrote a few songs—by way of contrast?—chiefly in the autumnal mood, the texts chiefly by Ludwig Rellstab, critic of the Berlin *Vossische Zeitung*. Schubert later returned to his poetry, but in March and April he set to music two remarkable songs, "Auf dem Strome" ("On the River"), with horn obbligato, and "Herbst" ("Autumn"), which undoubtedly inspired Brahms. Fischer-Dieskau observed of "Herbst":

Once again, Schubert's accompaniment is an independent musical statement which proclaims the sovereignty of music. The piano is frequently contrasted with the vocal line, so that we have a counterpoint which, if not strictly theoretical, nevertheless has its own inner logic. The sorrowing autumnal season is rendered by the musical transparency, the recollections of experiences, even the smell, all created by Schubert's sympathetic and sensitive genius.

In June Schubert began to compose a mass, his greatest, the sixth one, in E-flat major, working at it between the Symphony and the String Quintet. It follows the traditional structure of the mass, and Schubert may have written it because he thought he would once again apply for a regular post in the service of church music. If so, he was neither considered for official employment nor has the mass become a popular work. Yet it contains passages of both power and tenderness.

In August the fourteen songs, famous under the title *Swan Song*, were finished. Who gave it that title? It is sometimes stated that it was Schubert's title. I don't believe it. I believe that Haslinger gave the varied collection—one can hardly call it a "cycle"—the sentimental sobriquet when he published it in April 1829. Ferdinand Schubert approved. Seven use poems by Rellstab, six poems by Heine, one, added later, a poem by Seidl. By whatever name one calls them, whether one is cognizant of their history or not, one cannot fail to find here the light which will not dim as long as music has the power to disperse gray hours.

Heine's *Buch der Lieder* was brand new, having been published in 1827. It contained most of the poems which, musical in their poetry, urged that they be used for music. The pure tone of German lyricism is sounded in such famous poems as (one must quote them in the original) "Du bist wie eine Blume," "Leise zieht durch mein Gemüt," "Es war ein alter König," and of course "Lorelei." His poetry served many composers: more than 160 versions of "Leise zieht" are known. Schubert took a copy of the *Buch der Lieder* home with him, studied it, and emerged with six songs which give further testimony to a new mastery in vocal music. "Der Atlas" has the tragic weight of a Greek play: "I must bear the whole world of sorrow" contrasted with "You wished to be immeasurably joyful—or immeasurably miserable." "Ihr Bild" ("Her Picture") is the old theme of the rejected lover, but stated more sparsely with Harold Pinter silences. In "Das Fischermädchen" ("The Fishergirl") Schubert captures Heine's cozening and ironic tone. "Die Stadt" ("The

City") is another song of renunciation, lit by pale sunlight. "Am Meer" ("By the Sea") hides the lover's fear behind the deceiving calm of the sea; one thinks of the opening of the third act of *Tristan*. The last song is the most famous of all, "Der Doppelgänger." (How does one translate the word? Perhaps "The Second Self," though awkward, comes near the meaning.) This, strictly speaking, is no longer a song, at least not one with a defined melody; it is a sinister music-drama. Again one thinks of Wagner, on whom "Der Doppelgänger" made a deep impression. It was composed by the man who could not manage a good opera.

The seven Rellstab songs, though fine, are of smaller importance. The first, "Liebesbotschaft" ("Love's Message"), is charming, "Aufenthalt" ("Abode") is menacing and raging, and once again we hear in the piano the triplets of the "Erlkönig." "Ständchen" ("Serenade," No. 4) is one of Schubert's most-loved compositions; it is a "swan song" of a sweet melody which ends in an upbeat mood, "Come! Grant me joy."

The leaves were beginning to fall as Schubert finished the Quintet in C, op. 163, the one employing two cellos. This is Schubert's supreme work of chamber music, which is tantamount to saying that it is one of the supreme works of all chamber music. It is, so to speak, his *Jupiter* Symphony (and is in the same tonality). It is unsurpassable. Of the second melody of the first movement Maurice J. E. Brown has written:

> Its beautiful melody has been beloved by many musicians, but perhaps the strangest manifestation of this love is found in a small cemetery in South Norwood, England, where on a tombstone is carved the first six measures of the melody and beneath them these words:
>
> > So long as men can breathe or eyes can see,
> > So long lives this, and this gives life to thee.
>
> (From an essay for the recording by the Guarneri Quartet with Leonard Rose.)

The second movement, the adagio, makes one think of Shakespeare again: "The readiness is all." Readiness arrived at after struggle. The finale seems to me a reminiscence or a suggestion—but just a suggestion—of various forms of music with which Schubert had been preoccupied: the song, the dance, the impromptu, the sonata.

In September, the month in which the Quintet was completed, he composed as well the last three piano sonatas, the first in C minor, the second in A major, the final one, usually called the *Posthumous*—as if a good deal of his work was not published posthumously!—in B-flat major. It so happens that sketches for all three have survived and they show how carefully and extensively he worked. When in that astonishing final year did he find time to sleep? Yet several notations from Franz Hartmann and Bauernfeld, for example, show that he joined them for a get-together, and on September 27 he seems to have unexpectedly gone to a party at the house of the Viennese physician Dr. Ignaz Menz, where he played excerpts from the three sonatas, including the one in B-flat, which he had finished the day before.

All three of the last sonatas are works in which meditation, charm, wistfulness, sadness and joy are housed in noble structures. The A-Major Sonata in three movements is a vessel of beautiful tunes; when he alights on a specially lovely one, he won't let it go until he is good and ready. The Sonata is as well a taxing work which few pianists play and fewer still play well: one who does is Alfred Brendel, who finds that at the end Schubert leads us "into romantic regions of wonderment, terror and awe." But it is the last sonata which is the greatest. Claudio Arrau, who played it superbly, saw in it an ode on the intimations of mortality:

> The B-flat Sonata is a work written in the proximity of death. One feels this from the very first theme of seven bars in the dominant, the breaking off and the silence after a long mysterious trill in the bass. We hear the trill again and the silence, and then a restatement of the main theme *forte*. . . .
>
> The *Andante* . . . is one of the greatest movements of solitude and loneliness in music I know. In the opening bars of utter desolation the proximity of death is almost palpable . . . [from an essay written by him for the recording].

One performance I remember with a special intensity occurred in the winter of 1953. Horowitz, certainly not known as a Schubert specialist, had scheduled the B-flat Sonata for a concert in Boston. He had made a long study of the score, had played it privately but never publicly. Now he was going to try. His wife and I went with him by train, and from New Haven on he grew increasingly apprehensive, more so than usual— and that is saying a lot. Boston had been hit by a blizzard, and he was sure that nobody, "but nobody," was going to show up at the concert. Symphony Hall was filled to the last seat with an audience which had braved the storm. Inspired by that audience, he gave a performance in which the music "outsoared the shadow of our night." We sat and wept.

In October Schubert fulfilled a promise to a singer he admired, Anna Milder. He was not alone in his admiration. Beethoven was enchanted with her portrayal of Leonore in *Fidelio*. Napoleon was supposed to have been smitten by her. Long before, Milder had asked Schubert for a bravura song with which she could *épater les bourgeois* on her concert tours; now he composed "Der Hirt auf dem Felsen" ("The Shepherd on the Rock") for her. Perhaps a bit of self-interest was involved: he hoped that the famous singer would consent to play a role in the planned *Der Graf von Gleichen*. Death prevented him from hearing Milder sing "The Shepherd," that pastoral and lovely song with clarinet obbligato which is much more than a bravura piece. Ferdinand gave a copy of the manuscript to Vogl, who passed it on to Anna Milder. She was delighted with it and sang it often, as sopranos do today.

That he never heard a performance of this song nor of many of his other works, that his life was short, that he was chronically ill in his last six years, that he never moved beyond the frontiers of Austria, that all his operas were failures, that he never obtained an official position, that he had no sense of husbandry, that he never found a woman whom he could truly love—all that is sad, indeed. But before we become too lachrymose in the contemplation of his fate, we must remember two things. First, that he experienced the creator's satisfaction, which is uniquely rewarding. He knew this. Neither he nor any creator would exchange it for safety. And second, that he possessed the gift of laughter, a gift which was not in conflict with his melancholy, but which fused with it to produce a light which illumines us all.

I4

Summary

"THE MOST MISERABLE OF MEN"—IN THESE IDENTICAL WORDS BOTH Beethoven and Schubert described themselves. Most miserable and most fortunate. For whatever cruelties the fates bestowed on them, each to his own misery, of one gift they could be certain: they stood on the high peak of genius. Of their own immortality both proud Beethoven and modest Schubert were sure.

Schubert is a companion of those whose music means most to us, of Beethoven, Mozart, and Bach. His creation is more confined than that of the other three, less architectural, more intimate, the C-Major Symphony notwithstanding. He is very much of a personal friend. Not only in his songs but in his piano and chamber music he speaks to us more in the home than in the concert hall. And as many friends do in intimate conversation, sometimes Schubert runs on too long—he has so much to say; that is especially true of his finales. But that is a minor fault, compared with the wealth, benevolence, glow, ardor, pathos, fervor, humor, tenderness, piquancy of his achievement. Fundamentally he thought in terms of melody. Who has written more beautiful melodies? And don't all of us know that melody is the immediate advocate of music?

He was a highly trained musician. The belief that his knowledge of counterpoint and polyphony was deficient is absolute nonsense. He didn't warble as the birds do. The melodies of the songs seem unpremeditated, they sound so "natural." Not Nature produced them but thought, thought in the service of sense.

I am tempted to liken many of Schubert's songs which seem so spontaneous to the works of a different art and a different artist, Matisse. He strove to give his canvases and drawings an apparent spontaneity, an easy fluidity, a quality of improvisation. But this ease of Matisse or Schubert—and by the way, Matisse was fascinated by music and the dance—was the result of preliminary experiment, of trial and error. My comparison of Schubert to Matisse is merely a personal opinion, but when I look at Matisse's dancing figures I think of Schubert. In much of Schubert's instrumental music the dance is there, representing the grace and joy of life.

The fluidity of Schubert's melody gave Liszt the chance to interpret the songs for the piano. Of these transcriptions Sacheverell Sitwell writes in his biography, *Liszt* (1934), that "the most furious detractors of Liszt, the most severe critics of all his future works, are agreed that if he accomplished nothing else his transcriptions of Schubert's songs are masterpieces in their delicacy and appositeness. They do not hesitate to call these the one serious contribution made by Liszt to an art in which he, at least, covered more paper than any of his colleagues, past or future."

We have today a juster estimate of Liszt the composer than as a virtuoso and transcriber. Nonetheless what Sitwell wrote is true:

The problem that Liszt set himself to solve in the Schubert songs was the fusion of voice and accompaniment into an entity that retained the atmosphere and the characteristics of Schubert while it kept the form and manner of his own interpretation, just as if he was a great singer, or some famous actor who had his own unmistakable way of rendering a part. Liszt had a particular devotion all his life long for Schubert, whom he called "the most poetical composer who has ever lived," and he exercised a particular care and restraint where these songs were concerned. His customary magniloquence and his tricks of pianistic ornamentation are subordinated to the poetical directness and simplicity, the freshness and the free imagination of the songs. All their lovely qualities are transferred in a miraculous way from one medium into another, so that what was an impossibility without a singer became enlarged into the experience of many who had no other opportunity of hearing them. In themselves, they are miniatures of many different moods, inimitably expressed. Perhaps the transcription of *Auf dem Wasser zu singen* is the most beautiful of the lot, but then one remembers *Der Atlas, Ständchen* or *Meerestille*, and it is hopeless to decide upon their merits. All the beauties of the Romantic Age are present in them, and they are impregnated with all the sensitiveness of this extraordinary virtuoso who, at the time that he was setting them for his instrument, was at the very summit of his powers of interpretation.

Schubert's range of color and mood was extraordinary. Listening to him one sometimes has the impression of a walk through woods where the sunlight is dappled by shadow. In "Die junge Nonne" the storm is interspersed with the tinkle of the little cloister bell; the first movement of the Fifth Symphony swings back and forth in charming alternation; the first of the four Impromptus of op. 90 is a game of hide-and-seek, the second presents a kaleidoscope of unexpected modulations, the third is a "Song without Words," the fourth a classic scherzo with a classic trio. He is graceful, never bumpy; mellifluous, never turgid; so often easy, never tortuous. He appeals to the learned and the neophyte, but he never uses "tricks." Schubert's music is wide open. It gives us the kind of enjoyment which Schiller defined as "enjoyment which requires no appreciable effort, which costs no sacrifice, and which we do not repay with repentance" (*Essays, Aesthetical and Philosophical*, 1796). Schubert is an artist whom we need especially badly today in our fractured times. He introduces into our frantic mood that holy and liberating play without which we cannot feel ourselves human.

He made his way through twenty-one piano sonatas (not all of them complete) to the final three (Nos. 19, 20, 21), all composed in those crowded weeks of September 1828 and all published posthumously; these three are creations of the first rank, still rising to greater mastery and largeness of musical view in the last B-flat Major Sonata, which may measure itself against, or is at least a tribute to, the supreme conjurer of the form, Beethoven.

Aside from his songs, some of his incomparable music was composed for three, four, and one final work for five instruments. His finest piece of chamber music is the D-minor *Der Tod und das Mädchen* Quartet. I have referred to it, but I would like to add T. C. L. Pritchard's words:

He makes the work exceptional by maintaining the idea of the brevity of human life as a definite programme for it. . . . The shadow passes on its way; it has not the heart to enter here. There is no sigh of fragility or of languishment anywhere, no folding of hands in resignation to an impending fatality. The bracing energy of the beginning continues throughout and increases to the end. It is healthful music, for it is still the voice of unquenchable youth.

The Schubert Idiom.

The youthful Joseph of the multicolored coat—again one wonders what he might have done if . . . A sense of unfulfillment hovers over him stronger than even the regret we feel at Mozart's early death.

Equally healthful is Schubert's last chamber work, the C-Major Quintet with two cellos. It is an unfailing prescription against depression. Einstein loved the work:

> It is a work *sui generis* . . . so orchestral in conception and feeling that it scarcely comes within the scope of chamber music. . . . The Finale sounds as if two congenial spirits were strolling together, and as they walk they interrupt each other to point out new and enchanting beauties around them, or to draw each other's attention to strange, mysterious things. . . .

Joachim thought that only the Quintet in F Minor by his friend Brahms came near to Schubert's marvel. Brahms loved Schubert especially for his songs, being himself a composer of beautiful songs. Undoubtedly Schubert was the greatest song composer who ever lived. But he was more.

2.

I have attempted to show that several of the popular notions about Schubert are old-biographers' tales. The story, for example, that Schubert wrote a song on the back of a menu in a beer garden is silly. Not that it matters on what paper or where he wrote—but he didn't write in a beer garden. He may have been careless of his completed manuscripts, but he was not an alcohol-sodden poet like E. T. A. Hoffmann, jotting down finished works in a public place.*

He was neither uneducated nor totally unknown; his mind was not one-tracked, he was not unaware of the world, or—in his later years—ignorant of or indifferent to the prevailing efforts to climb from Napoleon's oppression and Metternich's restrictions to a clearer aura. Indeed,

---

*There does exist a four-page manuscript in the Library of the Gesellschaft der Musikfreunde in Vienna. Pages 1 and 4 contain Beethoven's song "Ich liebe Dich." On pages 2 and 3 are sketches for the slow movement of Schubert's Piano Sonata in E-flat Major, op. 122. Perhaps the Beethoven song served as a stimulant for the sonata—but that is just a guess.

he paid a price for these beliefs, as many of his friends did. He was responsive to poetry, literature, and the beauty of nature, which he was privileged to enjoy. Poor as he was, he was no beggar, and he was foolishly generous and extravagant when he did have money. Deutsch attempts to estimate Schubert's income from his compositions (not the income from his work as a teacher) at 7,638 florins A.C. He says rightly that the figure is conjectural. He compares it to the cost of Schubert's room near the Karlskirche of six florins, "which was considered dear," and to the price of daily nourishment, which came to about one florin. In modern terms his total earnings could be approximated at $30,000. "Even that," writes Deutsch, "seems to us little enough for him to make out of his work during his lifetime. There is but one consolation we may derive from the foregoing, partly speculative statement: Schubert never starved." He was, however, so maladroit a negotiator that, as we have seen, he sold Diabelli a whole group of compositions for 300 florins or less, when Sonnleithner proved that he could get him an average of 200 florins for each opus, and more.

However he may have undervalued his work financially, his "shyness" and "timidity" are another false legend, in my opinion. He knew his artistic worth. He delighted in demonstrating it. He did not hesitate to show his "wares." One instance among several: in 1827 young Ferdinand Hiller came to Vienna with his teacher, the composer, pianist, and conductor Johann Nepomuk Hummel. Hummel had long known Beethoven; Hiller, then sixteen years old, longed to see the dying man. In the course of their visit to Vienna, they spent an evening at the home of Katherina Laszny. Many years later Hiller described that evening.

I heard the songs of Franz Schubert for the first time. An old friend of my Master's, the once famous actress Buchwieser [the maiden name of Frau Laszny], at that time wife of a rich Hungarian magnate, invited Hummel and me a few times to her house. The charming lady still bore traces of her former beauty, but was in extremely poor health, scarcely able to move; her husband received the guests with friendly warmth. The rooms in which we sat were imposing and brilliant and breathed a deep, genuine, aristocratic calm. No one else was invited with us except Schubert, the favorite and protégé of our hostess, and his singer Vogl. A short while after we had left the luncheon table, Schubert sat down at the piano with Vogl at his side, we made ourselves comfortable in the large drawing-room, wherever we pleased, and a unique recital began. One song followed the other—the donors were tireless, the receivers were tireless. Schubert had little technique,

Vogl had little voice, but both had so much life and feeling, were so absorbed in their delivery, that it would have been impossible to perform these wonderful compositions with greater clarity or with greater sincerity. We thought neither of the piano playing, nor of the songs, it was as though the music had no need of any material sound, as though the melodies were revealing themselves like visions to ethereal ears. I cannot speak of my emotions or my enthusiasm—but my master, who after all had almost half a century of music behind him, was so deeply moved that tears were trickling down his cheeks.

Ferdinand Hiller, Aus dem Tonleben unserer Zeit, 1871

Let me cite an additional witness to speak of Schubert's mind. He is Anton Ottenwalt, Spaun's brother-in-law, who was in government service, reaching the position of Imperial Councillor; he was a serious and learned man, sensitive but by no means given to hyperbole. The reader may remember that Schubert and Vogl visited the Ottenwalts in Linz in the summer of 1825. One night Schubert and Ottenwalt were left alone:

We sat together until not far from midnight, and I have never seen him like this, nor heard: serious, profound and as though inspired. How he talked of art, of poetry, of his youth, of friends and other people who matter, of the relationship of ideals to life, etc.! I was more and more amazed at such a mind, of which it has been said that its artistic achievement is so unconscious, hardly revealed to and understood by himself, and so on. Yet how simple was all this! —I cannot tell you the extent and the unity of his convictions—But there were glimpses of a world-view that is not merely acquired, and the share which worthy friends may have in it by no means detracts from the individuality shown by all this.

That is why I am so glad that he seemed to like being near me and was inclined to show us that side of him, which one shows only to kindred spirits; and hence my desire to write to you about it.

Ottenwalt to Spaun, Linz, July 27, 1825 [DQ]

"Unity of conviction," "world-view," "amazed at such a mind" — this is a true portrait.

At his best Schubert was one of the most original composers who ever lived. Rembrandt was one of the most original painters who ever lived. According to Kenneth Clark, that means: "All great artists have studied the work of their predecessors and borrowed from it . . . but few have ranged so widely or shown such powers of assimilation as Rembrandt" (Clark, *Rembrandt*). How true that is of Schubert!

[234]

Making allowances for differences of mind and character, to a certain extent Schubert's fate could be compared to that of Rembrandt. They both experienced the ups and downs of success and failure. They were both destroyed, cruelly destroyed, one by infection, the other by drugs. Neither possessed the braggadocio of a Wagner, the swagger of a Rossini, the certainty of a Mendelssohn—or the haughtiness of a Picasso. Yet each was conscious of his singularity as a genius. Let us forget all "modesty" talk! An artist like Schubert or Rembrandt is *not* modest. He cannot be so and do the work that finally looks or sounds so right.

Judged by ordinary standards, their lives were circumscribed. Nothing sensational happened to Schubert as he made his rounds in Vienna and Linz. Rembrandt lived a little more in the world, as the political history of the Netherlands in the seventeenth century indicates. Neither was able to travel: Schubert never saw the ocean, Rembrandt probably never saw a mountain. Yet Schubert composed the beautiful seascape *"Meeresstille,"* Rembrandt painted the mystery of a mountain landscape as a background to "The Polish Rider." Schubert conjured up the antique legends—"Prometheus," *"An Schwager Kronos," "Die Götter Griechenlands"*—Rembrandt did it with "Aristotle Contemplating the Bust of Homer" and "Ganymede."

To their imaginations—one aided by the ear, the other aided by the eye, both aided by the mind—to those unique imaginations no bourn was set.

Both were famous: Schubert more for his songs than for his symphonies, Rembrandt more for his portraits than for his biblical inspirations. Both were "published" while they lived, but much work remained unpublished. Ferdinand had a heap of unpublished material to show Schumann. Kenneth Clark gives a list of some three hundred Rembrandt works unsold when an inventory was made in 1656.

In German there is a word, *Pechvogel*, for which no one-word equivalent exists in English. The word derives from the medieval practice of smearing branches of trees with lime or pitch to capture birds, and means "somebody pursued by ill luck." Schubert was a *Pechvogel*. Consider: during much of his adult life Vienna went through war and economic depression; wealth veered from the aristocracy which supported music to coarser interests; he was unable to find employment by church or Court, largely, I think, because of his and his friends' political views, but also because it was known that he disliked priests. Since he was impractical, the publishers took advantage of him and as yet no copyright laws existed to protect his works; at the very time he gave his successful 1828 concert it was doused by the excitement created by Paganini. And he was only five feet tall; had Nature granted him a half-foot more, he might have been more attractive to women and would have had no need to go to the Annagasse.

Was he then "the most miserable of men"? No, not if one measures the plus to offset the minus. He was given the inestimable joy of knowing that his work would be given immortality.

A Schubert Calendar

This calendar is not comprehensive. Its purpose is to help the reader to orient himself and to place Schubert's life and principal works within the framework of his times.

G.R.M.

DATE	LIFE AND PRINCIPAL WORKS	MUSICAL EVENTS	CULTURAL AND HISTORICAL EVENTS	POLITICAL EVENTS
January 31, 1797	Schubert born in Vienna.	Cherubini: *Médée*. Donizetti born. Haydn: *Emperor Quartet*	Hölderlin: *Hyperion*	Further Napoleonic victories against Austria. Peace of Campo Formio.
1803	Begins to show interest in music.	Beethoven: First performances, Symphony No. 2, Piano Concerto No. 3. *Kreutzer* Sonata. Berlioz born.		
1805–1808	In his father's school.	Beethoven: first version of *Fidelio*. Premiers of *Eroica* (1805), *Rasumovsky* Quartet (1806), Symphony No. 4 (1807).	Walter Scott: *The Lay of the Last Minstrel* (1805). Wordsworth: *Ode: Intimations of Immortality* (1807).	Napoleon crowned Italy (1805). Nelson's victory at Trafalgar. Napoleon occupies Vienna. Franz I becomes Emperor of Austria.
1808	Schubert becomes a member of the Imperial-Royal Seminary.	Beethoven: Symphonies Nos. 5 and 6.	Goethe: *Faust, Part 1* Canova: *Pauline as Venus* (sculpture) Ingres: *La grande Baigneuse*.	Napoleon's "Continental System." France invades Spain. Madrid capitulates.
1810	Takes lessons from Salieri. First attempts at composition.	Beethoven: *Egmont* music and Quartet op. 95. Chopin and Schumann born.	Scott: *Lady of the Lake* de Staël: *Germany*	Napoleon marries Marie Louise, daughter of Franz I.
1811	Songs "Hagars Klage" and other small compositions.	Beethoven: Symphonies Nos. 7 and 8 composed. Liszt born.	Jane Austen: *Sense and Sensibility* Fouqué: *Undine*	Austria devalues its currency, tantamount to bankruptcy. George III of England declared insane.
1812	At Seminary. Many songs, plus two string quartets. Operatic fragment, *Der Spiegelritter*.		Byron: *Childe Harold's Pilgrimage* J. and W. Grimm: *Fairy Tales* Goya: *Duke of Wellington* (painting)	Napoleon penetrates to Moscow. City burns. Then his retreat begins.
1813	Leaves Seminary. Becomes assistant schoolteacher. Flood of compositions, songs, quartets, dances. Composed the First Symphony.	Verdi and Wagner born.	J. Austen: *Pride and Prejudice* Shelley: *Queen Mab*	Leipzig Battle of the Nations: Napoleon is defeated.

Life and Principal Works	Musical Events	Cultural and Historical Events	Political Events
The great Goethe lieder begin: "Gretchen am Spinnrade." Mass No. 1. Symphony No. 2 (finished 1815). Opera: *Des Teufels Lustschloss.*	*Fidelio,* final version performed with great success.	Austen: *Mansfield Park* Byron: *The Corsair* Goya: *May 2* and *May 3* (paintings)	Napoleon, beaten, is exiled to Elba. Congress of Vienna begins.
"Erlkönig" makes him better known. Mass in G, No. 2. Operatic attempt: *Der Vierjährige Posten.* First two piano sonatas. Further Goethe songs—including "Heidenröslein," "An den Mond," "Mignon," and others. About 150 other songs. *"Die Freunde von Salamanka"—Singspiel* in two acts. String Quartet in G minor; Symphony No. 3. In love with Therese Grob. Meets Franz von Schober.			Bismarck born. Napoleon escapes, enters Paris, begins his rule of "The Hundred Days." Congress of Vienna ends. Wellington and Blücher defeat Napoleon at Waterloo. Napoleon shipped to Saint Helena.
Beginning of friendship with Schober. Symphonies Nos. 4 and 5. Productivity of songs continues.	Rossini: *Barber of Seville.* Beethoven Quartet op. 95.	Coleridge: *Kubla Khan* (published)	
Meets Vogl. Decides to relinquish schoolmastering. Piano Sonatas Nos. 4 to 9.	Rossini: *La Cenerentola.*	Hegel: *Encyclopedia of Philosophy* Byron: *Manfred*	
First public performance in Vienna (Italian Overture). First song printed ("Am Erlafsee"). To Zseliz, and Count Esterházy's, as teacher. Sixth Symphony.	Beethoven begins *Missa Solemnis.*	Keats: *Endymion*	

Date	Life and Principal Works	Musical Events	Cultural and Historical Events	Political Events
1819	Lives with Mayrhofer until 1821. *Trout* Quintet, piano Sonata No. 13. Mass No. 5 begun. Happy in summer excursions with Vogl.	Beethoven: "Hammerklavier" sonata.	Goethe: *Der West-östliche Divan* Schopenhauer: *The World as Will and Idea*	
1820	Comes with Senn under police suspicion of subversive behavior. *Die Zwillingsbrüder* performed. Wrote *Quartettsatz*.		Scott: *Ivanhoe* Pushkin: *Ruslan and Ludmilla* *Venus de Milo* discovered	
1821	Lives at Schober's. "Erlkönig" published as op. 1. Goethe's *Divan* songs.	Beethoven: Sonatas Nos. 110 and 111. Weber: *Der Freischütz*.	Heine: *Poems*	
1822	*Unfinished* Symphony. *Wandererfantasie*. Mass in A-flat. *Alfonso und Estrella*.	César Franck born. Rossini visits Vienna.	Pushkin: *Eugene Onegin*	
1823	Illness begins. Returns to parental home. *Fierabras*. *Rosamunde*. *Die Schöne Müllerin* song cycle.	Beethoven: *Missa solemnis*. Beethoven: Diabelli Variations. Weber: *Euryanthe*.		
1824	Schubert lives alone. Second visit to Zseliz. Octet. *Death and the Maiden* Quartet. Concentrates on chamber music, including A-minor Quartet, op. 29.	First performance of Beethoven's Symphony No. 9. Great ovation. Beethoven: String Quartet op. 127.	Byron dies at Missolonghi.	
1825	Visits Upper Austria with Vogl: piano Sonatas Nos. 15 to 17. A happy year.	Beethoven: Quartets Nos. 132 and 130. Johann Strauss, Jr. born. Chopin publishes Op. 1.	Pushkin: *Boris Godunov* Manzoni: *I Promessi Sposi*	
1826	Is refused post as second Court Kapellmeister. Goethe and Shakespeare songs. Quartet in G, op. 161. Happy visit to Graz to the Pachlers.	Beethoven: Quartet No. 135 and new finale for op. 130. Weber: *Oberon*. Mendelssohn: Overture to *A Midsummer Night's Dream*.		

TE	LIFE AND PRINCIPAL WORKS	MUSICAL EVENTS	CULTURAL AND HISTORICAL EVENTS	POLITICAL EVENTS
7	Many works being published. Fame increases. *Die Winterreise* song cycle. Four impromptus, op. 90. Trio in E-flat. All toward end of year.	Beethoven dies in March.	Heine: *Buch der Lieder* Ingres: *The Apotheosis of Homer* (painting)	
8	Year of great creations. Symphony in C major. Mass No. 6. String Quintet in C major. Three final piano sonatas (C minor, A major, B-flat major). "Schwanengesang" song cycle. Heine songs. Gives successful concert of his works (March 26), but newspapers ignore it. Moves to his brother Ferdinand's house. Falls ill in October. Dies November 19.	Paganini in Vienna.		

BIBLIOGRAPHY

Abraham, Gerald, Editor, *The Music of Schubert*. New York, 1947.
——, *Schubert: A Symposium*. London, 1947.
Barea, Ilsa, *Vienna, Legend and Reality*. London, 1966.
Barzun, Jacques, *Berlioz and the Romantic Century* (2 vols.). Boston, 1950.
Bates, Ralph, *Franz Schubert*. New York, 1935.
Bauernfeld, Eduard von, *Erinnerungen aus Alt-Wien*. Vienna, 1923.
Brion, Marcel, *Daily Life in the Vienna of Mozart and Schubert*. London, 1961.
Brockway, Wallace, and Weinstock, Herbert, *Men of Music*. New York, 1939.
Brown, Maurice J. E., *Schubert: A Critical Biography*. London, 1953.
Brusatti, Otto, Editor, *Schubert-Kongress Wien 1978*. Graz, 1979.
Butterfield, Herbert, *Napoleon*. New York, 1939.
Capell, Richard, *Schubert's Songs*. London, 1957.
Carse, Adam, *The Orchestra from Beethoven to Berlioz*. Cambridge, England, 1947.
Chandler, David, *The Campaigns of Napoleon*. New York, 1966.
Chorley, H. F., *Schubert and His Music*. London, 1854.
Copleston, Frederick, *A History of Philosophy, Vol. VI*. Westminster, 1960.
Crankshaw, Edward, *Maria Theresa*. New York, 1969.
Critchy, MacDonald, and Henson, R. A., Editors, *Music and the Brain*. London, 1965.
Dahms, Walter, *Schubert*. Berlin, 1912.

Deutsch, Otto Erich, *Mozart, a Documentary Biography*. Stamford, 1965.

——, *Franz Schubert's Briefe und Schriften*. Munich, 1919.

——, *Schubert: A Documentary Biography*. London, 1946.

——, *Franz Schubert: Die Dokumente Seines Lebens* (3 vols.). Munich, 1913.

——, *Schubert: Sein Leben in Bildern*. Munich, 1914.

——, *Schubert: Thematic Catalogue of His Works*. London, 1951.

Duncan, Edmond, *Schubert*. London, 1905.

Durant, Will and Ariel, *The Age of Napoleon (Vol. XI in "The Story of Civilization")*. New York, 1975.

Einstein, Alfred, *Schubert*. London, 1951.

Engel, Eduard, *Geschichte der deutschen Literatur* (2 vols.). Leipzig, 1917.

——, *Goethe*. Berlin, 1910.

Feigl, Rudolf, *Klar um Schubert*. Linz, 1936.

Ferguson, Donald U., *Masterworks of the Orchestral Repertoire*. Minneapolis, 1954.

Fischer-Dieskau, Dietrich, *Schubert's Songs*. New York, 1977.

Flower, Newman, *Franz Schubert, the Man and His Circle*. New York, 1928.

Friedenthal, Richard, *Goethe: His Life and Times*. Cleveland, 1963.

Friedländer, Max, *Franz Schubert: Skizze seines Lebens und Wirkens*. Leipzig, 1928.

Friedländer, Otto, *Letzer Glanz der Märchenstadt*. Vienna, 1969.

Gal, Hans, *The Golden Age of Vienna*. New York, 1948.

——, *Franz Schubert*. Frankfurt, 1970.

——, *Franz Schubert and the Essence of Melody*. New York, 1977.

Gay, Peter, *The Enlightenment: An Interpretation*. New York, 1966.

Groner, Richard, *Wien, wie es war*. Vienna, 1965.

Hadow, Sir W. H., *The Viennese Period*. London, 1931.

Hamerow, Theodore S., *Restoration, Revolution, Reaction*. Princeton, 1958.

Heindl, Gottfried, *Wien, Brevier einer Stadt*. Vienna, 1972.

Historic Museum, City of Vienna, *Vienna 1800–1850*. Vienna, 1960.

Holborn, Hajo, *The History of Modern Germany, 1648–1840*. New York, 1964.

Hutchings, A., *Schubert*. London, 1945.

Johnston, Wilhelm M., *The Austrian Mind*. Berkeley, 1972.

Kelly, Lindor, *The Young Romantics*. London, 1966.

Kerner, Dieter, *Krankheisten grosser Musiker*. Stuttgart, 1969.

Klatte, Wilhelm, *Franz Schubert*. Berlin, 1907.

Kobald, Karl, *Franz Schubert*. Zurich, 1921.

——, *Franz Schubert und seine Zeit*. Leipzig, 1935.

Kolb, Annette, *Franz Schubert: Sein Leben*. Stockholm, 1941.

Kralik, Heinrich, *The Vienna Opera*. Vienna, 1961.

Kreissle von Hellborn, Heinrich, *Franz Schubert*. Vienna, 1865.

Lang, Paul Henry, *Music in Western Civilization*. New York, 1941.

Landon, H. C. Robbins, *Mozart and the Masons*. London, 1982.

Liess, Andrees, *Johann Michael Vogl*. Graz, 1954.

Loesser, Arthur, *Men, Women and Pianos*. New York, 1954.

McGuigan, Dorothy Gies, *The Habsburgs*. New York, 1966.

Mann, Golo, *The History of Germany Since 1789*. London, 1968.

Margetson, Stella, *Leisure and Pleasure in the 19th Century*. New York, 1969.

Naumann, *Musikgeschichte* (2 vols.). Stuttgart, 1914.

Nicolson, Harold, *The Congress of Vienna*. London, 1946.

Mandyczewski, E., *Franz Schubert*. Leipzig, 1897.

Mayrhofer, Johann, *Gedichte*. Vienna, 1938.

Moore, Gerald, *The Schubert Song Cycles*. London, 1975.

Moscheles, Ignaz, *Recent Music and Musicians*. London, 1879.

Mowat, R. B., *The Romantic Age*. London, 1937.

Newman, Ernest, *From the World of Music*. London, 1956.

Ofner, Josef, *Franz Schubert und Steyr*. Steyr, 1973.

Ortner, Jakob, and Moisse, Gustav, Editors, *Schubertgabe*. Vienna, 1926.

Osterheld, Horst, *Franz Schubert*. Stuttgart, 1978.

Ovel, Alfred, *Schubert und Wien*. Vienna, 1928.

Pablé, Elisabeth, *Das kleine Schubert-Buch*. Hamburg, 1980.

Palmer, Alan, *Metternich*. New York, 1972.

——, *Napoleon in Russia*. New York, 1967.

Paumgartner, Bernhard, *Franz Schubert*. Zurich, 1947.

Perényi, Eleanor, *Liszt*. Boston, 1974.

Perfall, Jost, Editor, *Wien Chronik*. Salzburg, 1961.

Pleasants, Henry, *The Great Singers*. New York, 1966.

Priestley, J. B., *Literature and Western Man*. New York, 1960.

Radant, Else, Editor, *Die Tagebücher von Joseph Carl Rosenbaum, 1770–1829*. Vienna, 1968.

Reininghaus, Frieder, *Schubert und das Witshaus*. Vienna, 1978.

Schauffler, Robert Haven, *Franz Schubert, The Ariel of Music*. New York, 1949.

Schenk, H. G., *The Mind of the European Romantics*. New York, 1966.

Schindler, Anton Felix, *Beethoven As I Knew Him*. London, 1966.

Scholes, P. A., *The Oxford Companion to Music*. London, 1955.

Schonberg, Harold C., *The Great Pianists*. New York, 1963.

Schorske, Carol E., *Fin-de-Siècle Vienna*. New York, 1980.

Schurmann, Robert, *On Music and Musicians*. New York, 1948.

Sedgwick, H. D., *Vienna*. Indianapolis, 1939.

Silvestrolli, Anita, *Franz Schubert: Das wahre Gesicht eines Lebens*. Salzburg, 1938.

Sitwell, Sacheverell, *Liszt*. Boston, 1934.

Spaun, Josef, *Neues um Schubert*. Vienna, 1934.

——, *Die Wiener Oper*. Vienna, 1952.

Stein, Werner, *Kulturfahrplan*. Munich, 1946.

Sutherland, Donald, *On Romanticism*. New York, 1971.

Talmon, J. L., *Romanticism and Revolt, Europe 1815–1848*. London, 1967.

Thayer, Alexander Wheelock, *The Life of Ludwig van Beethoven* (E. H. Krehbiel, Editor, 3 vols.). New York, 1921.

Thomas, Henry, *Biographical Dictionary of Philosophy*. New York, 1965.

Thomas, Hugh, *History of the World*. New York, 1979.

Tovey, Donald Francis, *Chamber Music*. London, 1944.

Ulrich, Homer, *Chamber Music*. New York, 1948.

Vallotton, Henry, *Metternich*. Heide, 1906.

Waldegg, Richard, *Sittengeschichte von Wien*. Stuttgart, 1957.

Wandruszka, Adam, *Das Haus Habsburg*. Stuttgart, 1956.

Wechsberg, Joseph, *Schubert, His Life, His Work, His Time*. New York, 1977.

Weigel, Hans, *Das Buch der Wiener Philharmoniker*. Salzburg, 1967.

——, *Franz Schubert*. Vienna, 1960.

Weinstock, Herbert, *Rossini*. New York, 1968.

Wettzl, Leopold V., *Drei vergessene Lichtentaler aus Franz Schubert's Zeit*. Vienna, 1980.

Williams, Neville, *Chronology of the Modern World*. New York, 1966.

Wurzbach, Conrad, Editor, *Biographisches Lexikon* (60 vols.). Vienna, 1856–1891.

Ziese, Elly, *Schubert's Tod und Begräbins*. Grossdeuten, 1933.

INDEX